"*All Our Trials* offers us a robust history of late twentieth-century radical feminist antiviolence organizing. Thuma reminds us that the activism of the present is built upon an important legacy of work that traversed movements and prison walls. If we are to build an abolitionist feminist future, we would be wise to pay attention to the antiracist queer feminist politics of these activists. We owe a debt of gratitude to them for paving the way, and to Thuma for chronicling their struggles."
—Angela Y. Davis, University of California, Santa Cruz

"*All Our Trials* is a tour de force. It stands among the best books on the history of modern feminist politics and represents one of the most elucidating histories of the US carceral state produced to date. Emily Thuma centers criminalized women's ideas and organizing, providing graceful historical analysis that will undoubtedly influence current conversations about imprisonment, gender, and sexual violence. This history opens a fiercely urgent path toward an anticarceral feminist future."
—Sarah Haley, author of *No Mercy Here: Gender, Punishment, and the Making of Jim Crow Modernity*

"With deep compassion, Thuma offers one of the most compelling historical analyses of how feminist activism of Black, queer, and criminalized women has worked to resist the long and dangerous reach of the carceral state. *All Our Trials* is an important text in the growing fields of critical prison studies and anti-carceral feminism *and* a critical addition to activist reading lists."
—Beth Richie, author of *Arrested Violence: Black Women, Violence, and America's Prison Nation*

"*All Our Trials* transforms our understanding of both the history of feminism and of the carceral state. In her deeply compelling account, Thuma documents the work of activists who centered the lives of the most marginalized in their social justice imaginary and their political agenda, producing an anticarceral feminist politics and an expansive analysis of the interconnections between interpersonal and state violence. A crucial and timely read as we wrestle with gender, race, and violence today."
—Regina Kunzel, author of *Criminal Intimacy: Prison and the Uneven History of Modern American Sexuality*

All Our Trials

WOMEN, GENDER, AND SEXUALITY
IN AMERICAN HISTORY

Editorial Advisors:
Susan K. Cahn
Wanda A. Hendricks
Deborah Gray White
Anne Firor Scott, Founding Editor Emerita

A list of books in the series appears at the end of this book.

All Our Trials

Prisons, Policing, and the Feminist Fight to End Violence

EMILY L. THUMA

UNIVERSITY OF
ILLINOIS PRESS
Urbana, Chicago, and Springfield

Publication of this book was supported by funding
from the UCI Humanities Commons at the University
of California, Irvine.

Library of Congress Cataloging-in-Publication Data
Names: Thuma, Emily L., author.
Title: All our trials: prisons, policing, and the feminist
    fight to end violence / Emily L. Thuma.
Description: Urbana: University of Illinois Press, [2019]
    | Series: Women, gender, and sexuality in American
    history | Includes bibliographical references and index.
Identifiers: LCCN 2018038414| ISBN 9780252042331 (cloth
    : alk. paper) | ISBN 9780252084126 (pbk. : alk. paper)
Subjects: LCSH: Women prisoners—United States. |
    Abused women—United States. | Women—Violence
    against—United States. | Women—Crimes against—
    United States. | Feminist criminology—United States. |
    Criminal justice, Administration of—United States.
Classification: LCC HV9471 .T485 2019 | DDC
    365/.60820973—dc23 LC record available at https://lccn
    .loc.gov/2018038414

Ebook ISBN 978-0-252-05117-3

Contents

Acknowledgments

Many people have helped me conceive of, research, and write this book and it is an honor to recognize them here. My foremost thanks and deepest gratitude go to the activists whose organizing efforts to build a world free of violence are at the heart of this book. I am also extremely thankful for everything I have learned about justice, power, and social transformation from the activist communities and organizations in which I have participated. A special gratitude to former members of Communities Against Rape and Abuse who first inspired me many years ago to seek out and write a history of feminist organizing and the carceral state, and to the members of the California Coalition for Women Prisoners whose work has helped to propel me forward in the last stages of writing and revision. Along the way I have also learned a tremendous amount from the vision, strategy, and practice of Critical Resistance, Justice Now, Catalyst Project, and Survived and Punished.

I thank my undergraduate mentors at Western Washington University for a transformative education, and for sparking my desire to become a scholar and teacher: Larry Estrada, Connie Faulkner, Bill Lyne, and Midori Takagi. I owe a tremendous debt of gratitude to Lisa Duggan, whose exceptional mentorship and unflagging support were immeasurably important in the first stages of this project. Jennifer Morgan, Crystal Parikh, and Gillian Harkins were likewise remarkable guides who profoundly influenced my ideas and approaches. Other graduate teachers and mentors at New York University who indelibly shaped my thinking include Adam Green, Walter Johnson, José Esteban Muñoz, and Nikhil Pal Singh. Among my many graduate school peers in the Program in American Studies who constantly inspired and challenged me, I am especially thankful for the comradeship of Miabi Chatterji, Lezlie Frye, Rana Jaleel, Ronak Kapadia, and Ariana Ochoa Camacho.

I am grateful to the archivists, librarians, staffs, and volunteers at the various institutions where I conducted research. Particular thanks go to Deborah Richards who pointed me toward the Coalition to Stop Institutional Violence records at Northeastern University, and to Claude Marks at the Freedom Archives in San Francisco for his encouragement and engagement. Linda Burnham kindly opened up her home to me before the Third World Women's Alliance records made their way to the Sophia Smith Collection. I also benefited from the generosity of those who shared with me materials from their personal archives or their own scholarly research: Connie Breece, Cathy Cade, Donna Coker, Charoula Dontopoulos, Anne Gray Fischer, Marjory Nelson, and Joan Potter. I greatly thank the people I interviewed for sharing their memories and reflections with me. Among them, I am especially grateful to Diana Block, Connie Breece, Sunny Robinson, Loretta Ross, and Yvonne Swan. I would like to acknowledge the oral historians and activists who cocreated the Voices of Feminism Project at the Sophia Smith Collection, a meaningful archive of oral histories for this book.

This research was generously enabled by the Graduate School of Arts and Sciences at New York University's Dean's Dissertation Fellowship; the American Association of University Women Dissertation Fellowship; travel-to-collections grants from the Schlesinger Library at Harvard University, the Sophia Smith Collection at Smith College, and the Sallie Bingham Center at Duke University; the Center for Lesbian and Gay Studies at the CUNY Graduate Center's Heller-Bernard Fellowship; the University of California, Irvine Humanities Commons; and the University of California Hellman Fellowship.

I am very fortunate to work at the University of California, Irvine, where I have found an exceptional intellectual community and incredible students. I am thankful to my colleagues in Gender and Sexuality Studies for their indispensable support and engagement—Laura Kang, Lilith Mahmud, Catherine Sameh, Jeanne Scheper, and Jennifer Terry—and to those beyond my home department who have welcomed me to campus and provided advice and encouragement or opportunities for collaboration, including Jonathan Alexander, Sharon Block, Kaaryn Gustafson, Adria Imada, Arlene Keizer, Allison Perlman, Keramet Reiter, Damien Sojoyner, and Jane Stoever. I would also like to recognize the excellent colleagues and students I worked with at Western Washington University and the University of Washington, Bothell, where I taught before coming to UCI.

I am supremely grateful to the colleagues, mentors, and friends who read and provided feedback on portions or all of the manuscript at its various stages of development. They include Shana Agid, Dan Berger, Sharon Block, Jakeya Caruthers, Chris Dixon, Lezlie Frye, Christoph Hanssmann, Grace Hong, Sid Jordan, Regina Kunzel, Erica Meiners, Nick Mitchell, Liz Montegary, Soniya Munshi, Chandan Reddy, David Stein, and Alys Weinbaum. Dayo Gore, Sarah Haley, and Christina Hanhardt offered superb comments and guidance during an invaluable manuscript workshop. The astute and insightful feedback of two anonymous reviewers for the University of Illinois Press unquestionably strengthened the book. Grey Osterud's editorial advice was crucial and I thank her for helping me see the forest for the trees on more than one occasion and for teaching me to be a better writer. Christina Hanhardt, Gillian Harkins, and Sherie Randolph have stuck with me over the long haul of this project, and their critical readings and sage and generous mentorship have prodded me along. Alisa Bierria's incisive and supportive engagement, from idea to book, has made all the difference. Conversations and collaborations with many other friends, colleagues, and comrades have also inspired and pushed my thinking in ways that have enriched this book. I want to thank in particular Liat Ben-Moshe, Lauren Berliner, Angélica Cházaro, Aisha Finch, Rachel Herzing, Ren-yo Hwang, Adria Imada, Joseph Hankins, Mariame Kaba, Priya Kandaswamy, Mimi Kim, Colby Lenz, Sara Matthiesen, Cara Page, Romarilyn Ralston, Cassandra Shaylor, Amy Sonnie, Dean Spade, Craig Willse, and members of the Black Feminist Think Tank.

At the University of Illinois Press, I am grateful to my editor, Dawn Durante, for her steadfast encouragement and keen guidance; Nancy Albright, who copyedited the manuscript; and everyone who had a hand in the production process. I greatly thank Allison Dziuba for her assistance in preparing the manuscript for submission and Laurie Prendergast for providing the index. Small portions of chapters 1 and 4 were published in *Women's Studies Quarterly* and portions of chapter 2 have been revised from an essay published in *Feminist Formations*; I thank the Feminist Press of the City University of New York and the Johns Hopkins University Press, respectively, for permission to use this material. My gratitude also goes to the photographers, poster artists, and other makers whose work appears in this book, especially Juana Alicia, JEB (Joan E. Biren), Rachael Romero, and Ellen Shub. Lincoln Cushing generously facilitated access to several images.

Finally, my family and friends have helped sustain me throughout the many years I have worked on this project. I am grateful for the unwavering support and love of my parents, Mary Pat Thuma and Joel Thuma, my brother Alan, and my extended family, especially Marian, Mark, and Jen. More friends than I can name here have provided inspiration, encouragement, and respite. For their enduring companionship, especially deep thanks go to Christina Antonakas-Wallace, Makenzie Brookes, Belkys Garcia, Alex Guy, Molly McClure, Luke Newton, Holly Maeder Sheehan, Nadir Souirgi, Shannon Stewart, Amy Vanderwarker, and the dear friends and chosen family who appear earlier in these acknowledgments. There are no adequate words to express my gratitude for my partner, Sid Jordan, whose love, care, and brilliance have buoyed and awed me.

All Our Trials

Introduction

Washington, D.C.'s first-ever March to Stop Violence Against Women kicked off just after dusk on April 29, 1978. A boisterous crowd of roughly eight hundred people—diverse in age, race, class, gender, and sexual identity—snaked through the city's adjacent neighborhoods of Adams-Morgan and Dupont Circle. The marchers carried flashlights, whistles, and handmade signs, and their chants articulated the event's central message of "self-determination for women, power for women, [and] self-defense for women." An extensive list of principles and demands drawn up by the organizers advocated "community sanction" for rape and abuse and solutions "involving empowerment of women, education of men, and community action" rather than "criminal justice."[1] The demonstration represented a coalitional effort between three organizations: the D.C. Rape Crisis Center; the Task Force on Abused Women of the Women's Legal Defense Fund; and the "open-membership, action-oriented" D.C. Area Feminist Alliance. More than sixty other local groups endorsed the statement of principles and demands. The march was the culmination of the city's first annual Anti-Rape Week, a community education project organized by the black feminist leadership of the Rape Crisis Center.[2]

Once gathered at Dupont Circle Park, the demonstrators listened to an array of speakers and musicians. Among them was Linda Leaks, who delivered "revolutionary greetings" from Dessie Woods, a black woman serving a twenty-two-year prison sentence in the State of Georgia for killing an armed white man who had attempted to rape her and her friend. Leaks, a local member of Woods's national defense committee, told the crowd that the incarcerated woman's story belonged to a long legacy of white men's sexual violence against black women that was rooted in chattel slavery.[3] Just a month earlier, Rape Crisis Center staff members Deirdre Wright and Nkenge Touré had traveled to the Georgia Women's Institute of Corrections to interview Woods as part of the center's work to help disseminate her story and urge feminists and other progressive people to take action on her behalf.[4] To the organizers of the march, Woods's case, and others like it, exemplified the need for a feminist antiviolence agenda that took seriously the perilous entwinement of racism, classism, and sexism in the criminal legal system.

All Our Trials: Prisons, Policing, and the Feminist Fight to End Violence is a history of activism by, for, and about incarcerated domestic violence survivors, criminalized rape resisters, and dissident women prisoners in the 1970s and early 1980s. Across the United States, in and outside of prisons, grassroots women activists participated in collective actions that illuminated the interconnections between interpersonal violence against women and the racial and gender violence of policing and imprisonment. These mobilizations were spearheaded by radical women of color and antiracist white women, many of them lesbian-identified. They cultivated a distinctive left antiviolence politics that was defined by a critique of state violence; an understanding of race, gender, class, and sexuality as mutually constructed systems of power and meaning; and a practice of coalition-based organizing.[5] This book traces the political activities and ideas that constituted this anticarceral feminism and demonstrates that it shaped broader debates about the root causes of and remedies for violence against women. It also reveals the important role of this activist current in the making of a prison abolition movement in the 1970s.

Anticarceral feminist politics grew in the cracks of prison walls and at the interfaces between numerous social movements, including those for racial and economic justice, prisoners' and psychiatric patients' rights, and gender and sexual liberation.[6] Through the process of building coalitions that transected these social justice struggles, the activists at the center of this study produced a broad and layered understanding of "violence against women" that encompassed the structural violence of social inequalities, the violence of state institutions and agents, and interpersonal forms of violence, including rape, battering, and sexual coercion. This expansive analysis directly clashed with the "tough-on-crime" ethos of the 1970s and the mainstream women's movement's increasing embrace of criminalization as a frontline solution to interpersonal violence.[7] As this history demonstrates, violence against women was—as it still is—a highly charged political claim rather than a transparent descriptor, and the ascendency of a law-and-order feminism was a deeply contested process.

All Our Trials tells a story of resistance to violent policing and state repression of gender and sexual deviance and nonconformity. The chapters chronicle a series of organizing efforts forged by, and in alliance with, women whose social locations and practices placed them beyond the pale of dominant notions of feminine respectability and state protection and in the way of state harm: those who were black, indigenous, Latina, immigrant, poor, gender and sexual outsiders, labeled crazy or mad, or involved in the sex trade. Feminist coalitions that foregrounded criminalized and incarcerated women produced new knowledges. They analyzed the interrelationship of state abandonment and state violence in communities of color, the entanglements of carceral and psychiatric power, and the racial constitution of gender and sexual norms and their brutal modes of enforcement in locked institutions. As the veteran black feminist organizer Linda Burnham reminds us, "the struggle for social transformation [is] a powerful generator of theoretical insight," as it affords opportunities for "collective, mass-based inquiry."[8] Although this book focuses on activist formations and the theoretical understandings they engendered, it also documents numerous examples of individual marginalized women's—particularly black women's—bodily confrontations with institutional and interpersonal violence. From fighting back against a sexual attacker, to refusing to comply with a dehumanizing prison policy, to inscribing a testimony of personal violation in a radical prison newspaper, these everyday acts of survival helped constitute anticarceral feminist thought and practice.

This book, then, aims to offer a history of the carceral state from below. It recovers the political and theoretical contributions of grassroots activists who enacted solidarities across prison walls and seemingly discrete trials and struggles in their attempts to envision and create a violence-free world.[9] As the following chapters convey, this work was often arduous, and its results were uneven and messy. With varying degrees of success, activists strove to build coalitions that recognized rather than obscured differences of social power among women and centered those most vulnerable to the brutal, and sometimes lethal, nexus of interpersonal and state violence. In doing so, they put an intersectional analysis of structures of inequality and domination into practice. Critical race theorist Kimberlé Crenshaw coined the term *intersectionality* in the late 1980s to theorize the imbrication of racial and gender inequality in black women's lives and the incapacity of antidiscrimination law to address their multidimensional claims of employment discrimination.[10] Yet, as scholars and activists have pointed out, the larger theoretical insight that systems of racial, gender, economic, and sexual oppression are inextricably linked or "interlocking" has a long and collective history that includes black feminist and women of color feminist political organizing in the 1960s and 1970s. *All Our Trials* demonstrates how antiviolence mobilizations that focused on the lives of marginalized women were generative of an interwoven analysis of racism, sexism, heterosexism, and capitalism that pointed to the carceral state as a source of further harm rather than safety and redress.[11]

* * *

Over the last five decades, the U.S. carceral state has expanded dramatically. As is increasingly common knowledge, the country incarcerates a greater proportion of its populace than any other nation in the world. As of 2018, it confines nearly 2.3 million people in federal, state, military, and territorial prisons; local jails, juvenile jails, and reservation jails; immigrant detention centers; and state-run psychiatric hospitals and civil commitment centers, and it exerts control over the itineraries and behaviors of another five million people on parole or probation. While the number of people in women's prisons and jails continues to represent only a fraction of the incarcerated population, the rate of women's incarceration has more than octupled since the overall rate began to climb in the early 1970s. Black, Latinx, and indigenous communities are disproportionately represented throughout the country's vast system of lockups and hence disproportionately affected by the myriad social, political, and economic consequences of the mass incarceration crisis.[12]

Much scholarly and public attention has been devoted to grasping the multilayered political and economic roots of this massive prison boom. Whereas some scholars point to the Reagan administration's War on Drugs as the principal engine, others look further back to the pivotal moment of the 1960s War on Crime.[13] In 1965, amid black urban uprisings and insurgency and in the context of the civil and voting rights acts of 1964–1965 and President Lyndon B. Johnson's Great Society platform, Congress passed the Law Enforcement Assistance Act, which made local law enforcement a federal and increasingly militarized affair. Three years later, the Omnibus Crime Control and Safe Streets Act authorized the creation of the Law Enforcement Assistance Administration (LEAA) within the Department of Justice. It quickly grew into a sprawling federal agency and the infrastructural backbone of the new anticrime initiative. Under the tenets of restoring law and order and modernizing policing, the LEAA's principal function was granting millions of dollars to states each year to update and expand police weaponry, hire and train new personnel, and facilitate communication and coordination among local, state, and federal law enforcement. The LEAA played a decisive role in the buildup of carceral state power in the late 1960s and across the 1970s—most acutely exercised in low-income, urban, black communities—by shaping, seeding, and subsidizing tens of thousands of local- and state-level crime control initiatives.[14] These involved a diverse array of state agents: "the police, sheriffs, and marshals responsible for law enforcement; the judges, prosecutors, and defense lawyers that facilitate the judicial process; and the prison officials and probation and parole officers charged with handling convicted felons."[15] Just on the heels of unprecedented civil rights legislation intended to dismantle Jim Crow forms of racial exclusion and stratification, the racial state's capacity to surveil, police, and imprison swelled to new proportions.[16]

This immense influx of resources directly aided police and indirectly aided the FBI in criminalizing radical social movements in general and the Black Power movement in particular. As critical geographer Ruth Wilson Gilmore writes, "the disorder that became 'crime' had particular urban and racial qualities, and the collective characteristics of activists (whose relative visibility as enemies inversely reflected their structural powerlessness) defined the face of the individual criminal."[17] By the late 1960s, antiracist, new left, feminist, and gay liberation movements, to varying degrees, joined ranks with increasing frequency in expressions of solidarity. In response to this burgeoning opposition to the existing social order and with the direct aid of local law enforcement, the FBI expanded its existing counterintelligence program (COINTELPRO) and set out to "neutralize" these movements. Pervasive surveillance of organizations and individuals was the foundation for a barrage of tactics designed to disorganize groups from within, as well as to weaken their external appeal and credibility. These methods included leaking false information to the press, fabricating evidence for criminal prosecutions, planting infiltrators to act as provocateurs, and even facilitating the assassinations of dozens of activists. Though certainly not the sole cause of factional conflict and disarray among radicals, this campaign succeeded in demonizing the left, especially black activists. It generated thousands of arrests and produced hundreds of women and men political prisoners, dozens of whom remain imprisoned today.[18] This intense and targeted state-organized repression helped to make incarceration a core issue for the left. Communication and contact across prison walls increased, helping to spark the emergence of a radical prison movement.[19]

The precipitous growth of carceral state capacity not only placed more police in urban communities of color and aided in the repression of black and other radical activists, but it also created new political opportunities for the feminist antirape and battered women's movements that emerged in the early 1970s. Feminist efforts to politicize rape and abuse galvanized a multitude of local programs: by the middle of the decade, more than 500 feminist-run rape

crisis centers and refuges for abused women had been established throughout the country. These grassroots projects typically offered a combination of
peer-based counseling, support groups, hotlines, and shelter; some included
self-defense classes and community education programs. All embraced a
philosophy of radical self-help and mutual aid, and many included staff who
self-identified as rape survivors and formerly battered women. The resources
needed to provide around-the-clock shelter and other forms of crisis support
led many activists to pursue government funding, and one of the most readily available sources was the LEAA. Feminists who built these institutions
from the ground up weighed the possibilities and contradictions of relying
on criminal justice funds to keep their doors open. Some advocates evinced
a fundamental mistrust of law enforcement and pointed to persistent patterns of institutional racism, class bias, and the repression of left-wing social
movements. Most were concerned about the potential for such a relationship
to undermine values and strategies that they had fought to prioritize, such as
survivor self-determination, layperson expertise, and participatory decision-
making structures. And those working to amend rape and domestic violence
laws questioned the strategic value of developing a client relationship with
the state as they sought to reform the police and courts. Police and prosecutors often dismissed accusations of rape and battering, blamed victims for
inviting assault by dressing or acting provocatively, exposed women's entire
sexual histories to public scrutiny to degrade their credibility, avoided "domestic disturbance" calls, and, as was the case with Dessie Woods, prosecuted
women who used violence in self-defense.[20]

Scholars have argued that feminist movements contributed to the making of mass incarceration through support for "get tough" policy making
in response to rape and domestic violence.[21] Feminist advocacy efforts in
the 1970s helped to put sexual and domestic violence on the national crime
control agenda by advocating more punitive responses, such as preferred
and mandatory arrest policies and stiffer sentencing, and by narrowly framing domestic violence as a social problem that could be most effectively
addressed by granting battered women "the protection afforded to other
victims of crime."[22] Sociologist Beth Richie points to the significance of the
antiviolence movement's early rhetoric of *it can happen to any woman*—what
she and others refer to as the everywoman construction—to this process of
state incorporation. Grassroots activists initially developed this formulation
to make plain that rape and battering were pervasive cultural phenomena and
not matters of individual pathology. By deploying it, they sought to debunk
racist, classist, and imperialist stereotypes that such violence was inherent
in and confined to particular "races," classes, or nations. Yet, as feminists

"won the mainstream but lost the movement" between the 1970s and 1990s, as Richie puts it, this construction inadvertently took on a new valence—it can *even* happen to white, middle-class, gender- and sexual-conforming women—and helped to reroute resources and energies into improving law enforcement and judicial interventions and away from a community organizing approach.[23]

The passage of the 1994 Violence Against Women Act (VAWA) is perhaps the starkest example of how the claim to crack down on individual perpetrators of violence against women became a critical lever of legitimacy for expanding the carceral state. The new law earmarked unprecedented federal funding for improving the prosecution of sexual and domestic violence as well as providing services for victims. Yet VAWA was just one component of the largest crime bill in U.S. history. The Violent Crime Control and Law Enforcement Act allocated nearly 10 billion dollars for new prison construction, put 100,000 more police officers on the street, applied the three-strikes-and-you're-out rule to a variety of federal crimes, and terminated government funding for prisoners to pursue postsecondary education. Hence, an act promising to curb violence against women simultaneously authorized the expansion of institutional violence against the nation-state's racial and economic others, including many victims of domestic and sexual violence.[24]

All Our Trials complements and extends these indispensable accounts of the making of "carceral feminism" by demonstrating that, in tandem and in tension with feminist advocacy for criminal justice–based approaches to rape and battering, activists also explicitly challenged criminalization and explored nonstatist approaches.[25] It offers an alternative history of feminism and the carceral state by shifting the focus to spaces and places at the edges of the mainstream antiviolence movement: prisoner defense campaigns, women's prisons, multi-issue coalitions, and radical print culture. Indeed, the various organizing efforts and debates tracked in this book constitute important evidence that the process of state cooptation through "liberal law-and-order" was neither unchallenged by some activists nor unwitting on the part of others.[26] The terrain of feminist antiviolence organizing in the 1970s and early 1980s was experimental and conflicted, and the dialectical relationship between this organizing and the state not only yielded "incorporative reforms" but also compelled emergent expressions of a prison abolitionist feminism.[27]

By homing in on this understudied current of late-twentieth-century radical activism, this book contributes to the overlapping fields of carceral history and critical prison studies. To date, scholars have provided illuminating analyses of prison and jail rebellions, prison activist cultures, and the writings and cultural production of imprisoned radicals in the 1960s and 1970s, but very few of these studies focus on organizing and collective action inside and outside of women's prisons and jails.[28] *All Our Trials* builds on these works as well as on a growing scholarship that examines how gender and sexuality are entwined with race and class in the history of the modern carceral state.[29] Placing feminist prison organizing at the center of historical analysis does more than recover examples of various women's participation in the radical prison movement of the 1970s. It invites a rethinking of the movement's allies and influences, strategies and targets, geography and durée. For instance, freedom campaigns for women of color such as Dessie Woods drew together activists affiliated with a variety of movements and helped to make gender violence an arena of anticarceral organizing. Similarly, the campaigns to oppose the construction of new maximum-security behavior modification units for women prisoners that I explore in chapter 2 took shape at the interface of feminist, psychiatric patients' liberation, and prison movements. Gender and sexual nonconforming or "queer" feminist radicals, both white and of color, brought their personal encounters with psychiatric coercion to bear on their analyses of the prison system, impelling their demand for the end of all forms of caging.

This study of antiracist queer feminist activism joins a vibrant scholarship that illuminates the diverse participants, contentious politics, and manifold fronts of struggle that defined the so-called Second Wave of U.S. feminism. By centering the activism of women of color, working-class and poor women, and queer and trans women, or by focusing on the politics of multiracial and cross-class coalitions and alliances, this body of work has demonstrated the "messy multiplicity" and broad horizons of feminism in the 1960s and 1970s.[30] *All Our Trials* is particularly indebted to scholarship that emphasizes the permeable boundaries and interchanges among postwar liberation movements, either by recovering the itineraries of individual activists who traversed these movements—and transformed them in the process—or by zeroing in on particular local spaces, places, and coalitions in which the boundaries of feminism were constructed and contested.[31] As it brings our attention to feminist organizing at the nexus of criminalization, imprisonment, and violence against women, it especially heeds historian A. Finn Enke's argument that "feminism exceeded feminist identification."[32] While numerous radical and progressive women of color and working-class and poor women embraced and defined feminist identities for themselves in this period, many others eschewed this label because of the racism and class bias of white feminisms, or they opted to use other terms to express their gender politics. Hence the genealogy of activism drawn in this book represents the efforts of self-described black, indigenous, Native American, Chicana, Latina, Asian American, socialist, and lesbian feminists as well as people who were not identified with the moniker of feminism.

*   *   *

All Our Trials traces the making of anticarceral feminist politics by a translocal, loose collection of activists and groups that spanned the country. I have structured the book's chapters around particular forms, or genres, of collective action, rather than around geographic locations or case studies. This arrangement brings into focus the development and circulation of ideas and organizing models and conveys the breadth and variety of people and groups that contributed to this feminist formation. I provide a close look at particular groups and coalitional spaces, as well as trace conversations in activist print media that brought together people and organizations in different places. The publications I explore not only linked but transformed existing organizing efforts while catalyzing the emergence of others. As Maylei Blackwell argues in her study of 1970s Chicana feminism, "movement print culture functioned as a mediating space where new ideas, theories, and political claims were constructed, negotiated and contested."[33]

Print culture was a particularly vital organizing forum for prison activists, as it enabled their ideas to breach carceral walls and helped to form political communities that included many people who were not allowed to meet face to face. Researching the history of women prisoners' organizing presents particular challenges since its archive is inherently evanescent. Incarcerated women who led sit-down strikes and uprisings, drafted and circulated petitions, or smuggled uncensored mail in or out of the prison risked a range of punishments, including solitary confinement, transfer to a higher security prison, and denial of parole, as well as unofficial retribution by prison staff in the form of verbal and physical abuse and the destruction of their personal belongings. The threat and reality of reprisal effectively suppressed access to written records of the necessarily clandestine organizing done by dissident prisoners. The transient quality of much of this organizing and the inaccessibility of prison records renders the surviving archive even more opaque. At the same time, prisoner activism centers on piercing the isolation and invisibility that shields institutional authorities from scrutiny and accountability.[34] As they do today, prison activists on both sides of the bars in the 1970s and 1980s turned to alternative media and created their own newspapers and newsletters to circulate information, confront dominant ideologies of crime and punishment, and participate in political communities that traverse institutional and local boundaries. The three chapters of this book that detail examples of inside-outside prison organizing analyze letters, communiqués, and prose collected in "underground" and alternative media as an unauthorized archive of the political activities and ideas of incarcerated women.

Writing a grassroots and translocal history of feminist radicalism presents difficulties that are inherent in documenting small groups that typically operated on shoestring or nonexistent budgets and were sometimes short-lived. Concerns about state surveillance may also have prompted groups to encourage anonymous authorship and to avoid keeping records of their activities. Hence, the book draws on primary sources scattered across a wide array of state, university, community, and personal archives. These include organizational records and newsletters, activist ephemera and propaganda, personal correspondence, speeches, photographs, and mainstream and alternative newspapers. Ephemeral materials such as leaflets, pamphlets, and posters that I repeatedly found in diverse archives were integral to my research process, both as cultural texts that I interpret as performing intellectual work, and as indicators of how and where locally produced knowledges traveled. I surveyed a variety of creative works that were independently produced or published by movement activists, including films, chapbooks, memoirs, and multigenre anthologies. Oral history interviews, conducted by myself and others, augment these archival and media sources and help me to reconstruct the histories of particular formations.[35] The campaigns, organizations, and activist periodicals that garnered the brightest spotlight in this study are those for which I was able to trace a more substantial paper trail. For each one chronicled here, there were a half-dozen more that left only small archival fragments and whose stories remain to be told.

Chapter 1 examines the role of participatory defense campaigns in the making of a feminist politics that conceived of the struggle against the abuses of the carceral state and the struggle to eradicate sexual and domestic violence as indivisibly linked. It focuses on four contemporaneous campaigns for racialized women who killed a sexual assailant: Dessie Woods, Joan Little, Inez García, and Yvonne Wanrow. In a range of locales, black, indigenous, Latina, and white radical women helped to link these mobilizations ideologically and practically. For these activists, the indictments, murder charges, trials, and imprisonments faced by each of these four women concretely exemplified and publicly symbolized the ways in which the carceral state compounded rather than redressed violence in the lives of those whom antiracist leftists identified as "US Third World women." The chapter pays particular attention to the Free Joan Little campaign, the most renowned of the four, and shows how it became a coalitional space for black liberation, feminist, and prison movements that, in turn, transformed leftists' understandings of who should be considered a political prisoner and galvanized support for the other three criminalized women. This cohort of freedom campaigns pivotally influenced debates about law enforcement funding in the rape crisis center movement. By placing the criminalization of low-income, racialized women's self-defensive violence at the forefront of conversations about social movement strategy, it forced a reckoning with the contradictions of pursuing a crime-control approach to sexual violence under racial capitalism.

The mobilizations that I explore in chapter 1 fueled the development of new organizations focused on imprisoned women in such places as North Carolina's Triangle Area, New York City, Seattle, and the San Francisco Bay Area. Chapters 2 and 3 explore the political strategies and thought of groups that prioritized organizing between the bars of women's prisons and what many prisoners called "the free world." In chapter 2, I examine how women prisoners and their activist supporters analyzed and resisted the escalating use of medicalized forms of behavior modification in federal and state prisons during the 1970s. I focus specifically on the Coalition to Stop Institutional Violence (CSIV), a broad-based, feminist-led alliance in Greater Boston that represented a coming together of diverse organizations and constituencies, from those advocating for the rights of prisoners and mental patients to the Prostitutes' Union of Massachusetts and the Boston Committee to End Sterilization Abuse. The chapter details the coalition's successful campaign to block the construction of a locked treatment center for "violent women" prisoners at a state mental hospital, showing how activists theorized the gendered, racial, and economic dimensions of what they termed the "prison/psychiatric state" and identified this interlocking network of jails, prisons, and mental hospitals as a facilitator of violence against marginalized women. Through its organizing strategies and writings, CSIV interrogated the pathologization of women prisoners' acts of noncompliance, refiguring them as acts of survival and political resistance in an abusive prison regime. The chapter also explores the nascent blueprints for community-based alternatives to incarceration that the coalition generated and how these informed its organizational structure and culture. Making the means of organizing reflect the liberatory ends they desired was a central aspiration of many feminist activists, as well as of the fledgling movement for prison abolition that CSIV helped to advance.

Chapter 3 analyzes women's prison newsletters as constituting a counterpublic sphere. It explores how feminist prison activists made alternative media production an elemental part of their organizing, allowing prison activists to forge lines of communication among those incarcerated in myriad institutions and disrupting the invisibility of women's prisons and prisoners in mainstream and leftist political milieus. I focus on the conversations that took shape among imprisoned and nonincarcerated contributors within two key newsletters, *Through the Looking Glass* and *No More Cages*, which were produced and circulated from the mid-1970s to the mid-1980s and independently published by feminist collectives in Seattle and Brooklyn. I read the newsletters as archives of what anthropologist James C. Scott would call "hidden transcripts" of prisoners' everyday resistance to the violence of incarceration.[36] As they facilitated counterpublic communications within and across institutional walls, these grassroots publications attacked the isolation that was (and still is) a key strategy of social control in prisons. This print culture incubated trenchant critiques of the chasm between a prisoner rights movement focused on men's institutions and a feminist antiviolence movement increasingly enmeshed with the criminal justice state. In the process, activists produced new knowledge about the gendered and sexual dimensions of the racial carceral state.

Chapter 4 provides a close look at coalition-building efforts in Boston and Washington, D.C., in the late 1970s and early 1980s that simultaneously addressed gender, racial, and economic violence. On both of these highly segregated and stratified local terrains, black feminist organizations emerged as intellectual and organizational leaders of alliances that crossed lines of race, class, gender, sexuality, and neighborhood. The chapter begins in Boston with an examination of the origins, ideology, structure, and strategy of the Coalition for Women's Safety, a multiracial feminist alliance forged in response to the murders of twelve black women and girls within a few months in the winter and spring of 1979. I highlight the leadership of the Combahee River Collective in the Coalition for Women's Safety, demonstrating the pivotal influence this group of self-described black lesbian feminist socialists had on the coalition's intersectional analysis of power, and its theorization and method of violence prevention. In Washington, D.C., I focus on the political strategies and thought of a cohort of black women radicals at the helm of the capital city's Rape Crisis Center (RCC) in the late 1970s and early 1980s. In addition to serving as a force of interconnection between local feminist and black liberation movements, the RCC organized and hosted the First National Third World Women and Violence Conference in 1980, an unprecedented gathering of black, Latina, Asian American, and indigenous activists. The intersectional coalitions explored in this chapter reoriented local discourses of violence against women around a critique of state harm and a mandate for alternatives to criminal justice. In so doing, they expanded the purview of what was considered "antirape work" and confronted its growing containment through the requirements of government funders.

In the more than forty years since Dessie Woods was tried in court and sentenced to prison, the need for a transformational antiviolence politics has only become more acute. Despite the growing chorus of activist groups, advocates, and scholars that has demonstrated the contradictory consequences of pursuing tough-on-crime approaches to sexual and domestic violence in a "prison nation," it has been enormously difficult to dislodge the notion that law enforcement and incarceration are the keys to safety from gendered forms of violence.[37] Indeed, the promise to protect women, children, and LGBTQ people from violence remains the alibi par excellence for expanding U.S. carceral power.[38] *All Our Trials* returns to the first years of the making of the contemporary carceral state to excavate the ideas and actions of activists who imagined otherwise.[39] As the epilogue suggests, the culture of opposition they created resonates with and offers a usable past for activists working in today's prison abolition, antiracist, and feminist movements.

1. Lessons in Self-Defense

From "Free Joan Little" to "Free Them All"

I'm only one out of a thousand. Don't forget it.
—Joan Little (1975)

So these four cases—Dessie Woods, Joanne Little, Inez García, Yvonne Wanrow—were cases that raised national attention and brought out a lot of the contradictions, the conflict, you know, was played out and so, it was a very educational process for people who were paying attention.
—Nkenge Touré (2005)

On Saturday morning, November 16, 1974, a crowd of demonstrators assembled outside the gates of the North Carolina Correctional Center for Women (NCCCW) in southeast Raleigh. In the back of a pickup truck with a bullhorn in hand stood Celine Chenier, a black community activist in her thirties from nearby Durham and cofounder of a newly formed local group, Action for Forgotten Women. When she shouted, "Can you hear me, sisters?" to the more than 400 people held captive in the prison, cheers erupted from behind the fence. Chenier, along with Brooke Whiting, a young black student at the University of North Carolina at Chapel Hill who was also a cofounder, had called the demonstration to help their fledging grassroots group recruit new allies for the state's women prisoners, including a particular NCCCW prisoner by the name of Joan (pronounced Jo-Ann and sometimes spelled JoAnne and Joann) Little. The twenty-year-old black woman had recently been charged with the murder of a white jail guard.

Activists from throughout North Carolina's Triangle area and beyond—including members of the Winston-Salem group Mothers for Black Liberation, the Black Panther Party, and the Triangle Area Lesbian Feminists—joined

Action for Forgotten Women that morning to support Little and to denounce the deplorable conditions at the prison. The incarcerated women's grievances included involuntary and unpaid labor, overcrowding, an abysmal health care system, scant educational and vocational training opportunities, and a library nearly empty of books. Those assigned to work in the laundry, a principal industry at the institution, reported having to lift heavy loads of unsanitary clothing from the prison and nearby hospitals and sanatoriums in temperatures as high as 120 degrees. Activists inside and outside also condemned the institutional violence of routine vaginal and rectal searches. The protesters, mostly black and white women, held handmade signs that read "Free Joan Little!" and "Abolish Women's Prisons!" as they chanted along with Chenier: "Free Our Sisters, Free Ourselves!"[1]

Little had begun serving a seven-to-ten-year sentence for burglary and larceny in the Beaufort County jail in the state's Coastal Plain region that summer. In the early morning of August 27, sixty-two-year-old Clarence Alligood was found dead in Little's cell. According to the autopsy report, the night jailer's "shoes were in the corridor, his socks on his feet. He was otherwise naked from the waist down. . . . Extending from his penis to his thigh skin was a stream of what appeared to be seminal fluid."[2] Little would later testify in court that Alligood had held an icepick to her head as he forced her into oral sex. She managed to gain control of the tool he was wielding as a weapon and stabbed him with it multiple times. Traumatized, terrified, and unaware that the wounds could be fatal, she fled from the jail.[3] One week later, with the help of an activist attorney, Little emerged from hiding and surrendered to police on the condition that she would not have to complete her sentence at the same county lockup. She was taken to the women's prison in Raleigh, and a grand jury swiftly handed down an indictment for murder in the first degree, which could carry the death penalty.

By the close of Little's trial the following summer, thousands had participated in a national campaign to save her life, and countless others had become familiar with her name, if not the details of her plight. The far-reaching mobilization of civil rights, Black Power, prisoner rights, and other left-wing and feminist activists helped to secure her exoneration in what some at the time dubbed the "trial of the decade," making her the first woman in the United States to be acquitted for wielding deadly violence to protect herself from rape.[4]

Joan Little's murder trial was one of several causes célèbres in the 1970s that involved a black, brown, or indigenous woman who killed her or her child's sexual assailant. The cases of Inez García, Yvonne Wanrow, and Dessie Woods inspired significant numbers of activists to work together to raise

Action for Forgotten Women demonstration at the women's prison in Raleigh in November 1974. Photographer unknown. Appeared in *Break de Chains of Legalized U.$. Slavery*, edited and published by the North Carolina Women's Prison Book Project, 1976. Courtesy of the Freedom Archives.

funds for legal costs and to engage in direct action and education to raise public consciousness about women's right to resist sexual violence. The Wanrow and García decisions set legal precedents, allowing the courts to consider the history of a battering relationship in cases where women killed abusive partners.[5] All four defense campaigns brought diverse social-movement actors, ideologies, and agendas into contact, exchange, and at times contention with one another.

More than a legal strategy, "self-defense" was a shared and galvanizing rhetoric that transected the radical social movements of the era. The breadth and efficacy of these four campaigns were made possible by the extent to which each woman's story of violation and resistance came to symbolically represent multiple and intersecting struggles for racial, gender, and economic justice. As American Studies scholar Rebecca Hill suggests in regard to the history of defense organizing in the United States, "campaigners assert the value and strength of their own people, their own ideas, and their own movements, and they create a popular history of America as a struggle between forces of repressive terror and heroic defiance."[6]

This chapter demonstrates the catalytic role that defense organizing played in the emergence of an expressly anticarceral feminist agenda in the 1970s. It uncovers the intellectual and organizing work of activists who established connections between the coalitional campaigns for Little, García, Wanrow, and Woods.[7] This labor produced an understanding of the four cases as a collective symbol of the intersecting race, gender, class, and colonial politics of using self-defensive violence, and as a cautionary tale for feminist antirape activists about the dangers and costs of aligning with the state. I begin with the Free Joan Little campaign, which played a critical role in generating political momentum for the other three mobilizations. I trace how it expanded the boundaries of who was considered a "political prisoner," made the coercion of incarcerated women visible, and contested a "single-axis analysis" of rape as a matter of gender power alone.[8] I then turn to the other three defense campaigns, focusing primarily on the ways they overlapped in time, political milieu, and participants, as well as in the new perspectives they articulated and propagated. Finally, I explore how these four cases figured in debates about whether, in what ways, or to what ends feminist antiviolence activists should accept criminal justice funding and prioritize criminal legal reform. Radical women of color and antiracist white women in multiple locales engaged with these cases and developed and circulated arguments against a criminal justice–centered approach. In the process, they produced an intersectional account of the sources of violence in women's lives as well as a nascent feminist politics of prison abolitionism.

The Crossroads of the Free Joan Little Movement

Upon Joan Little's indictment for murder, her newly assembled legal team quickly realized that an activist groundswell would be necessary to save her from a death sentence. The local papers in Beaufort and surrounding eastern counties cast Little as a calculating, Jezebel-like seductress who lured Alligood, "a man who gave his life in the line of duty," into her cell as part of an escape plot.[9] Her attorneys anticipated that the prosecution would construct a narrative of "a sexually deviant delinquent who murdered Alligood in cold blood," and they feared that Little's biography provided ample fodder for the state's ploy.[10] She routinely ran away as a teenager, eager to escape a stressful home environment, and, when she dropped out of school at age fifteen, a judge ordered her to a nearby training school for delinquent girls. Because Little had not earned a high school diploma or GED, she had great difficulty finding steady and decently paying work. By nineteen, she had a reputation as a "bad girl" and rumors flew that she and her older boyfriend were the organizers of local theft and prostitution rings. Prior to her indictment for burglary and larceny in March 1974, she had been arrested several times for shoplifting, though none of the charges stuck due to lack of evidence. The young woman's nonconforming behavior not only earned the condemnation of local whites but also violated the standards of black middle-class respectability.[11]

As several historians have demonstrated, Little's case must be situated in the context of unfinished struggles for racial and economic justice in the Tar Heel state.[12] The violent white supremacist power structure remained in place ten years after the civil and voting rights acts of 1964 and 1965. The Ku Klux Klan, which had a resurgence in the 1950s and 1960s, was thousands-strong. Racism and economic oppression remained starkly intertwined. Black North Carolinians fought pitched battles with whites in the streets and in courtrooms over school desegregation, voting rights, and police brutality. Moreover, Christina Greene has recently reconstructed Little's earlier encounters with the criminal justice system: jailed as a youth, harassed by police, failed by a public defender, and sentenced at age twenty to seven-to-ten years in prison for confessing to stealing $1,300 worth of property. Greene argues that these experiences reflected a widespread "pattern of racially discriminatory policing, judicial, and sentencing practices" and were perhaps fueled as much by Little's reputation as a wayward girl as "by any alleged criminal activity on her part."[13] Not merely vestiges of Jim Crow, the forces of racial criminalization in North Carolina were emboldened by federal sponsorship from the Law Enforcement Assistance Administration (LEAA) beginning in the late 1960s, and by 1980 the state incarcerated more people per capita than any other in the country.[14] Like Little, the majority of North Carolina's prisoners were black, indigent, and had not graduated high school. Moreover, black women comprised two-thirds of the women's prison population but only one-fourth of the state's citizenry.[15] Little's lawyers and grassroots campaigners alike sought to draw national attention to entrenched racial and economic inequality in the state, especially in its criminal justice system.

In September 1974, Little's legal team—which included Jerry Paul, a prominent white civil rights attorney, and Karen Galloway, an African American recent graduate of Duke University Law School—along with several local and seasoned civil rights, Black Power, and women prison activists, promptly established the Joan Little Defense Fund, the organization that anchored what soon became a national campaign.[16] Through publicity materials and speaking engagements, Defense Fund members laid the groundwork for a multivocal understanding of the case, intended to draw the broadest pos-

Joanne Little Defense Fund poster, circa 1974–1975. Courtesy of the Center for the Study of Political Graphics.

sible array of supporters. They suggested that the case raised and connected several critical issues, including "the very right of a woman to defend herself against sexual attack; prison conditions for women, including misuse of prison guard authority to obtain sexual gains; the discriminatory use of the death penalty against poor people and blacks; the selection processes which fail to produce juries of true peers; [and] the right of a poor person to an adequate defense."[17]

In Durham, North Carolina, where the defense fund was headquartered, the campaign's eclectic and predominantly African American base included university students and professors, everyday working and unemployed people, and organizers for regional and national racial justice organizations.[18] Defense committees sprouted up in numerous cities around the country, including Atlanta, Boston, New York City, Oakland, Pittsburgh, and Washington, D.C. They were encouraged to "follow their own initiative" while keeping Durham apprised so that their strategies could be shared through the growing communication network.[19] A central task for these campaigners was fund-raising. In addition to putting together Little's massive bail bond of $115,000 ($562,000 in today's dollars), the Defense Fund needed tens of thousands of dollars to defray legal, publicity, and campaign expenses, including those associated with the effort to get the trial moved from eastern to central North Carolina. The coastal counties had exceptionally few registered black voters, so few black citizens were prospective jurors, and polling data showed strong support for the death penalty among whites. Thanks in no small part to the national mobilization, the legal team ultimately won an unprecedented change of venue to Wake County, home to the capital city of Raleigh and the university cities of Chapel Hill and Durham.[20] A jury comprised of six African Americans and six whites, the majority of whom were women, ultimately heard the case and unanimously voted to acquit Joan Little after only seventy-eight minutes of deliberation.

The campaign became a common cause among antiracist, feminist, and leftist organizations at the regional and national levels as well. It drew support from prominent civil rights organizations such as the Southern Christian Leadership Conference, National Association for the Advancement of Colored People (NAACP), and Urban League; the more recently established Southern Poverty Law Center; and antiracist and anticapitalist organizations such as the Black Panther Party, National Alliance Against Racist and Political Repression, and Young Socialist Alliance. It also garnered endorsements from women's organizations, ranging from the equal rights–oriented American Association of University Women and National Organization for

Women (NOW) to the left-wing and antiracist Black Women's United Front, Third World Women's Alliance, National Black Feminist Organization, and Women's International League for Peace and Freedom.[21] The decidedly decentralized character of the mobilization meant that these campaigners created and circulated different narratives of Joan Little as they wrote fund-raising appeals, convened teach-ins, and staged rallies: she was a target of a racist, classist, and draconian southern criminal justice system, a victim of male violence, a militant rape resister, a political prisoner. To some activists, she was indivisibly all of these things.

The defense movement drew upon and extended a long history of black women's antirape activism, and veteran organizers from previous struggles participated directly in the Little campaign. The renowned southern civil rights organizer Rosa Parks helped to found a Joan Little Defense Committee in her new home city of Detroit. Parks's antirape activism dated back to the 1940s, when she led a campaign to demand that a group of white men in Abbeville, Alabama, be prosecuted for raping a young black woman. The mobilization for Recy Taylor was only one of several civil rights coalitions in the 1940s and 1950s to demand criminal accountability for white men's sexual violence against black women.[22]

Little's case resonated most poignantly with that of Georgia sharecropper Rosa Lee Ingram in the late 1940s and 1950s, which had brought unprecedented activist and media attention to the state's long-standing practice of criminalizing and imprisoning black women who defended themselves against rape and domestic violence.[23] Ingram, a widowed mother of twelve, and her two teenage sons were sentenced to death by an all-white jury in January 1948 for the murder of John Stratford, a white local landowner. She maintained that Stratford had, on multiple occasions, made unwanted sexual advances toward her, and that in November 1947, her two sons had come to her defense in the face of the man's armed sexual attack. The NAACP lent vital legal support, filing several appeals and staving off the executions until the courts ultimately reduced the death sentences to life in prison. According to one scholar, "no issue galvanized black women in the black left more than the Ingram case" during the 1950s.[24] Black women activists spearheaded two national organizations that endorsed Ingram's claim of self-defense and fought for the family's freedom by organizing demonstrations, collecting signatures, visiting the Ingrams in prison, and drumming up publicity. The Women's Committee for Equal Justice of the leftist Civil Rights Congress took up the cause, and the Sojourners for Truth and Justice placed Rosa Lee Ingram at the forefront of its work, unequivocally asserting "self-protection as a right for all black women."[25] Despite these efforts, the Ingram family spent more than ten years in prison before being released on parole in 1959. Several veteran black women activists in the Raleigh-Durham area who had campaigned for the Ingram family's freedom helped to found Concerned Women for Justice in 1974 to raise money for the Joan Little Defense Fund among black church congregations across the state. The group also visited Little and other women imprisoned at NCCCW.[26]

As it built upon the efforts of previous generations of black women activists, the campaign brought a new level of visibility to state-sanctioned sexual violence in southern prisons and jails. The National Association of Colored Women had first exposed the ubiquity of prison abuse more than a half-century earlier through its campaign to abolish the convict lease system.[27] In the 1960s, black women civil rights activists affiliated with the Congress of Racial Equality and the Student Nonviolent Coordinating Committee drew national attention to a culture of sexual violence in the region's jails. The Mississippi freedom fighter Fannie Lou Hamer testified on national television at the 1964 Democratic National Convention about the sexualized brutality that she and four other black women endured in an Alabama county lockup in 1963. The five were among many black women activists who were jailed for their participation in nonviolent direct action campaigns and faced beatings and sexual assaults at the hands of guards. Along with Hamer, dozens of women courageously recounted stories of violation to their families, fellow activists, and movement leaders.[28]

As part of Little's defense team's investigation, her lawyers interviewed dozens of women, the vast majority of whom were African American, who had previously been held in the women's section of the Beaufort County Jail.[29] The nearly one hundred media correspondents who descended upon Raleigh to cover the July–August 1975 trial reported the testimonies of several of the women who took the stand to recount being sexually harassed and abused by guards, including Clarence Alligood.[30] Their stories cohered into a collective account of chronic verbal and physical sexual abuse at the facility. An Atlanta attorney pressed reporters to take note that there were "a thousand Joan Littles all over the South. . . . What happened in North Carolina is typical."[31]

After the trial concluded, Little's defense attorneys began working with the Southern Poverty Law Center to lay the groundwork to sue the state for mistreatment of women in custody. They had received calls from numerous women beyond those they interviewed who also reported their experiences of sexual abuse in North Carolina prisons and jails.[32] Speaking to *New York Times* journalist James Reston, Celine Chenier of Action for Forgotten Women and the defense fund declared: "Joan's courage has inspired people to come forward now."[33]

"Power to the Ice Pick"

The Free Joan Little campaign was forged within a 1960s–1970s left political culture in which questions and tactics of armed resistance to state violence, as well as issues of government repression, were central. Around 1970, as the FBI counterintelligence program (COINTELPRO) escalated its assault on leftists and black radicals, increasing numbers of activists were incarcerated for their political work. In turn, violence by law enforcement became a central issue for the radical left, prisoner defense campaigns emerged as a key mode of activism, and the walls separating radical social movements from the country's prisoners grew increasingly permeable. Both locally and nationally, Black Power and prison activists joined the forefront of the Little campaign, helping to situate it within a broader narrative of racist political repression and state violence. Simultaneously, they celebrated Little's violent self-defense against a man who embodied the white supremacist power structure as an expression of a long tradition of black armed resistance.

The Black Panther Party, a staunch participant in the Free Joan Little movement, was perhaps the most visible and controversial proponent of armed self-defense in the Black Power era. Yet in North Carolina and throughout the South this strategy had been a through-line of "the ethics and politics of living and overcoming Jim Crow," to borrow a phrase from American Studies scholar Nikhil Pal Singh.[34] Indeed, with a touch of prophetic vision, fifteen years before Black Power and feminist activists donned shirts and held signs that read "Power to the Ice Pick" in front of the Wake County courthouse, the iconic militant activist and North Carolinian Robert F. Williams argued that armed resistance was both a right and a necessity for black people in the face of unrelenting white supremacist violence, and that they "must make use of the gas bomb, the lye can, *the ice pick*, the switchblade, the axe, the hatchet, the razor, the brick and the bullet"—the same arsenal of weapons that whites routinely used to terrorize African Americans.[35] In founding the Black Panther Party in Oakland, California, in 1966, Huey P. Newton and Bobby Seale looked to the Jim Crow South as they developed their practices and aesthetics of armed resistance. Yet, as scholars of the party have demonstrated, the organization cast self-defense broadly to include not only its notorious armed surveillance of the police, but also its various community survival and self-help initiatives, such as free health clinics and freedom schools, which resisted the structural and institutional violence embedded in the normative social order.[36]

In tandem with and influenced by the Black Panthers, the Puerto Rican Young Lords and pan-indigenous American Indian Movement adopted equally capacious understandings of self-defense. The Young Lords, for example, pledged to defend Puerto Ricans living in the barrios of U.S. cities "from greedy businessmen, racist teaching systems, rats and roaches, disease, police brutality, robbery and murder."[37] These organizations conceived of U.S. imperial militarism and U.S. domestic law enforcement as intertwined elements of the same power structure, and they defined racially oppressed communities and indigenous peoples in the United States as a "Third World within." For radicals of the U.S. Third World left, self-defense signified a critique of the state's claim to a monopoly on legitimate force.[38]

Black women had long been leaders in this tradition of armed self-defense; its foremost spokeswoman was the legendary antilynching crusader and journalist Ida B. Wells. Yet, as many women involved in the Black Power movement charged then and later, sexism too often circumscribed the "construction of the revolutionary, of the militant leader with transformative agency, [as] masculine."[39] The political organizing and theorizing of groups such as the Third World Women's Alliance (TWWA) helped to create a political imaginary that eschewed masculinist protection and asserted the right of racialized and colonized women to take up arms in defense of their own bodily integrity as well as the integrity of the collective body of the oppressed.[40] The TWWA concluded an extensive document on the organization's mission and politics with a statement on self-defense: "Whereas the struggle for liberation must be borne equally by all members of an oppressed people, we declare that third world women have the right and responsibility to bear arms. Women should be fully trained and educated in the martial arts as well as in the political arena. Furthermore, we recognize that it is our duty to defend all oppressed peoples."[41]

The TWWA began as the Black Women's Liberation Committee of the Student Nonviolent Coordinating Committee, based largely in New York. In 1970, it became an independent organization of black, Latina, Asian, and Native American women that understood the "struggle against racism and imperialism" and the "struggle for women's liberation" as interdependent.[42] As cofounder Frances Beal recollects, "What we were trying to deal with was the integration of race, gender, class, in consciousness, and not like just put one above the other, because we didn't think it actually operated as one is more important than another."[43] By 1972, the organization had a strong chapter in the San Francisco Bay Area and a fledgling one in Seattle. The TWWA's stance on armed self-defense informed its decision to make women political prisoners, and imprisoned women more generally, an organizational priority. The group participated in the 1970–1971 international defense campaign for the black radical activist and scholar Angela Davis, who was jailed for nine months on trumped-up charges stemming from her ties to imprisoned Black Power militants. TWWA helped to draw attention to the cases of Joan Bird and Afeni Shakur, two women members of the New York chapter of the Black Panther Party who were arrested and jailed along with nineteen of their male comrades (altogether known as the Panther 21) on false charges of planning to bomb several government buildings. The group used its bimonthly newspaper, *Triple Jeopardy*, to highlight the "struggle in the prisons" and to facilitate communication with imprisoned women.[44] Joining the freedom campaign for Joan Little in 1974–1975 was an organic extension of this work.[45]

The far-reaching fights to "Free the Panther 21" and "Free Angela Davis" were important precursors to the Little campaign. Members of the National United Committee to Free Angela Davis, including Davis herself, created the National Alliance Against Racist and Political Repression (NAARPR) in the wake of their victory. This new formation played an instrumental role in generating support for Little throughout the country. In particular, Davis used her media prominence to shine a light on the case and helped Little and her attorneys prepare for trial, while alliance director and veteran black radical organizer Charlene Mitchell traveled to North Carolina from California more than once over the course of the yearlong mobilization to help build its local base.[46] North Carolina held particular significance for NAARPR members. One of the alliance's cofounders, Reverend Ben Chavis, was himself imprisoned in the Tar Heel state. In 1971 he and nine other civil rights activists were arrested and convicted on fabricated charges of arson and conspiracy to commit arson. The group, which included eight black youths and one middle-aged white woman, became known as the "Wilmington Ten" and attracted international attention.[47] The NAARPR organized a 10,000-strong "March on Raleigh" that took place on July 4, 1974, seven weeks before Joan Little's flight from the Beaufort County jail. With the highest death row population per capita in the country and more than a dozen black activists behind bars, North Carolina's criminal justice system was a strategic target for the newly launched alliance.[48]

Another key contributor was the Attica Brothers Legal Defense, the anchor organization for a broad movement in support of the sixty-two prisoners indicted for their participation in the infamous 1971 rebellion at the New York State prison. As historian Devin Fergus observed, the composition of Little's defense team "ensured that the case's connection to other New Left causes was more than rhetorical": taken together, lead attorney Jerry Paul and consultants William Kunstler and Marvin Miller had defended Attica prisoners, American Indian Movement leaders, and members of the Black

Panther Party.[49] Affiliates of the Attica Fair Jury Project traveled from Buffalo, New York, to North Carolina in early 1975 to teach volunteers with the Joan Little Defense Fund the methods of data collection and statistical analysis they had used to prove that the Attica defendants would not receive a fair trial in the same county as the prison. The social-scientific survey the group administered demonstrated "extremely high levels of racial bias" in the state's eastern counties and helped to win the change of venue for the trial.[50]

Over the course of the yearlong mobilization, many local defense committees sponsored events that linked Little's case to the cases of activists imprisoned for their political organizing and to those of prisoners facing reprisal for their participation in prison strikes. The lineup of speakers at the "Joann Little Solidarity Day Rally" in New York City, for instance, included black feminist lawyer Florynce "Flo" Kennedy, Puerto Rican independista and former political prisoner Carlos Feliciano, and Herbert X Blyden of the Attica Liberation Faction.[51] In Louisville, the Southern Organizing Committee for Social and Economic Justice organized "Free Joann Little Week," drawing connections between Little's case and that of the Wilmington Ten and locating both within "a fabric of repression that has made North Carolina notorious across the U.S."[52] In Oakland, hundreds gathered on the weekend before the trial began to hear Elaine Brown, chairperson of the Black Panther Party; Maria del Drago of the NOW's recently established Task Force on Minority Women; Angela Davis on behalf of the NAARPR; and William Tate of the San Quentin Six situate the case in the context of a broader pattern of racist repression, historical forms of racialized sexual violence, and a "racist and sexist" judicial system.[53]

The defense campaign refigured the political prisoner as a black woman with no previous history of participation in the era's social justice struggles who engaged in armed resistance against state-sponsored sexual assault. As Angela Davis argued in *Ms.* magazine on the cusp of the trial, Little's self-defense was not a singular act of fighting off Alligood before dawn on August 27, 1974. Rather, it was a sequence of actions that included her flight from the jail to avoid becoming "just another number in the statistics surrounding prison deaths" and her decision to remain in North Carolina and tell her story to the court and the jury.[54] Though not all leftists understood Little to be a bona fide political prisoner, she was, indisputably, a *politicized* prisoner. A poem she penned in early 1975 and shared with campaigners affords a window onto her self-understanding of her insurgent actions: "I, a black woman, stood proudly up for self, For without pride, dignity, what is there left; I struggled in self-defense; now I'm caged, behind a prison fence."[55] While Little was out on bail in the months leading up to her trial, she told

Joan Little speaking at
Northeastern University,
1975. Photograph © Ellen
Shub 2018.

audiences about the squalid medical, hygiene, and housing conditions she
endured at the North Carolina Correctional Center for Women in Raleigh.[56]
As she explained to supporters at a Washington, D.C., rally, "My ordeal has
changed me in that I am now more concerned about the conditions received
by prisoners." She expressed her determination to call attention to prison
conditions that affected countless other women "just like her."[57] And yet, as
historian Genna Rae McNeil importantly heeds, Little was also wary of being
reduced to a political symbol, telling journalists, "I am nobody's cause, . . . I
am on trial for my life."[58]

Action by and for "Forgotten Women"

The North Carolina Correctional Center for Women (NCCCW) became
a center of gravity for the campaign in its own right. Imprisoned women
in Raleigh enlisted new allies from among the defense movement's ranks,

helping to expand activist efforts both inside and outside the state's women's prison. Action for Forgotten Women (AFW) staged the boisterous rally outside the gates of NCCCW in November 1974 to draw attention to the prisoners' demands for improved conditions of confinement as well as Little's legal plight.[59] The small but determined crowd of protestors reflected the growing base of the defense campaign: AFW cofounders Celine Chenier and Brooke Whiting had worked with the Defense Fund from its inception, and many of the demonstration's cosponsoring organizations had pledged their support for Little.[60]

Just weeks before the trial, roughly half of the more than 400 women imprisoned at NCCCW participated in a spontaneous sit-in. This direct action began on Sunday, June 15, when they gathered in the courtyard and refused an order to return to their dormitories for lockup. AFW members responded swiftly to a last-minute telephoned request, from one of the protest leaders, to assemble outside the prison gates and keep a watchful eye. Demonstrators had filed numerous grievances about the paltry health facilities, unsafe working conditions, and lack of educational and occupational training programs, but to no avail.[61] Moreover, they alleged that many women had been subjected to unnecessary and compulsory pelvic examinations, and complained that infirmary staff frequently engaged in racist commentary.[62] The deputy and acting directors of the Department of State Prisons addressed the women that night and listened to their indictment of the institution, but made no promises to change these conditions. Early the following morning, guards forced the women into the gymnasium. Once inside, some women armed themselves with anything they could find, from riot sticks to broomsticks, and fought their way back out and into further clashes. More than a dozen injured women were taken to the hospital.

Over the next several days, the protest evolved into a full-fledged strike, forcing the laundry to close. State troopers guarded the prison's main gate, where reporters, people from the surrounding predominantly black working-class neighborhood, and activists from throughout the Triangle area gathered each day. Formal negotiations between corrections officials and demonstrators began and ended on Thursday, when prison guards and police officers from across the state used nightsticks and tear gas to quell the protest. Dozens of participants were placed in segregation or temporarily transferred to the state's maximum-security men's prisons.[63] One AFW member wrote in the Triangle Area Lesbian Feminists' newsletter, *Feminary*, "I have witnessed the state arrogance and police violence that caused Attica, the Chicago Police Riots, and now the disturbance at Women's Prison."[64]

Two weeks after the June demonstration, Celine Chenier, Joan Little, and

Karen Galloway shared a stage at the University of North Carolina in Chapel Hill where they addressed a crowd of several hundred about the uprising and retaliation at the prison. Little gave an extemporaneous talk about conditions at NCCCW and urged the audience to pledge their support for her own case and those of "all political prisoners."[65] Those imprisoned at the correctional center reciprocated Little's solidarity. As Chenier later recalled, "All the women there supported Joan a hundred percent. I got stuff in the mail saying 'give my love to Joan.' They would correspond with her."[66] An imprisoned contributor to the July issue of *Feminary* affirmed: "We all are with her even though we are locked up. I believe hell will break loose in the prison if any shit gets flaky at that trial." In August, an incarcerated contributor commented on the acquittal: "Oh wow, sister Joann's victory has renewed old strength and given to the non-believer new strength. . . . If you see her, congratulate her for me and give her many thanks from her struggling comrades. As the power of the people has freed sister Joann, so shall it free the many brothers and sisters of the dehumanizing conditions and treatment we are currently forced to endure."[67]

The imprisoned activists sought to capitalize on the media attention Little's trial brought to Raleigh that summer. Journalists helped to disseminate images of imprisoned women "just like Joan" objecting to their conditions of confinement through individual and collective acts of resistance. Prisoners who spoke to reporters critiqued the structural violence of the institution, from exploitative working conditions to medical neglect, as well as expressing their concern about the welfare and return of those transferred off site or put in solitary confinement as a result of the June uprising.[68] Eighteen of the thirty-three women who were illegally transferred to the men's prison in Morganton brought a class action lawsuit with the assistance of the National Conference of Black Lawyers and AFW.[69] Grasping the window of opportunity the trial afforded, one activist expressed the hope that the suit might be expedited "while the attention is still on the system."[70] The bad press helped to compel officials to agree to modest versions of some of the prisoners' demands, and it prompted them to promise enforcement of an existing law that required female matrons in every state lockup facility that held women. As activist Marjorie Marsh suggested, however, improvements at NCCCW were more cosmetic than substantive: "We did not ask for a softer bed, a night stand, a locker, etc., we asked for life! i.e., someone qualified to operate these various aids to medical attention. A new dental chair with no dentist is useless. . . . New equipment only makes the hospital *appearance* more pleasant."[71] Joan Little's own victory was also circumscribed. Although the defense campaign succeeded in saving her from being killed by the State of North Carolina, it stopped short of securing her freedom. Her appeal on the original conviction for burglary and larceny was heard and denied, and the court ordered her back to NCCCW to continue serving the seven-to-ten-year sentence.

Contesting the "Everywoman" Narrative

One of Joan Little's most ardent supporters was Bernice Johnson Reagon, a civil rights activist and founder of the renowned black women's vocal ensemble Sweet Honey and the Rock. Reagon took to song to chronicle Little's story of resistance and persecution and swell the ranks of the campaign, composing "Joanne Little" in the thick of the mobilization. She began and ended with the same line: "Tell me, who is this girl, and what is she to you?"[72] Who saw Little as a "sister," and on what basis? Framing the Joan Little case as paramount to a women's rights agenda was a key rhetorical strategy on the part of the Defense Fund, which generally encouraged a capacious, multiracial and cross-class understanding of the Little case as "symbolic of the struggle of all women."[73] A fund-raising letter penned by Senator Julian Bond on behalf of the Southern Poverty Law Center described Little's story as "one of the most shocking and outrageous examples of injustice against women on record."[74] While clearly a strategy of expediency in order to save her life, expressions of what sociologist Beth Richie has called the "everywoman analysis" also drew criticism for obscuring the particular social, political, and historical conditions of the case.[75]

The most widely circulated refutation of a universalizing feminist analysis of the case was Angela Davis's essay, "JoAnne Little: The Dialectics of Rape," published in June 1975 in *Ms.* magazine. It was a pressing appeal to the feminist publication's estimated three million readers—particularly white women and those involved in antirape organizing—to dedicate themselves to the campaign for Little's freedom, and, equally importantly, to grasp the "sociohistorical context" of her circumstances. She began the piece with a different black woman's story: that of Cordella Stevenson, raped and murdered by a white lynch mob in Columbus, Mississippi, in 1915. "Little, one of the most recent victims in this racist and sexist tradition, is the cultural grandchild of Cordella Stevenson," Davis declared. Alligood's attack on a prisoner was part of a history of white male sexual violence against black women that reached back to chattel slavery and its cultural and legal construction of black women as licentious and sexually available to all white men. This history, Davis argued, could not be pulled apart from the formidable racist narrative of the black beast rapist that had provided ideological cover for lynching in the Jim

Crow South. Both represented tools in the "arsenal of racism." Little's case afforded yet another object lesson in the "rape-racism nexus": when white feminists treat rape as solely an issue of male supremacy and demand a "get tough" response from the police and courts, they will not only fail to stem rape but strengthen a criminal justice system pervaded by racism and class bias—the same system that ensnares and harms women like Little. Indeed, Davis emphasized that the specificity of Little's social location as a young, indigent, black woman had shaped the trajectory of events, beginning with the circumstances that led to her imprisonment in the Beaufort County jail in the first place. The essay urged feminists involved in the burgeoning anti-rape movement to proceed from a recognition of the reciprocal relationship between "racism and male supremacy" in the context of sexual violence.[76]

Several southern white socialist feminists who participated in the cam-paign, including the well-known antiracist organizer and journalist Anne Braden, seized the opportunity offered by the high-profile case to address the women's movement about what they viewed as the problems inherent in framing rape primarily as an object of criminal justice. The Socialist Women's Caucus of Louisville interpreted Little's story as confirmation of "common knowledge that the worst offenders are white policeman and jail guards—be-cause they are so often in a situation where Black women are at their mercy."[77] Braden, a member of the Louisville group, pointed out in an open letter to other white women in 1976 that, while many white women in and beyond the South joined in the black-led movement for Little's freedom, significantly fewer white feminists were willing to "struggle against the racist use of the rape charge." Braden was among those who had joined a campaign coter-minous with Little's to drop the charges against Delbert Tibbs, an African American man convicted of rape and sentenced to death in Florida despite the fact that the prosecution was not able to place him within 150 miles of the crime scene. White feminists' silence on the Tibbs verdict, along with other concurrent cases involving false charges of rape brought against black men, confirmed for Braden, Davis, and others the contradictions of an ev-erywoman ideology that "tears rape from its social context."[78]

Yet even Joan Little met with ambivalence among southern white feminists, particularly in North Carolina. Out of fear of rebuke by family, employers, law enforcement, or other whites, or their own belief in her guilt, white women involved in local feminist groups did not join the mobilization in meaningful numbers. Support was most robust among the memberships of the leftist Women's International League for Peace and Freedom, which organized its own events to raise funds and awareness, and the relatively new Triangle Area Lesbian Feminists (TALF). Several members of the predominantly white and middle-class TALF joined the black-led group AFW, and the organization circulated information about Little's case as well as the upheavals at NCCCW through its newsletter *Feminary*. The editors urged readers to view Little as a victim of the criminal justice system for asserting her right to defend herself against Alligood's attack, no matter her criminal status or her sexual interests, practices, or past, and more generally for being a woman "who violates their norm (women are passive and submissive)."[79] In this way, they imagined an affiliation rooted in a shared gender and sexual nonconformity between themselves and Little, who lived beyond the pale of both white and black standards of respectability.[80] The political influence of the Little campaign and the NCCCW uprising on organized lesbian feminist communities in the Triangle area was visible in the increasing emphasis they placed on what they described as the "interrelatedness of all oppressions," as well as on differences of "class, lesbianism, age, race, and political affiliation" within the ranks of TALF, *Feminary*, and a third affiliated organization, the Triangle Women's Union.[81] While AFW appears to have disbanded sometime in 1976, that same year TALF collaborated with the North Carolina Hard Times Prison Project to publish a collection of writings, drawings, and poetry by women prisoners involved in the June 1975 rebellion.[82]

Aside from these organizations, public support for Little remained relatively rare among white feminist women in North Carolina. Several white feminists with a history of involvement in racial justice organizing found their way from New York to the Triangle area in the spring and summer of 1975 through their connections to the Attica Fair Jury Project (FJP) and the NAARPR. Among them was Marjory Nelson, a graduate student at the State University of New York, Buffalo, whose daughter had taken a temporary assignment with the FJP. Early in July Nelson attended the first major socialist feminist conference in Yellow Springs, Ohio, where, she recently recalled, "everybody was talking about Joan Little." When her daughter told her about the merely nominal participation of local white feminists in North Carolina, she decided to go see how she could be of use. Particularly dismaying to Nelson was the news that only six of 150 people on the mailing list of the Raleigh Rape Crisis Center responded positively to a mailer about the campaign. During her two-week stay she worked with the NAARPR; her task was to organize other white women to attend the local demonstrations surrounding the trial. In addition to the Rape Crisis Center, she focused her energy on NOW.[83]

While the newly established NOW National Task Force on Rape, as well as NOW's National Task Force on Minority Women, endorsed the campaign as early as the fall of 1974, support for Little among the organization's North

Carolina members remained uneven and tenuous. Fortuitously, a statewide NOW meeting took place in Raleigh on the weekend prior to the start of Little's trial. As card-carrying members of the organization, Nelson and another visiting white feminist organizer from Chicago Women's Liberation attended, determined to recruit local members to take action. The two joined several black women and two dozen white women at a black feminism workshop on Saturday. Aware that the state-level "leadership did not want the issue raised," the group decided to present a resolution in support of Little to the "whole convention" at the final plenary session that evening. Scattering themselves around the room to create the impression that support for Little came from "everywhere," they "swung the organization" in favor of their resolution and a proposal that NOW hold a press conference the next morning to publicly declare its solidarity with Little. Notably, the resolution passed by just one vote. Thirty members assembled on the Raleigh courthouse steps on Sunday, holding signs that read "Black and White Women Together" and "None Are Free Until All Are Free." Despite the small turnout, the NOW-sponsored press conference represented an important victory for the ad hoc group.[84]

Just on the heels of the trial, Susan Brownmiller published her book *Against Our Will: Men, Women, and Rape* to popular acclaim. The feminist activist and accomplished journalist offered a sweeping critique of male violence against women across a multiplicity of historical and cultural contexts that culminated in a clarion call for promoting arrests and stiffening penalties for sexual assault. As one antiracist feminist writer wryly observed of the book's mainstream appeal, "Never before has the media been so friendly to radical feminism."[85] In a review of the book published in *Freedomways*, Angela Davis noted that it was the Little case that piqued her interest in the burgeoning feminist booklist on rape. Although she found that the majority of this literature had a "decidedly racist edge," it was Brownmiller's tome that she found most guilty of both reproducing the racist myth of the black-beast-rapist and disavowing "the systematically ruthless ways in which Black women have been subjected to sexual violence by white men."[86] In the Free Joan Little movement was the analytical brick and mortar for an antirape movement that challenged, rather than collaborated with, racial criminalization.

"Inez Will Be Free because Joan Is Free": The Defense Campaigns Coalesce

On the other side of the country and just a month after Joan Little fled from the Beaufort County jail, a California jury found a thirty-one-year-old Latina woman guilty of murdering her rapist. On March 19, 1974, Inez García

was beaten and raped outside her home in the Central Coast town of Soledad by Miguel Jimenez and Luis Castillo. Once she made it back inside her
apartment, the men telephoned and threatened to kill her if she told anyone
about the assault. Approximately twenty minutes later, García took a rifle
in her possession and went out in search of her assailants, whom she found
beating her roommate nearby. When Jimenez threw a knife at her, she shot
and killed him. García, who was of Cuban and Puerto Rican descent, had
moved to the Monterey County area from New York in 1971 to live near her
husband, who was incarcerated at Soledad prison. She supported herself and
her young son by laboring in the local lettuce fields; in contrast, Jimenez's
"large and influential family . . . owned a labor camp on which many local
workers depended."[87] While in jail awaiting trial, she disclosed to her husband
that she had been raped. On his recommendation she contacted San Francisco activist attorney Charles Garry, "well-known to Soledad inmates for
his radical defense of Black Panthers."[88] Another client of Garry's suggested
the formation of a defense committee.

In August, a small group of feminist activists in the San Francisco Bay Area
set to work building a grassroots campaign. The Berkeley-based Inez García
Defense Committee (IGDC) organized daily carpools throughout the Bay
Area and the coastal cities near the town of Salinas where the September–October trial took place, ensuring that the gallery was packed with supporters,
in addition to the many reporters covering the event.[89] The judge instructed
the jury that the question of whether García was raped prior to the shooting
was irrelevant, ruling out the matter of self-defense. Moreover, when García
took the stand she refused to perform remorse. "I'm not sorry I did it . . . I'm
only sorry I missed Luis [Castillo]," she declared before defiantly walking out
of the courtroom in the face of the prosecutor's cross-examination.[90] Predict-
ably, the jury handed down a verdict of second-degree murder. Afterward
García told reporters: "Nobody gets justice, but I've already won. A lot of
women know about my trial now and a lot of women believe in the action I
took."[91]

Two weeks later, García was sentenced to five years to life in the California
Institution for Women, an hour east of Los Angeles. At the sentencing hearing, "Viva Inez" campaigners turned out in the hundreds. Activists rallied
outside the Monterey courthouse, chanting "Stop Racism in the Courts!" and
"Free Inez! Free All Political Prisoners!" IGDC members read statements of
solidarity from well-known feminist writers such as Gloria Steinem, Simone de Beauvoir, Marge Piercy, and Kate Millett, and organizers such as Flo
Kennedy and Margaret Sloan of the National Black Feminist Organization,
and Maria del Drago, former chairperson of NOW's Task Force on Minority

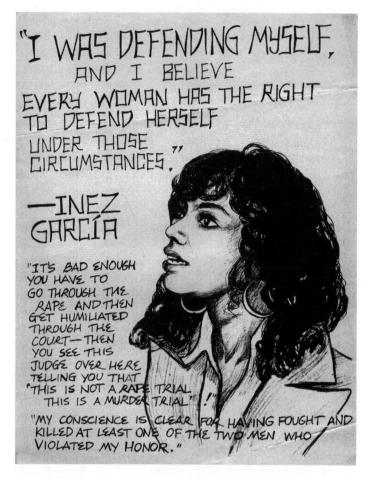

Inez Garcia flier, circa 1975. Louise Merrill papers, Courtesy of the Gay, Lesbian, Bisexual and Transgender Historical Society.

Women and a member of IGDC. The leading sex worker rights activist Margo St. James had challenged her colleagues in the sex industry to make that day "National No-Nookie Day." According to the IGDC, demonstrations took place throughout California and in Seattle; Chicago; Iowa City; Washington, D.C.; and several Florida cities, as well as at the U.S. embassies in London and Paris.[92]

While the Inez García Defense Committee was a predominantly white and Bay Area–based group, the Viva Inez campaign was a much broader, decentralized movement that attracted a wide range of participants and endorsers, including the Third World Women's Alliance, the San Francisco–based Latina feminist organization Concilio Mujeres, the National Conference of Puerto Rican Women, and the San Francisco gay men's group Combating Sexism, as well as members of the Black Panther Party and the United Farm Workers.[93] Like Joan Little's defenders, Viva Inez campaigners as well as García herself encouraged a capacious understanding of the case's social and legal implications and promoted an analysis of the intertwined workings of racism, sexism, and classism within the criminal legal system. A testament to the campaign's high visibility, García appeared on the glossy cover of *Ms.* magazine in May 1975. Inside its pages, Maria del Drago wrote about the collective significance of García's testimony for all survivors of rape, and for Latina survivors like herself in particular: "Inez freed me with her defiance, her shouted insistence on her own right to self-defense. She freed me, and untold numbers of other women, to speak of our own past without shame."[94] A fact sheet circulated in 1976 proclaimed that "her struggle is the struggle of all oppressed people against the racist, sexist, and class-oriented system that exploits and oppresses brown, black, red, yellow, and poor white women, children, and men."[95] Like Little, García spoke to reporters while out on bail about the galvanizing effects of the defense campaign on her own politics: "I have changed in that I want to get involved in helping other women like me—getting involved in the people's movement and trying to help other people. There are a lot of changes that need to be done in the system—not only about rape. We have all types of different oppression, different rapes."[96]

Campaigners increasingly drew links between García's and Little's cases and made them a platform for addressing the politics of gendered imprisonment in the Golden State more generally. In February 1975, roughly 250 activists in San Francisco marched from Union Square to the State Building to present Governor Jerry Brown with more than 2,000 signatures for "justice for Inez García and other women prisoners." The petition demanded that the governor pardon García, recognize a woman's right to self-defense against rape, and establish a "multi-racial women's commission . . . to review the convictions of all women presently serving prison or probation sentences in CA. The cases of women convicted of murder or manslaughter must receive first priority." The demonstrators occupied the building's lobby, filling the space with the sound of their chants, songs, and wooden clackers. An activist with a bullhorn provided an update on the Joan Little campaign. Under threat of arrest, all but thirty-eight protestors left the building after an hour. The thirty-two women and six men remaining were arrested and charged with trespassing, marking the start of their own legal battle that persisted until the end of that year.[97] In Washington, D.C., black and white women affiliated with the D.C. Rape Crisis Center and the newly launched Feminist

INEZ GARCIA   JOAN LITTLE

TWO SISTERS ONE STRUGGLE   DOS HERMANAS UNA LUCHA

"Inez Garcia and Joann Little: Two Sisters, One Struggle/Dos Hermanas, Una Lucha." Poster © Juana Alicia, 1975. All Rights Reserved.

Alliance Against Rape formed the D.C. Coalition for Joan Little and Inez García, which raised funds, collected petitions, and sponsored teach-ins that placed the two women's stories in dialogue. "Inez will be free because Joan is free" became a popular refrain after Little was acquitted in August 1975.

García, too, saw her own and Little's stories as interdependent aspects of the same struggle.[98] With the aid of a new attorney, feminist Susan Jordan, and a steadfast defense campaign, García won her appeal for a new trial in 1976, and in March 1977 she was acquitted on the ground of self-defense.[99] After the victory, Louise Merrill of the IGDC sent a note of thanks to those who gave money to the campaign in which she expressed "hope that Inez's victory will help to hasten a victory for Yvonne Wanrow and for Dessie Woods, whose cases are as important to all women as Inez's was."[100]

Immediately following Joan Little's trial in July 1975, the State of Georgia charged Dessie Woods with first-degree murder and armed robbery. Woods was a thirty-year-old, working-class black woman with two children, as well as an activist and a practicing Muslim.[101] She and her friend Cheryl Todd, also a young, working-class black woman, had traveled from Atlanta to the Georgia state prison in Reidsville on June 14, 1975, to advocate for Todd's brother, who was in need of medical care. Not only were they denied access, but when Todd fainted from heat exhaustion in front of the prison the police arrested both women for public drunkenness (without administering breathalyzer tests) and jailed them for three days. They were hitchhiking home to Atlanta after this harrowing experience when Ronnie Horne, a white insurance salesman impersonating a detective, offered them a ride. He then entrapped them in his car in a deserted area. As Todd and Woods resisted his armed sexual attack, Woods shot Horne with his own gun. The women took money from Horne's wallet and made their way toward Atlanta; they were arrested the next day.[102]

Todd was ultimately given a five-year sentence, of which she served four months, whereas Woods was found guilty of manslaughter and robbery and sentenced to twenty-two years in prison. She was tried in the rural town of Hawkinsville in south-central Georgia in February 1976. The judge had acted preemptively to avoid the media blitz that accompanied Little's trial in Raleigh the previous summer by issuing a court order that severely curtailed media access and activist demonstrations in the courthouse area. Additionally, dozens of state troopers were dispatched to the town to augment the local police force.[103] "The whole trial was unjust," she later told members of the D.C. Rape Crisis Center. "Because I was a black woman they put me in prison. . . . And my case came right behind Joann Little and they would not allow two women to be acquitted in a row."[104]

For the six years until she was finally released in July 1981, the National Committee to Defend Dessie Woods (NCDDW) coordinated local, regional, and national fund-raising, educational, and direct action efforts.[105] The group was formed and led by women and men affiliated with the African People's Socialist Party, a revolutionary black nationalist organization established in the southeast in the early 1970s that advocated a Black Power politics of community self-defense and Pan-African solidarity.[106] Defense committees were formed in Florida, California, Illinois, Kentucky, and elsewhere, and campaigners sold a multitude of Dessie Woods buttons, posters, and T-shirts that generated both necessary funds and visibility. The campaign traversed prison walls, and letters of solidarity came from numerous activists behind bars, including imprisoned women in Raleigh. By 1980, Woods had gained supporters in Paris, London, Berlin, and Geneva.[107]

Activists worked to intervene at Hardwick prison where Woods routinely endured abuse in the form of beatings, death threats, solitary confinement, and denials of mail and visitors.[108] She, in turn, funneled information to her supporters beyond the prison walls about conditions of confinement, including ubiquitous sexual abuse. More than once she was transferred to a mental hospital in Milledgeville where she was drugged and beaten. "They destroyed my records at Central State," Woods told a feminist reporter. "People from all over the world called to have me released and yet there is nothing."[109] In the face of extreme and unrelenting abuse at the hands of authorities, Woods continued to advocate not only for her own freedom but for the rights of other prisoners.

In September 1977, a national day of action brought together hundreds of demonstrators from "virtually every progressive sector" in both Atlanta and San Francisco.[110] The crowd of 500 in Atlanta that marched in the rain to the State Capitol building included former Joan Little campaigners from North Carolina, and Inez García was one of the featured speakers at the rally. In a press release, the NCDDW declared: "After the case of Joann Little, it had been hoped that such cases as Dessie Woods's would diminish. . . . Inez García, Yvonne Wanrow, and Dessie Woods, are three of the cases we know of. There are probably others which have not got the publicity and therefore are unknown to us. . . . The NCDDW is committed to smashing such attacks on Black women once and for all."[111] Feminist organizers with the recently victorious Viva Inez campaign helped to mobilize hundreds to rally for Woods's freedom in San Francisco, where Yvonne Wanrow addressed the crowd.[112]

While Little's attorneys and the Defense Fund had especially encouraged a kaleidoscopic narrative of her case, the NCDDW employed the rhetoric of *colonial violence* against black women and emphasized racial capitalism as the primary contradiction. This frame reflected the African People's Socialist Party's theoretical orientation of "internal colonialism," which held that the United States' political and economic subjugation of black communities within its borders constituted a colonial relationship.[113] Committee members acknowledged and celebrated the fact that securing Woods's freedom would "be a major setback for the reactionary anti-woman attitude and forces," but they also called upon white feminists to adopt a political framework of anticolonial and antiracist solidarity rather than solely one of antisexism.[114] The campaign's rhetoric linked Little, García, Wanrow, and Woods as "colonized women who have shown by their heroic actions that they will no longer tolerate the subjugation of their people, of women, and the tactics used to maintain that subjugation."[115] This narrative not only militated against the everywoman frame but asserted an alternative view: the common bond shared by these four defendants was their victimization by, and resistance to, a colonialist, capitalist, racial state that condones sexual violence as a tool of suppressing U.S. Third World women. Woods also stressed the specificity of gendered antiblack racism in her case: "It's not just that a woman defended herself against a man, it's that a black woman defended herself against a

"Free Dessie Woods! Smash Colonial Violence" poster, 1978. Courtesy Lincoln Cushing/Docs Populi Archive.

white man. This is a racial issue. By convicting me, the U.S. government said that a black woman does not have the right to self defense."[116] These political and rhetorical differences from the Little and García campaigns combined with the media blackout of the trial help to explain why Woods received far less mainstream media attention and attracted far fewer white liberal feminist supporters. The unwavering revolutionary black nationalism of her defense committee did, however, resonate with Yvonne Wanrow's claim of self-defense against white settler-colonial patriarchy.

Although Wanrow was arrested before Little, García, and Woods, her legal appeals extended through 1979, and her case attracted growing notoriety and activist energy through its connection with the others. Wanrow, a member of the Sinixt/Arrow Lakes Nation of the Colville Federated Tribes, was living in Spokane, Washington, in August of 1972 when she fatally shot a white man who broke into her friend's home. William Wesler, who had a prior arrest for child molestation, had recently threatened her nine-year-old son with a knife and sexually assaulted her friend's seven-year-old daughter; the two women had contacted the police earlier that day but were told there was nothing to be done. Significantly smaller in size than Wesler and on crutches and in a leg cast at the time of his break-in, Wanrow maintained that she acted instinctively to protect the children in the house when she fired her own registered gun first at Wesler and then at his friend, who sustained a minor injury: "When Wesler headed towards one of the children, I screamed for help. Wesler, who was drunk out of his mind, turned, lurching toward me. So I shot him. I immediately called the police to report what had happened. They arrested me and put me in jail. I feel all I was guilty of was being a mother who loves her children."[117] In May of 1973, she was convicted of first-degree assault and second-degree murder by an all-white jury and sentenced to twenty-five years in prison.[118]

The trial took place in a general climate of virulent anti-Indian racism in eastern Washington and against the particular backdrop of the American Indian Movement's (AIM) seventy-one-day occupation of the small town of Wounded Knee in South Dakota, the site of a U.S. Army massacre of several hundred Lakota people in 1890. The occupation was front-page news during her jury trial, and the coverage was overwhelmingly disparaging of the occupiers. "All Native Americans were seen as militants and extremists," Wanrow later recollected.[119] By 1973 AIM had identified criminalization and imprisonment as priority concerns. It was the first activist organization to rally behind Wanrow and work with her and her family to launch a national defense campaign. Through her involvement with AIM she came to secure representation from feminist lawyers with the New York–based Center for Constitutional Rights (CCR) in 1975.[120]

Over the next several years a growing number of Native American, feminist, and civil rights activists joined the effort, and defense committees emerged in the Pacific Northwest, California, Midwest, and Northeast. Out on bond throughout the six-year appeals process, Wanrow headed her own defense campaign. She traveled around the United States meeting with activists and participating in solidarity events, not only for herself, Inez García, and Dessie Woods, but also for several other lesser-known black and indigenous women in comparable legal predicaments, and for imprisoned AIM leader Leonard Peltier.[121] In 1976 she took part in the historic International Tribunal on Crimes Against Women in Brussels, and in 1978 she joined a delegation of indigenous peoples in the Americas that traveled throughout West Germany, helping to circulate her story and mobilize supporters internationally.[122] "I'm fighting as a woman, I'm fighting as a Third World person, and I'm fighting as a Native American," she told audiences.[123] She regularly stressed that her case was "not unique" but rather "just one blatant example of brutality that has been perpetrated towards Native people in this country."[124]

Wanrow and her multitude of supporters achieved a victory in 1977 when the Washington State Supreme Court affirmed her right to claim self-defense.

Yvonne Wanrow at a political prisoner speak-out in New York City, November 1975. Photograph © Bettye Lane.

After the court denied a request for a rehearing, however, the prosecutor brought new charges. Facing another trial in Spokane, Wanrow and her team expanded their organizing efforts there. Under the modest sponsorship of CCR, former Joan Little campaigner Marjory Nelson and her lover at the time, Polly Taylor, traveled to Spokane in 1977 to drum up additional support for Wanrow among non-indigenous people. The two helped to build an eclectic defense committee that included religious leaders, civil rights activists, students, and teachers with the goal of demonstrating to Spokane residents and eventually a jury that "this isn't just an isolated little case." Wanrow gained another powerful base of support in Women of All Red Nations (WARN), a coalition of more than two hundred activists, many with ties to AIM, that formed in 1978 and made reproductive rights, imprisonment, and environmental degradation key priorities.[125] As a prospective prisoner, Wanrow was fighting not only for her right to protect her children but to continue parenting them, and in this way her case dovetailed with contemporaneous campaigns by WARN and other indigenous women against forced and coercive sterilization and the removal of indigenous children from their families and communities.[126] In 1979 Wanrow decided against enduring another trial and accepted a plea bargain that reduced her crime to manslaughter in self-defense. She was sentenced to five years of probation.[127]

I STAND IN SOLIDARITY WITH THE STRUGGLE OF MY PEOPLE AND WITH ALL SISTERS WHO LIKE JOANN LITTLE AND INEZ GARCIA CHOOSE RESISTANCE OVER PASSIVITY.

YVONNE WANROW

Yvonne Wanrow poster, 1976. Courtesy Lincoln Cushing/Docs Populi Archive.

As in the other three defense campaigns, activists pressed for a rethinking of violence to include the structural and institutional forces that produced the moment in which Wanrow killed Wesler. As one organizer put it: "In Yvonne's case, the refusal of the police to provide protection was an act of violence. The continuing effort of the prosecutor to go after her—after 5 years—is an act of violence. A prison system that locks up a Joanne Little for theft for 8 years and lets Watergate criminals go free is violent. . . . We need to go a lot further back into the chain of violence to reach the real source."[128] For many campaigners, Wanrow's struggle for her freedom symbolized indigenous resistance to the institutional racism and sexism of the criminal legal system, as well as to the gendered structural violence of the settler colonial relationship between the United States and indigenous communities within its borders.

The Antiviolence Pedagogy of the Campaigns

The four defense campaigns unfolded amid the burgeoning of the rape crisis movement and quickly came to figure in contentious debates among activists about the future of "feminist-controlled" antiviolence programs. As Nkenge Touré of the Washington, D.C., Rape Crisis Center later reflected, the mobilizations for Little, García, Wanrow, and Woods became an extended self-defense classroom that "brought out a lot of the contradictions, the conflict" surrounding intersections of race and gender and interpersonal and state violence within the feminist antirape movement.[129] Joan Little was indicted for murder just two years after feminists founded the country's first rape crisis centers (RCCs) in Washington, D.C., Seattle, and the San Francisco Bay Area. By 1974, hundreds of community-based antirape projects were in operation, and questions of "co-optation" and "professionalization" already loomed large. Many activists worried that the requirements and expectations imposed on feminist antiviolence programs as conditions for the receipt of public funds pushed them toward a more hierarchical organization directed by credentialed staff and toward a more exclusive focus on direct service provision rather than advocacy. The most readily available government funding source for RCCs was the sprawling and deep-pocketed federal LEAA agency, the linchpin in the dramatic expansion of the state's capacity to surveil, police, and imprison across the 1970s.[130] Perspectives on criminal justice sponsorship and partnership increasingly diverged, stimulating heated debates in feminist conferences, newsletters, and anthologies. The self-defense cases of women of color offered activist critics of a criminalization-centered antirape movement a "moral and ideological discourse" that emphasized the capacity of the criminal legal system to facilitate rather than stem violence against women of color and advocated an intersectional, rather than an everywoman, analysis of rape.[131]

Sexual violence had first become a focal point of the predominantly white women's liberation movement around 1970, and the question of "self-defense for women" saturated early conferences and speak-outs by rape survivors.[132] Many activists reasoned that it was "justifiable to deal with the problem in extralegal fashion."[133] San Francisco Women Against Rape (SFWAR), for example, initially saw little promise in criminal legal responses since the "police, laws, and courts all have been set up to serve the ruling men in power in the country." In addition to establishing a hotline, emergency shelter, and community education program, the group "envisioned community self-defense as a militant, collective alternative to reliance on the police."[134] Other organizations made self-defense training their sole focus, offering affordable classes taught by feminist instructors. Self-defense teachers and students saw women's physical fear and sense of vulnerability as an important basis of "the power structure between men and women." Training in self-defense focused not only on "growing strong" but also on transforming the "mind set" of powerlessness.[135] The feminist press celebrated women who fought back against their sexual assailants. One of the most iconic images of the feminist antirape movement, designed by Betsy Warrior, a member of the

Boston-based radical feminist group Cell 16, boldly proclaimed that physical self-defense tactics that "disarm rapists" are necessary to "smash sexism," indicating that self-defense training was more than a "liberal strategy" of individual empowerment.[136] As historian Pamela Haag has argued, "this strain of the feminist imagination followed a certain leftist and militant logic of . . . insurrectionary violence."[137] For example, the feminist newspaper *off our backs* reported in 1974 that "Dallas women . . . are pursuing an alternative means to ensure justice, both swift and righteous, for rape or attempted rape victims" by forming Women Armed for Self Protection, which promoted "immediate and drastic retaliation against all rapists."[138] Importantly, however, these forms of antirape militancy did not necessarily translate into a total rejection of legal reforms. Rather, militant self-defense was more often conceived of as a grassroots alternative to abusive men and an unresponsive state.[139]

In 1974, a small collective of primarily white and working-class women inaugurated the *Feminist Alliance Against Rape Newsletter* (*FAAR News*). Its editors envisioned a forum for dialogue and strategizing among feminist activists who were concerned that "the rape issue was being co-opted" by government funders and law-and-order politicians, as well as by "non-feminist professionals."[140] In 1978, FAAR merged with the battered women's movement's National Communications Network and the Alliance Against Sexual Coercion to become *Aegis: Magazine on Ending Violence Against Women*. *FAAR News* and *Aegis* played a central role in bringing the cases of Little, García, Wanrow, and Woods to bear on feminist antiviolence discourses in the mid-to-late 1970s. This counterpublic space provided readers with consistent coverage and analysis of these cases and a forum for debate about criminalization, imprisonment, and state cooptation into the mid-1980s, when *Aegis* ceased publication.

FAAR founders dedicated their second issue to the theme of incarceration, in which they contended that "encouraging women to prosecute a rape [helps] to reinforce the legitimacy of the criminal justice system. . . . We should begin to actively seek alternatives."[141] An article on García's unfolding trial followed one written by the founders of Prisoners Against Rape, a self- and peer-education program organized by a group of black men convicted of rape and incarcerated in Lorton, Virginia. The decision to problematize criminal justice interventions provoked a critical response from SFWAR, published in the next issue, wondering whether *FAAR News* was "feminist in name only" since it advocated "male rapists' needs and rights."[142] Clarifying their stance, the editors responded: "What we are saying is that we don't believe increasing the conviction rate will lead to the elimination of rape. Therefore, we question whether we as feminists should devote our energy to

Dessie Woods on the cover of *Aegis*, July–August 1979. From
the Women's and LGBT Periodicals Collection, Sallie Bingham
Center for Women's History and Culture, Rubenstein Library,
Duke University.

winning individual convictions, or whether we should examine alternatives
which may have a greater influence on society as a whole."[143]

FAAR and the D.C. Rape Crisis Center were both instrumental in forming
the D.C. Coalition to Support Inez García and Joan Little.[144] Activists utilized
the newsletter to help galvanize national attention and financial support for
both Little and García—and later for Wanrow, Woods, and others—by calling on its burgeoning readership to publicize the cases through their local
networks. Moreover, they highlighted what they viewed as the race and class
implications of these self-defense cases for feminist antirape agendas. A fall

1974 editorial argued that the criminal legal system offered few prospects for redress, let alone transformational justice. Police officers, prosecutors, and judges base their decisions on their "white male experience," and "because men are rarely, if ever, subject to rape, they cannot identify with the feelings of a rape victim."[145] In concrete terms, this analysis translated into taking a neutral stance on prosecution when counseling rape victims, as well as a thematic focus in the newsletter on developing "alternatives to the criminal justice system."[146] In February 1975, the coalition sponsored a teach-in featuring Yvonne Davis, a core member of the Joanne Little Defense Fund, and Lourdes Miranda King of the National Conference of Puerto Rican Women. Both speakers situated the cases in broader frames of economic marginalization, racialized and gendered images, and structures of state violence. An *off our backs* reporter wrote: "The experiences of the speakers with the police and courts hardly pointed to these institutions as our source of defense. Yet, when a woman in the audience told us that she had been receiving phone calls from a man threatening her with murder, the first response was 'call the police,' followed by an air of bewilderment which hung over the rest of the conference."[147] This observation suggests the ways the Little and García cases were thought to exemplify what was wrong with "the system," as well as pointing to the yawning gap between theorizing alternatives to the law enforcement system and successfully putting them into practice.

Informed by these critiques, the largely white, socialist feminist group Santa Cruz Women Against Rape (SCWAR) utilized *FAAR News* to circulate its "Open Letter to the Anti-Rape Movement" in 1977. Following Angela Davis and other critical voices, the organization lambasted a higher conviction rate for rape as a misguided goal: "The system is racist through and through. Prisons are used to keep *all* Third World people down. We cannot turn our backs to the racism of the system when a Black man is being prosecuted and expect that same racism not to be used against Joann Little, Yvonne Wanrow, Inez García, etc."[148] Several years later, artists and activists affiliated with SCWAR produced a docudrama entitled *The Confrontation: Latinas Fight Back Against Rape*. Promoted as a representation of "what can happen when women unite against racist and sexist violence," the film features the story of a young Chicana teacher, Marta, who is raped by a white male acquaintance after a party. In the face of police indifference, Marta and her friends confront the man at his place of work.[149] The Inez García Defense Committee also took aim at liberal feminist proposals to expand the number of women police officers, arguing that "they will just throw a few more poor white and Third World men in jail, and leave rapist upper-class and white men free to terrorize us as always."[150] In addition to confrontations, these two groups promoted self-defense classes, increasing community-based sanctions through public education, and publicizing descriptions of men known to have raped women.

Nonstatist and antistatist antiviolence strategies were the subject of the 1981 activist anthology *Fight Back! Feminist Resistance to Male Violence*, a 400-page sourcebook of essays, letters, interviews, poetry, photography, and art by nearly sixty activist contributors that crossed lines of race, class, sexuality, and gender expression. Its capstone is a directory of approximately 1,200 organizations, including crisis centers, shelters, self-defense schools, newsletters, and legal aid organizations. Coeditors Frédérique Delacoste and Felice Newman forthrightly asserted in their preface: "We cannot unwittingly become tools of racism by looking to the state for solutions to male violence. We must be conscious that giving unlimited power to a racist, classist and violent judicial system perpetuates our own oppression." Several contributors assessed the challenges, strategies, and significance of prisoner defense work, and one remarked that antiviolence activists "too often forget all the women inside [prison] who never found a shelter or who could not wait for the larger changes." Others described examples of direct-action-style, militant interventions: groups of feminists who would move into an abused woman's home to pressure the batterer to move out or to prevent his return; small squads that stalked men who stalked women, "effectively intimidating the man into a change of behavior"; guerilla groups that posted detailed descriptions and the names of men who raped women in the perpetrators' neighborhoods; "dyke patrols who have been known to respond on the spot, tailing a man on foot or by car, verbally embarrassing him or roughing him up"; and ad hoc groups like the one fictionalized in *The Confrontation* that accompanied survivors to face their sexual assailants at their homes or places of employment.[151]

As various defense committees organized events that linked the cases of criminalized rape resisters to those of political prisoners from the Black Power, Red Power, Chicano/a, and Puerto Rican independence movements, discourses of "self-defense for women" and "racist and political repression" interacted and influenced one another. Some antirape activists came to view all women imprisoned for killing their sexual assailants and batterers as political prisoners, regardless of their political histories or the particular circumstances of their cases.[152] FAAR member and self-defense instructor Sue Lenaerts wrote in *FAAR News* in 1976 that "attitudes reflecting sex, race, and class bias cloud the judgment of both judges and juries. It is likely that only in a society where rape did not exist could a woman get a fair trial for a self-defense killing. Thus, by this contradiction, we consider women found guilty of murder in a self-defense case to be political prisoners." As greater numbers of women faced conviction for using lethal violence to defend themselves from rape and battering, Lenaerts argued, it was the responsibility of antiviolence activists to accept the "politically crucial" challenge of increasing the scale and efficacy of prisoner defense work.[153] Noting that the primary organizational vehicle for addressing this contradiction was the "individual defense committee or defense fund," she suggested forming a "national network for the defense of all women who are prosecuted for killing their attackers" that would thread through crisis centers and "self-defense schools." At the same time, Lenaerts acknowledged that most centers were "ill equipped to fully shoulder the responsibility of a full fledged defense committee." Indeed, FAAR's unsuccessful attempt in 1974–1975 to build a membership-based organization of local "feminist-controlled anti-rape projects" alongside and in relation to publishing its newsletter suggests that the "hand to mouth" existence of most rape crisis centers limited their engagements with these high-profile cases and the urgent and broad-based coalition-building efforts they engendered.[154]

Members of SFWAR were divided over these issues. Cofounder Diana Block reflected: "We had to come up with a way to balance a woman's right to determine her own options with our own political distaste for the police as the enforcement arm of a system we abhorred. We decided to explain what a woman's options were and, if she decided to go to the police, we would accompany her in order to assure that she was correctly treated. Many women ended up choosing this option and inevitably this drew us into dealing more and more with the police."[155] News of Inez García's upcoming trial surfaced just as members were grappling with this predicament in 1974. While Block expected that SFWAR would participate actively in the defense campaign, the demands of direct service provision left some staff wary that publicly endorsing García would compromise "the fragile working relationship" the agency was cultivating with law enforcement.[156] Ultimately, according to Block, very few SFWAR affiliates worked on the campaign. For her and a number of other radical white women in the San Francisco Bay Area who joined the mass defenses of Little, García, Woods, and Wanrow, these campaigns moved them to channel their feminist activism into antiracist, anti-imperialist solidarity organizing.[157]

Unlike SFWAR, the D.C. Rape Crisis Center (RCC) functioned as a hub for defense work in the mid-to-late 1970s. "We always intentionally lifted up these cases of women of color who lived at the intersection of violence against women and the criminal justice system," former RCC director Loretta Ross recently recollected.[158] In addition to its involvement in the D.C. Coalition to Support Inez García and Joan Little, the RCC became a significant ally to the National Coalition to Defend Dessie Woods. Staff members traveled to Georgia to visit Woods in prison and helped disseminate information about her case in *Aegis* and through local public education efforts and direct actions. After her release in 1981, the RCC sponsored Woods's visit to Washington where she participated in Anti-Rape Week, an annual political education event organized by the center.[159] Significantly, the RCC avoided LEAA funding and sustained a central focus on grassroots organizing and coalition-building into the early 1980s. A group of primarily young, white women involved in the local women's liberation movement founded the organization in 1972, and several of them went on to establish FAAR. By the RCC's third year of operation, Black Power feminist and community organizer Nkenge Touré had become the center's first paid director, and over the next several years increasing numbers of women of color joined the staff, board of directors, and volunteers.[160] In 1980, the center's leaders identified the Little, Woods, and García cases as having pivotally "exposed the injustices of the criminal justice system as it related to Third World Women," and, at the same time, galvanizing more women of color to join the rape crisis center movement.[161]

By and large, however, few RCCs appear to have incubated, anchored, or even endorsed these campaigns. These institutional silences likely had diverse and multiple causes, ranging from racism and class bias to the depoliticizing effects of crisis center–criminal justice collaborations and the rigorous demands of everyday crisis intervention work. Rather than emanating from within the rape crisis center movement, the four defense campaigns pressed this movement to engage in critical and reflexive dialogue about the path forward for RCCs, given their increasing entanglement with the criminal legal system.

From defense committee meetings to the pages of *Aegis*, activists discussed the daunting challenge of how to mobilize support for countless other women who had been criminalized and imprisoned for fighting back not only against strangers, acquaintances, and authorities, but also against their intimate partners. By the late 1970s, a feminist movement for battered and abused women—distinct from, but modeled upon, the rape crisis movement—spanned the country, comprised of local programs providing emergency shelter, peer-based counseling, and other forms of emotional and practical support to women negotiating or leaving abusive relationships and organized through statewide and national alliances. Radical feminist newspapers and newsletters did their part to educate readers on the ubiquity of such cases by regularly pairing updates on García, Little, Wanrow, and Woods with news of

Cassandra Peten Defense Fund poster, circa 1978. Courtesy
Lincoln Cushing/Docs Populi Archive.

numerous other women—who were primarily of color or indigenous, more
than occasionally disabled, and almost always working class or poor—in
comparable circumstances who were supported by a local defense committee. Wanrow's feminist attorneys from the Center for Constitutional Rights
helped to launch the Women's Self-Defense Project in 1978, whose affiliates
"consulted on more than 100 cases, most of them involving women charged
in the deaths of an abusive intimate partner or ex-partner."[162]

One particularly salient, albeit short-lived, attempt at scaling up defense
campaign organizing was the Bay Area Defense Committee for Battered
Women (BADC). Formed by women activists with ties to U.S. Third World,
women's, and gay liberation movements, this multiracial feminist group

sought to trade on the visibility and pedagogical work of the four well-known defense campaigns to generate support for other women imprisoned for killing their intimate partners. The committee understood the activism these cases engendered as having helped to situate "third world women in a pivotal position—to forge the links between the white women's movement and third world communities."[163] BADC intended to coordinate multiple defense campaigns for women of color, especially battered women who endured "the repressive power of the state machinery," seeing these campaigns as a strategic pressure point for "transforming our intimate social relations as well as the society we live in."[164] The group initially came together around the case of Cassandra Peten, a young African American mother and shipyard worker from Oakland who was convicted of killing her abusive husband. Over its two-year existence, the organization coordinated education, publicity, and fund-raising efforts for more than a half-dozen battered women of color who had injured or killed their intimate abusers. Ultimately, this work proved too difficult to sustain with a relatively small group and on a meager budget. In an application to the progressive foundation Vanguard, project coordinator Amma Price acknowledged the transformative power of the "few celebrated cases" of women of color who killed their sexual assailants, yet emphasized that the four represented only the "mere tip of the iceberg."[165]

* * *

In the mid-1970s, the cases of Joan Little, Inez García, Dessie Woods, and Yvonne Wanrow engendered powerful grassroots campaigns that illuminated the interconnections of gendered violence and racial criminalization. The four cases had cumulative effects, not merely because of their "calendrical coincidence,"[166] but primarily because activists made analytical, rhetorical, and practical connections among them. These mobilizations functioned as coalitional spaces where multiple liberation movements interfaced and cross-fertilized. Indeed, defense organizing provided key opportunities for developing coalitional consciousness and practice.

Campaigners drew on the moral power and momentum afforded by Little's cause, which itself built upon a long history of black resistance to sexual exploitation and racialized punishment. The campaign combined a civil rights organizing tradition of collectively resisting interracial sexual violence with Black Power critiques of policing and imprisonment, and fused multiracial feminist rebukes of respectability with the embrace of sexual self-determination and autonomy. Despite the meaningful differences between Little's case and those of García, Wanrow, and Woods, activists insisted that the four—and the multiple forms of violence they represented—should be linked together.

The debates and initiatives that grew out of these organizing efforts reveal the great urgency that propelled activists and the difficulties they confronted as they attempted to develop a social movement strategy that prioritized those most vulnerable to violence in its myriad structural, institutional, and interpersonal forms. As the following chapters demonstrate, the organizing and theorizing propagated by the cases of Little, García, Wanrow, and Woods stimulated feminists to consider alternatives to reliance on the coercive power of the state to protect women against sexual and domestic violence. They also informed and spurred feminist organizing efforts that confronted the institutional violence of imprisonment itself.

2. Diagnosing Institutional Violence

Forging Alliances against the "Prison/Psychiatric State"

They write us up, or send us to seg [solitary] if we refuse to take a needle of drugs that destroy our minds and spirits.
—Carol Crooks (1975)

Ultimately, then, our goal is to dismantle the whole violent system.
—Coalition to Stop Institutional Violence (1977)

On October 1, 1977, nearly a thousand demonstrators took to the streets of downtown Boston to protest the planned opening of a center for "violent women" at a Massachusetts state mental hospital in Worcester. Organized by a local alliance called the Coalition to Stop Institutional Violence (CSIV), the march culminated at the Boston Common in front of the State House, where spokespersons outlined their objections to the center. Worcester State Hospital, which was already the subject of investigation for its mistreatment of incarcerated patients, would function as an institutional outpost of the Massachusetts Correctional Institution at Framingham (MCI-Framingham), the state's women's prison. The center was the latest in a series of proposals issued by the state's departments of corrections and mental health to establish a secure facility for Framingham prisoners deemed a threat to themselves or others. Activists focused their protest on correctional authorities' opaque use of the designation *violent*, suggesting that it veiled the highly political nature of the center. They argued that the center would be used discretionarily against imprisoned women who protested their conditions of confinement, and that women of color and lesbian women would be especially vulnerable.

Coalition to Stop Institutional Violence rally at the statehouse in Boston, October 1, 1977. Photograph © Ellen Shub 2018.

Critiquing the euphemistic language of "treatment," they contended that dissident prisoners might be subject to a range of physically and mentally invasive behavior-modification techniques, including psychotropic drugging, sleep deprivation, electroconvulsive shock, and psychosurgery. Turning the language of "violent women" on its head, the demonstrators carried signs that read "Stop the Violent Unit!" and "Stop Violence Against Women."[1]

CSIV grew out of an organizing effort in 1973–1975 that prevented the Department of Corrections from building a similar maximum-security unit for women prisoners at Bridgewater Hospital for the Criminally Insane, a men's institution notorious for flagrant abuses. The coalition represented a coming together of diverse organizations from across Greater Boston. At its center was a coordinating body of feminist women who crossed lines of race, class, sexuality, and direct experience with institutionalization. The metropolitan area was a hub of several widespread, translocal movements that challenged custodial, medical, and intimate violence and emphasized strategies of self-help and mutual aid, including movements for battered women, mental patients' liberation, radical feminist health care, and prison reform and abolition, making it a particularly good place to forge an alliance to confront what CSIV activists called the "prison/psychiatric state." In their work to challenge the expansion and medicalization of women's imprisonment in the Commonwealth of Massachusetts, CSIV leaders reached beyond the grassroots and radical left to engage sympathetic legislators and civil liberties advocates seeking to ameliorate prison conditions. This breadth proved instrumental to the coalition's success in 1978 in preventing the creation of the Worcester center.

This chapter offers a detailed study of CSIV's political organizing and theorizing. Through its "practical activities of social contestation," the coalition advanced a critique of the power of the carceral state and of psychiatry to define legitimate and illegitimate violence, and normal and deviant gender behavior.[2] Resonating with political scientist Cathy Cohen's call for a "politics of deviance," the group's rhetoric, writings, and campaigns centered on those who were the most stigmatized and most vulnerable to state and structural violence, refiguring these women's modes of "acting out" as signifying agency rather than pathology.[3] Activists blended existing analyses of the prison and the mental hospital as irredeemable institutions designed to confine racial and economic "Others" with a critique of the policing and punishment of nonnormative forms of gender and sexual expression. This politics combined the multiple strands of political thought represented by the alliance's diverse membership. As activists fought to "stop the violent unit," they elucidated the structural and social conditions of violence in imprisoned women's lives, ranging from racial, economic, and gender oppression to the process of institutionalization itself. CSIV's understanding of incarceration as gender violence also propelled it to advocate noncarceral, socially transformative approaches to preventing interpersonal violence against women.

The proposal for a satellite unit for unruly MCI-Framingham prisoners epitomized a broad national trend toward medicalizing the techniques used to control those incarcerated in state and federal prisons in the late 1960s and 1970s. As prisoner uprisings proliferated throughout the country, corrections professionals increasingly championed and relied upon segregation, psychotropic drugs, invasive psychiatric treatments, and the threat of transfer to another institution to maintain control. Dissident women prisoners and their allies in California, New York, North Carolina, West Virginia, and elsewhere fought these practices and challenged the construction of units analogous in form and function to those proposed in Massachusetts. After examining this national context, the chapter then turns to the particular case of CSIV, tracing the coalition's origins and formation, detailing its successful campaign against the Worcester center, and exploring its theoretical insights about the medicalization of violence and punishment in women's prisons. It concludes with a look at how CSIV activists debated and formulated ideas about alternative structures of safety, accountability, and healing in a post-capitalist, postprison society, as well as attempted to put their radical politics into practice in their organizational culture.

The "New Rebellion": Behavior Modification in National Context

The attempts by the Massachusetts departments of corrections and mental health to establish formal pipelines between MCI-Framingham and the state's high-security mental hospitals reflected a broader categorical shift in corrections policy making toward the expansion and medicalization of administrative segregation in what historian Alan Eladio Gómez calls the 1960s-1970s "dialectic of prison rebellions and repression."[4] Accounts of this transformation have primarily focused on men's prisons. The case of MCI-Framingham and several other initiatives demonstrate that women's prisons also served as sites through which the logics and practices of behavior modification were developed and contested in the 1970s. Prison activists in a variety of locales criticized behavior-modification programs for women, objecting to both their involuntary character and their harmful consequences. At stake was the propensity of corrections officials to enlist biomedical knowledge and practice in the service of quelling dissent and eroding constitutional safeguards for prisoners' rights.

Medical humanities scholar Jonathan Metzl has shown that cultural and political discourses about racial protest were imprinted on medical diagnoses of mental illness in the 1960s and 1970s, and "new 'psychochemical' technologies of control merged with concerns about the 'uncontrolled' nature of urban unrest."[5] As activists involved with the black liberation, Puerto Rican independence, antiwar, and Red Power and Brown Power movements were sent to jails and prisons on charges linked to their political activities, prison administrators registered an acute sense of concern that prisoner dissent was aided and abetted by imprisoned radicals and the larger social movements with which they were affiliated.[6] For example, the warden of McNeil Island Federal Penitentiary in Washington State, speaking at a 1969 meeting of the American Correctional Association, identified the "fomenters" of what he called the "new rebellion" as "former prisoners, militants, far-out liberals, subversives, and even a few clergymen, educators, and social workers."[7] Prison administrators identified special control units (which in some cases were called "alternative program units") and attendant behavior-modification regimens as a frontline strategy for suppressing dissent. Black, Latina/o, and indigenous prisoner organizers were routinely targeted for isolation and treatment. Prison psychiatrists underwrote the expansion of these practices by investing control units with medical expertise. As sensory deprivation, psychotropic drugs, and electroconvulsive shock therapy eclipsed the psychoanalytic and education-based approaches that had predominated in the 1950s, they "muddled commonplace distinctions between what constituted punishment, rehabilitation, and torture."[8]

Behavior modification contributed to what the sociologist Alondra Nelson refers to as the "biologization of violence" in the late 1960s and early 1970s.[9] In 1967, psychiatrist Frank Ervin and neurosurgeons William Sweet and Vernon Mark, all affiliated with the Boston-based Neuro-Research Foundation, argued in the *Journal of the American Medical Association* that, in addition to the structural inequalities that spurred the black urban uprisings of the mid-1960s, "brain disease" was also to blame for "urban violence."[10] In 1971, these proponents and practitioners of psychosurgery received a combined total of $600,000 ($3.6 million in today's dollars) from the National Institute for Mental Health and the Department of Justice's Law Enforcement Assistance Administration to "develop a way to identify and control persons who commit 'senseless' violence, as well as those 'who are constantly at odds with the law for minor crimes, assaults and constantly in and out of jail.'"[11] That same year, Boston newspapers reported that geneticists from Massachusetts General Hospital had collected fingerprints and blood samples from selected women prisoners at MCI-Framingham as part of a screening program designed to detect women's genetic capacity for violence.[12] Although the racial identities of these prisoners were not disclosed, the fact that black women were disproportionately incarcerated and disproportionately subjected to punitive segregation meant that the study reflected the recent and historical context of medical experimentation on black prisoners and pathologization of blackness in American science and medicine.[13] On the West Coast, a broad coalition led by Black Panther Party members prevented the creation of a similar research initiative at the University of California at Los Angeles in 1972.[14]

As women's prison organizing burgeoned around the country, activists—captive and free—mobilized against behavior modification and institutional transfers similar to those proposed in Massachusetts. At New York's Bedford Hills prison in the mid-1970s, administrators regularly labeled black activist prisoners "mentally ill" and "violent" and targeted them for segregation and transfer. Carol Crooks, a well-respected leader among her peers, successfully sued the prison in August 1974 for violating her right to due process when she was beaten by a group of guards and thrown in solitary confinement that February.[15] Shortly after she returned to general population on the court's order, she allegedly struck another prisoner and resisted when a team of guards attempted to take her back to solitary. The officers "drug her down the hallway, like a rag, and literally threw her down these concrete steps," remembers fellow prisoner Cindy Reed.[16] The following day, women protested in a nonviolent takeover of two buildings and a recreation yard that later became known as the "August Rebellion." Administrators, who alleged that the prisoners took seven officers hostage for several hours, called in more than 200 state troopers and guards from neighboring men's prisons to quash the demonstration. In the aftermath, Crooks and twenty-two women who participated in the rebellion were transferred to the Matteawan Complex for the Criminally Insane where they were locked down for twenty-three hours a day and "forced to take high doses of behavior modifying drugs such as Thorazine and Prolixin."[17] Matteawan served as a Bedford Hills outpost again in 1976 when the warden obtained permission from the New York DOC to classify ten activist prisoners as "mentally disturbed."[18] As sociologist Juanita Díaz-Cotto suggests, "the medical establishment not only stigmatized women who rebelled as being mentally ill, but also perpetuated further psychological and physical abuse through forced medication."[19] In 1977, members of the Brooklyn-based group Women Free Women in Prison reported that Bedford had implemented a new behavior modification initiative known as the Satellite Program: "Behind locked steel doors, out of reach, hearing and sight from the general population, . . . the administration places women they label 'mentally disturbed,' 'dangerous,' etc."[20]

California women prisoners and their allies fought the creation of an Alternative Program Unit at the California Institution for Women (CIW) in the mid-1970s. Located roughly forty-five miles east of Los Angeles, CIW was the state's sole women's prison and the nation's largest. Officials proclaimed that the unit would "provide more structure, control, and special program attention for those who have difficulty adjusting to general rules, guidelines and expectations at the prison,"[21] while opponents charged that it would "segregate women who do not conform to prison authorities' definition of a proper prisoner or a well-behaved woman."[22] Moreover, the protestors expressed concerns about the malleability of classifications like disruptive, difficult, or maladjusted, and the possibility that women of color and lesbian women would be disproportionately targeted. Nearly a thousand people affiliated with women's and prisoners' rights groups traveled to Sacramento in March 1976 to attend a hearing on the prison, stage a rally outside the capitol building, and deliver a petition with more than 2,000 signatories, including 400 of the 700 CIW prisoners. Demonstrators packed the hearing and, as one local reporter put it, the crowd "turn[ed] what might have been a fairly dry hearing on proposed rules to govern California prisons, into a lively, three-hour discussion of conditions at CIW."[23] At the rally afterward, several former prisoners addressed the crowd, including Lia Stahrlite, who described how imprisoned activists had organized a "successful strike at CIW in 1973" that led to the shutdown of a similar behavior modification facility called the Intensive Program Unit.[24] The groundswell in Sacramento reflected the activist base cultivated through the Santa Cruz Women's Prison Project (SCWPP), a program that brought hundreds of volunteers from the Greater Bay and Los Angeles areas into CIW between 1972 and 1976 to teach university-level courses and facilitate other educational and cultural programs. The project also organized monthly gatherings to cultivate a support network among women paroled to the Bay Area and those affiliated with SCWPP.[25]

In addition to battles at state prisons, the National Prison Project of the American Civil Liberties Union (ACLU) spearheaded a campaign in 1976 to oppose the construction of a maximum-security unit at the Federal Reformatory for Women at Alderson, West Virginia. The prison held the dubious distinction of caging the country's "most dangerous women."[26] Despite this provocative reputation, many of those it confined were District of Columbia residents, nearly all of them African American, serving long sentences for low-level offenses because crimes committed in the capitol city counted as federal violations. Others who found themselves at Alderson, such as black liberationist Assata Shakur, were never convicted of a federal offense but had been transferred there from prisons in other states in accordance with the terms of an interstate compact agreement; such transfers typically took place under the justification that a prisoner required a higher level of custody than was available at the sending institution.[27] In a front-page story in the *New York Times* in 1977, spokespersons for the Federal Bureau of Prisons claimed that the nationwide expansion of MSUs was correlated with an increase in the number of women committing violent crimes, yet the FBI's own statistics showed that this rate was declining since the early 1970s. Upon its opening in 1978, the MSU's function was swiftly made clear. While there were no transparent criteria in place for release from the unit, a policy statement from the bureau stated explicitly that a record of previous "involvement in subversive organizations" was just cause for preventative detention, and ACLU researchers documented a pattern of officials transferring prisoners who filed grievances or otherwise fueled dissent. When she arrived at Alderson in April 1978, Shakur was immediately placed in the MSU: "It was surrounded by an electronic fence topped by barbed wire, which in turn was covered by concertina wire (a type of razor-sharp wire that had been outlawed by the Geneva Convention). It was a prison within a prison."[28] ACLU staffers, along with grassroots activists and several of the unit's former prisoners, mounted enough public pressure to shut down the unit later that year. Campaigners highlighted what they viewed as the "actual purposes" of MSUs: to quell prisoner activism by removing political organizers from the general population and by threatening more severe conditions of confinement for those who might question or challenge institutional authority. This kind of retribution, the NPP efficaciously argued, was a clear violation of prisoners' constitutional rights.[29] Among the cosignatories of this campaign to close the Alderson unit was the Coalition to Stop Institutional Violence.[30]

"At Framingham Prison, the Women Fight Back"

Massachusetts' women's prison sits at the edge of the town of Framingham, roughly thirty miles west of Boston. Founded in 1877, it was one of the first separate women's institutions in the country. For more than ninety years, it—at least partially—reflected the aspirations of nineteenth-century women reformers who fought for the creation of gender-segregated prisons to reform so-called fallen and wayward women through a program of "maternal uplift, in bucolic, cottage-style reformatories that offered a strong dose of domestic training."[31] Until security was tightened in the 1960s, MCI-Framingham's thirty-acre campus of brick buildings looked like a girls' reform school, with its unbarred living quarters, modest fencing, and nearly all-female staff. Under Miriam Van Waters, who served as superintendent from 1932 to 1957, education and job training programs and counseling and medical services all expanded considerably, as did the institution's indenture program through which women worked for substandard wages in nearby laundries, restaurants, and homes during the daytime.[32] Her platform of "maternal justice" and relaxed custodial regime attracted numerous liberal admirers and boosters, yet it increasingly drew sharp criticism from conservative corrections department officials and politicians. According to historian Estelle Freedman, several converging developments at mid-century paved the way for a more punitive Framingham in the post–Van Waters era. These forces included a rising rate of incarceration among African Americans in the Northeast that fueled white anxieties about "black criminality"; an increasingly popular narrative—stoked by the Cold War "lavender scare"—about female homosexuality running amok in women's prisons; and the rising number of women serving sentences for "crimes against property and the person, rather than against public order."[33] By the 1960s, staff had received training in using tear gas inside the walls; a maximum-security program had been implemented; programming and medical care had suffered cuts; and physical isolation (often called either "administrative segregation" or "solitary confinement") was a more common response to prisoners' acts of noncompliance.[34]

The origins of the proposed center for violent women at the Worcester State Hospital lay in a turbulent period at MCI-Framingham that began in the wake of the 1971 Attica prison uprising. Like their counterparts in numerous prisons and jails, Framingham prisoners organized to demand better treatment from their keepers. The Massachusetts prison contained roughly 130 women in the early 1970s, more than a third of whom were African American. Prisoners' concerns about the lack of health care and poor labor conditions were compounded in December 1971 when a new superintendent, Gloria Cuzzi, expanded the number of male custodial staff and enforced dress codes much more vigorously than her predecessor. These inaugural administrative acts of what activist prisoners would come to call the "Cuzzi regime" prompted nearly half of the imprisoned women to participate in a sit-in, out of which grew a prisoner grievance council. Just a few weeks later, correctional officers found groups of women partaking in unauthorized New Year's celebrations and drinking "home-brew" in their living quarters. In response, administrators called in roughly fifty guards from the state's men's prisons to help turn Framingham upside down in search of contraband. By evening on New Year's Day, thirty people had been locked in the prison's maximum-security cells and another ten were transferred to the Worcester County House of Correction, including several of the grievance council members.[35] Rather than quell rebellious behavior, these transfers ignited prisoner organizing.

In March 1972, more than fifty prisoners, the majority of whom were black, staged a strike against the administration. It began on a Monday when activists occupied Cuzzi's office. Despite the peacefulness of the sit-in, the superintendent once again dispatched several dozen guards from the men's prisons to Framingham.[36] Over the next several days, the protesters convened in the gymnasium where they itemized their grievances and drew up proposals for institutional change, making decisions by consensus.[37] At a press conference, spokespersons alleged that the facility's medical provider refused to treat people experiencing urgent symptoms on the grounds that they were hysterical rather than physically ill, while encouraging and performing medically unnecessary hysterectomies. As a major prison industry was sewing flags, one prisoner wryly asked, "How long must we be Betsy Ross?" Another key point of concern was harassment and brutality from male guards. Tina Williams testified, "I was in maximum and witnessed seven male guards beating up a woman."[38] Other grievances outlined for the press included paltry education and job training programs and censorship of the Black Panther Party's newspaper and other publications deemed "politically inflammatory."[39] Among the group's chief proposals were that their "shipped sistuhs be returned"; medical care, educational, and job-training programs be improved; the recently hired male guards be removed; additional Spanish-speaking and African American staff be hired; and finally, that the new superintendent be dismissed.[40] "We've been patient for a very long time but now we're tired of going unheard," Candace Bonds told reporters.[41]

MCI-Framingham prisoners challenged the conditions of their confinement in the context of a nationwide wave of prison protest that was symbolized as well as fueled by the Attica rebellion.[42] Nearly every one of Massachusetts' prisons was shaken by demonstrations in 1971 and 1972.[43] Men at MCI-Norfolk, MCI-Walpole, MCI-Concord, and Suffolk County House of Correction at Deer Island all staged strikes, most often to demand greater access to visitors and more opportunities for education and parole and to protest abuse by guards. Just prior to the March sit-in at Framingham, a riot at Walpole caused an estimated $1.6 million in damage to the facility. Weeks later, 200 state troopers descended upon MCI-Norfolk to put down a protest involving roughly forty prisoners.[44]

Just as the New York prison massacre inspired activists inside and outside of prisons to declare that "Attica is all of us," it moved politicians and corrections officials in Massachusetts and elsewhere to vow to prevent "future Atticas." In 1972, an unprecedented consensus was achieved in the Commonwealth among a sizable cross section of politicians, high-ranking corrections officials, and community activists that a comprehensive overhaul of corrections policy was needed. With the wind at his back, the moderate Republican governor, Francis Sargent, unveiled a reform agenda at the end of 1971 that included new safeguards for prisoners' rights, a new vision of replacing the state's custodial institutions with a broad system of "community corrections centers" and halfway houses, and a new corrections commissioner. Many activists saw Sargent's appointment of John Boone as commissioner as especially promising, for Boone was a nationally known reformer who had voiced support for doing away with large prisons and expanding opportunities for parole. He was the first African American to assume control of a major state department of corrections. During the first half of 1972, Boone worked with the governor's office and in consultation with the Ad Hoc Committee on Prison Reform, a collection of representatives from nearly two dozen community organizations, to develop legislation that promised a substantial expansion of work and education release and furlough programs.[45] The Ad Hoc Committee was a motley, sprawling, and politically diverse group composed of people one member described as "lawyers, ministers, writers, poor people, and most importantly ex-cons."[46]

Despite this breadth of support for a sea change in corrections, the reform movement—and Boone in particular—encountered implacable opposition from corrections officials. Over the course of his brief eighteen-month tenure, Boone contended with several superintendents and a multitude of correctional officers who viewed his decarcerative philosophy and proactive support of prisoners' rights to due process and grievance proceedings as threats to their authority, safety, and long-term job security. Close to 200 guards from MCI-Framingham, MCI-Walpole, and MCI-Bridgewater staged a "sickout" on the heels of the spate of protests in March and April to register their grievances against Boone.[47] The commissioner also battled with Superintendent Cuzzi that spring over disciplining dissident prisoners and her desire to expand Framingham's maximum-security unit. That June, he fulfilled one of the activist prisoners' demands when he fired the warden. The reform agenda met even greater organized resistance on the part of guards after Governor Sargent signed the Omnibus Prison Reform Act into law in July. Many refused to implement the new policies Boone ordered, helping to generate and disseminate an image of the system as out of control and plagued by violence and unrest.[48] This strategy temporarily backfired on the guards at Walpole in the spring of 1973 when they walked off the job *en masse* to protest reforms, leaving the prisoners at the maximum-security prison to fend for themselves. As Jamie Bissonette Lewey (Abenaki) documented in her book, *When the Prisoners Ran Walpole*, for a three-month period the prisoners practiced collective self-government and enacted their own reforms: they instituted a part-time work schedule, created new educational programs, and opened up the prison to community observers.[49] Several years later the Massachusetts Research Center assessed the implementation of the Omnibus Prison Reform Act and found that the legislation had only marginally succeeded in ameliorating conditions in the system.[50]

In this volatile political context, MCI-Framingham officials began pressing for the creation of an off-site facility that had the capacity to "deal with" a small number of "violent women" prisoners in a "total and planned sense." At the same time, initially unbeknownst to the corrections commissioner, they transferred several prisoners deemed "serious management problems" to Bridgewater State Hospital for the Criminally Insane, which was a regular practice of their counterparts in the state's men's prisons.[51] Situated on the sprawling 1,400-acre grounds of MCI-Bridgewater, a maximum-security facility an hour south of Boston, the hospital was the sole correctional facility under the purview of both the Department of Corrections (DOC) and the Department of Mental Health (DMH). Bridgewater was the largest of the state's correctional institutions, housing a population of approximately

1,000 in the early 1970s. The complex included an alcohol and drug treatment center, a treatment center for "sexually dangerous persons," a diagnostic center for pretrial psychiatric observation, a protective custody unit for those deemed at risk of harm from other prisoners, and segregation units for prisoners transferred from other institutions. In its 1974 report on the conditions facing the small number of youth detained there, the Massachusetts Office for Children explained Bridgewater's function as providing "maximum security to persons whom not only our communities, but even our institutions, refuse to tolerate."[52] The deplorable conditions at the maximum-security hospital had recently been made infamous by filmmaker Frederick Wiseman's 1967 documentary exposé, *Titicut Follies*.[53] As the chairperson of the Walpole Lifers Group wrote in the *Boston Globe* in 1972, "the thought of a ride down to Bridgie is enough to knock your spirit right out of you."[54]

The Women's Prison Collective, a feminist group that grew out of the MCI-Framingham protests, helped to politicize the transfers by emphasizing their illegality: MCI-Bridgewater was defined by statute as an exclusively male institution. Collective members mobilized prisoners' rights and feminist organizations in the Boston area to fill the courtrooms when judges heard the transferees' appeals. Although the courts ultimately ruled in favor of the prisoners, the DOC and DMH formalized a partnership in the fall of 1973—characterized by those opposed to the transfers as an "unholy alliance"—when they established a task force to explore the possibility of rewriting the institution's statutes so as to construct a new maximum-security unit for women prisoners at Bridgewater. The unit would be used for pretrial examinations, determinations of competency to stand trial, hospitalization of those labeled mentally ill, and segregating women from Framingham on an "emergency basis."[55]

Among those who supported the prisoners' appeals was Sunny Robinson, a thirty-year-old white civil rights and feminist activist who had recently been hired as director of education and training at the Prison Health Project, which grew out of the prison reform initiatives of 1972 and received funding from the federal Office of Economic Opportunity (the infrastructural center of what remained of 1960s War on Poverty programs). When the task force solicited the Prison Health Project's approval for the Bridgewater women's unit, Robinson and several other progressive staffers strongly objected, but to no avail. As Robinson recently recalled, "not knowing exactly how to address this, but feeling that it had to be challenged immediately, I simply said: 'over my dead body!'" Her outspokenness led to her dismissal, which prompted five other disaffected staff members to quit in protest shortly thereafter. She remembered that she "immediately went home and started identifying people in the women's movement, in the prison movement, in the mental health justice movement, and at the ACLU to come together and find a way to learn more about this proposal and to figure out some strategies to try and address what they were proposing."[56]

Between 1974 and 1975, the nascent coalition sponsored public demonstrations, petition drives, and behind-the-scenes lobbying efforts in its campaign to defeat a series of bills that proposed authorization and allocation of funds for the maximum-security unit at Bridgewater. This grassroots mobilization benefited from both the relationships built through the 1972 Ad Hoc Committee on Prison Reform and the hospital's severely compromised reputation, soured not only by the criticisms that followed the revelations of *Titicut Follies* but also by three recent federal lawsuits brought against the institution on behalf of incarcerated patients. The Bridgewater unit failed to gain the backing of the state legislature. The next year, however, DOC and DMH officials produced an alternative proposal for a center for "violent women" at Worcester State Hospital, stimulating their opponents to officially declare themselves a "Coalition to Stop Institutional Violence."[57]

Forging a Coalition in Greater Boston

The proposal for a center for women at Worcester State Hospital galvanized a broad cross section of activists in Greater Boston to join ranks to challenge this fusion of the "therapeutic state" and the carceral state.[58] Notably, these activists coalesced within a racially and economically stratified metropolitan area, carved out by two decades of "white flight" and discriminatory housing policy and market practices, and exacerbated by an acute period of national economic stagflation in the 1970s.[59] The Bridgewater and Worcester center struggles unfolded in the wake of the 1974 court-ordered desegregation of the city's schools and the resulting groundswell of white backlash euphemistically known as the "Boston busing crisis."[60] The individuals and organizations that composed CSIV occupied diverse social and structural positions in relation to the medical and legal establishments and the criminal justice system. They also represented a wide span of activist sectors, including movements for battered women and women's health, decarceration and prisoners' rights, and psychiatric deinstitutionalization. Reflecting this social and ideological diversity, CSIV's antiviolence politics braided together multiple strands of political thought.

During its years of peak activity (1975–1978), CSIV functioned as a network of roughly fifteen groups and several hundred people that transected the "women's, mental patients' liberation, and prison abolition movements."[61]

A smaller core group of twelve to twenty that coordinated and carried out the everyday work of the organization was limited to self-identified feminist women; some members represented the coalition's affiliated organizations, and others made CSIV their primary activist endeavor. The core group, which fluctuated over time, included ex-mental patients and former prisoners; African American, Asian American, and white women (including a significant number of white Jewish women); lesbian, transgender, and heterosexual women; and working-class and middle-class women. The handful of women who remained most involved from beginning to end were predominantly white, lesbian-identified paraprofessionals in their twenties and early thirties.

CSIV drew leaders, supporters, and political inspiration from several different local feminist networks. Among the most influential were grassroots activists in Cambridge, Dorchester, Roxbury, Somerville, and the South End who founded numerous shelters and safe-home projects, rape crisis centers, and "women-controlled" free or low-cost health clinics as part of their attempts to challenge what they viewed as negligent, paternalist, or abusive public systems. By 1976, Transition House in Cambridge and Casa Myrna Vasquez in Boston's South End had opened their doors to battered women and their children, and both the Boston Area Rape Crisis Center and the Women's Community Health Center were in their third year of operation. These institutions, and the translocal movements of which they were a part, championed radical egalitarianism, peer education, survivor and layperson expertise, and mutual aid, even though these values could be only partially realized in practice.[62] Many of these projects intersected through the Cambridge Women's Center, which was also a "home base" for CSIV's leadership core. Located in a building owned by Harvard University, the center grew out of an International Women's Day march in 1971 that culminated in a takeover of the vacant space. It provided a meeting place and other resources to a variety of groups that emerged from the primarily white and college-educated or student base of women's liberation in Cambridge and, to a lesser extent, from multiracial, working-class neighborhoods of Cambridge and Boston.[63] The coalition gained endorsements from the Prostitutes Union of Massachusetts, the socialist feminist organization Wages for Housework, and the Committee to End Sterilization Abuse, which worked to curb coercive practices that denied women their right to bear children and were used disproportionately against poor women, women of color, and indigenous women.[64]

Boston was the point of origin for the Combahee River Collective (CRC), a renowned black lesbian socialist feminist group that formed in 1974. Though the collective did not formally join CSIV, members of the CRC and CSIV worked together in several coalitions in the second half of the decade. CRC cofounder Barbara Smith and CSIV's Sunny Robinson and DeCourcy Squire were active in a multiyear defense campaign for Ella Ellison, a poor African American woman from Dorchester who was falsely convicted of murder in 1974 for her alleged participation in a robbery that resulted in the death of a police officer. Ellison spent several years at MCI-Framingham before her conviction was overturned.[65] Both Smith and Robinson also joined the defense campaign for Willie Sanders, an African American man falsely accused and later exonerated of raping several white women in 1979. Additionally, CSIV and CRC members worked together in Boston's Take Back the Night Coalition and in the Coalition for Women's Safety, a broad alliance of community organizations that formed in response to a spate of twelve murders of black women in the winter and spring of 1979. Through its community organizing work and its widely circulated writings, particularly "A Black Feminist Statement" (1977), the CRC's analysis of "interlocking" oppression and critique of single-issue politics made an indelible imprint on feminist discourse on violence in and well beyond Greater Boston.[66]

Groups such as the Boston Bail Project (BBP), Families and Friends of Prisoners, the Prison Book Program, and the Worcester Correctional Change Group all anchored the CSIV network in local prisoner support and anti-incarceration efforts.[67] The BBP was a founding organizational member of CSIV. The collective had a day-to-day mission of raising funds to post bail for women awaiting trial and a long-term vision of ending pretrial detention. As studies showed that the likelihood of conviction and prison time both increased exponentially for people who could not afford bail, the BBP identified pretrial detention as a key economic and constitutional injustice that disproportionately affected women of color.[68] When the group formed in 1973, its attention was focused on the Charles Street Jail in the central city where women arrested in Suffolk County were held. A few months later, a U.S. district court ruled in favor of a class of pretrial detainees, finding that the jail conditions violated constitutional rights and ordering the facility closed within three years.

In an effort to expedite the process of emptying the decrepit jail, the DOC opened a new Awaiting Trial Unit (ATU) at MCI-Framingham where women detainees in Suffolk, Middlesex, and Essex counties would now be incarcerated.[69] While most spent a week or less there, the BBP estimated that roughly one-fourth of the hundreds of women who passed through the ATU in a given year spent upward of six months at the prison. Isolated from Framingham's general population, they sat idle with no programming, little recreation time, and little clarity on their circumstances. One former ATU detainee said, "I think it was the waiting and not knowing what was going to happen was the worst."[70] BBP members began visiting women at the ATU each week in the spring of 1974, informing people of their legal rights and collecting and publicizing information about conditions there. In January 1980, the collective organized letter-writing campaigns to public officials concerning the lack of social workers at the ATU. The group also called attention to a reported sexual assault by a corrections officer on a woman whom he was driving from the courthouse to the prison.[71] Although the group remained committed to a two-pronged strategy of raising bail for as many individual women as possible and making the conditions at Framingham's ATU widely known, members argued that "the problem is not in the conditions of any particular pre-trial jail, but in the existence of pre-trial detention itself." For DeCourcy Squire and other members of the BBP who dedicated themselves to the campaign against the Worcester center, the prospective unit posed a direct threat to their constituents in the ATU since "already there has been an influx of women at the ATU labeled 'mental health referrals.'"[72]

Among CSIV's closest organizational partners was Families and Friends of Prisoners, founded in 1974 by community activists in Dorchester, a working-class, multiracial area of Boston and a stronghold of civil rights activism since the 1960s. A mutual aid organization led by working-class and poor black and white women, the first issues of Families and Friends' monthly newsletter, *Doing Time*, made it plain that it was "not a group of social workers. We are people who have loved ones imprisoned in Massachusetts and who suffer everyday because of it."[73] The group grew out of an earlier organization called Citizens and Relatives Concerned about Prisons.[74] Families and Friends' principal goals included "helping other families and friends to survive during the time of incarceration" and supporting former prisoners through a range of volunteer-powered, grassroots-funded initiatives that together were known as the Survival Center. Between 1974 and 1982, these programs included transportation to the state's many prisons, a child care cooperative, a clothing cooperative, a clearinghouse on prison regulations and prisoner rights, peer counseling, and assistance in finding housing and work. Feminist economic justice activist Kip Tiernan, board member of Families and Friends and founder of Rosie's Place, a shelter for homeless women, aptly captured the significance of the Survival Center several years later at an International Women's Day rally: "One of the peripheral perks of hanging out with such assorted folks in Dorchester are the new ways of looking at old problems, and out of that comes the *alternative structures*. They are the structures we create, because if the existing ones don't work too well for all of us, *we* help create new ones."[75] In tandem with the self-help arm of the organization, Families and Friends spearheaded and joined campaigns for prison reform and public education efforts.[76] Staunchly abolitionist, the group was a sustaining force in the local radical prison movement; most important, it ensured that those intimately harmed by prison had a place at its forefront.[77]

Ironically, it was a federally funded program that afforded CSIV members a direct channel of communication with Framingham prisoners during the Worcester campaign. Beginning in September 1975, the U.S. Department of Health, Education, and Welfare funded the University of Massachusetts Boston—Framingham Prison Project (FPP), an eighteen-month pilot program that coordinated a range of activities prisoners had identified as needed, from university courses and educational release opportunities to prenatal workshops and a creative writing program.[78] Connie Breece, a recent graduate of UMass Boston and a core member of CSIV from 1975 on, was the lead staffer for the project and a crucial conduit between the coalition and the prison. Participants in the writing program collectively produced several plays as well as a short-lived magazine entitled *Turning Point.* "Our main objective is to let you know what is happening to and with the minds of imprisoned bodies (mainly ours)," wrote the magazine's editor B. De'Love, "so enter our world for a short time. You may find answers here that aren't available anywhere else. Come on! Come in Peace and go with KNOWLEDGE!" Under the auspices of UMass Boston, hundreds of people from Greater Boston visited the prison during the years that CSIV campaigned against the Worcester unit—as co-participants in seminars, as audience members for women prisoners' poetry readings and plays, and as cultural workers who taught writing or performed their music. Framingham prisoner Ella Ellison's case was already a local cause célèbre by the start of the FPP, and in 1976, the well-known antiwar militant and lesbian feminist Susan Saxe was sentenced to the prison for her part in a 1970 bank robbery in which a Boston police officer was killed.[79] As Breece remembers, "it was just on everybody's tongue in terms of getting out to MCI-Framingham. . . . And we would load busloads of women from Central Square and drive out to the prison for the performances."[80]

Additionally, the coalition found allies at the local office of the American Friends Service Committee (AFSC), a pacifist Quaker organization committed to prison reform. From its inception in the Progressive Era, the organization advocated on behalf of imprisoned conscientious objectors; by mid-century, its advocacy work had expanded to include everyday prisoners. In the 1970s, the AFSC sponsored a voter registration project in Massachusetts prisons, as well as promoting a nationwide call for a moratorium on new jail and prison construction.[81]

Finally, CSIV reflected the vibrant local movement for deinstitutionalization. The coalition drew leaders and supporters from the Mental Patients

Cover of *The Turning Point* magazine, 1976. Courtesy of the
University Archives & Special Collections Department, Joseph P.
Healey Library, University of Massachusetts–Boston: Framingham
Prison Project records.

Liberation Front (MPLF), a grassroots self-help organization founded in
1971 that engaged in media production, peer-directed support, and direct
action organizing. Judi Chamberlin, a renowned leader (and later grassroots
historian) of the mental patients' liberation movement and a self-described
ex-mental patient, joined both MPLF and CSIV upon her arrival in the city
in 1976. She helped to start the Elizabeth Stone House in the Jamaica Plain
section of Boston, a "patient-controlled" residential alternative to state-spon-

"Stop Forced Drugging of Psychiatric Inmates!" Poster © Rachael Romero, San Francisco Poster Brigade, 1978.

sored institutions for women and their children and another organizational member of the CSIV network.[82] Organizations such as MLPF, New York's Mental Patients Liberation Project, Portland's Insane Liberation Front, San Francisco's Network Against Psychiatric Assault, and Philadelphia's Alliance for the Liberation of Mental Patients formed a decentralized, primarily urban-centered network that advocated for the self-determination of current and former mental patients and the abolition of psychosurgery, electroshock therapy, and locked institutions. This far-flung movement convened every year beginning in 1973 at the Conference on Human Rights and Psychiatric Oppression. Notably, MPLF hosted the annual conference in Boston in 1976. In addition to the San Francisco–based *Madness Network News* ("all the fits that's news to print"), Somerville's own *State and Mind* (formerly *Rough Times*) helped to circulate activists' analyses of the "psychiatric state" and campaign updates, including those of CSIV. Chamberlin later reflected, "We used the term 'mental patients.' We said that we have to use that term, not in the sense that we acknowledge that there's an illness, but in the sense that that's what the world calls us. . . . Not embracing the ideology behind it, but embracing the term."[83] These groups extended the scrutiny of psychiatric practice that emerged in the broad countercultural context of the 1960s and 1970s.[84] As historian Michael Staub has argued, "A significant portion of the populace . . . believed madness to be a plausible and sane reaction to insane social conditions, and that psychiatrists served principally as agents of repression."[85] The view that madness was social and structural rather than individual and biological prevailed in the leftist milieu of Greater Boston.

The Campaign to "Stop the Violent Unit"

In the spring of 1976, DMH and DOC officials successfully placed their proposal for the center for violent women at Worcester State Hospital on the agenda of the State Senate's Ways and Means Committee. It called for a three-to-one ratio of custodial and medical staff to prisoners and projected an operating budget of approximately $60,000 per prisoner, per year ($250,000 in today's dollars). Although the committee approved an initial $150,000 for a diagnostic team of Worcester State Hospital employees to screen prisoners for "clinical pictures of violence," it made approval of additional monies for the center contingent on the creation of an advisory body that included members of concerned community groups.[86] When their expected invitations to join the new body failed to materialize, CSIV members declared it "a public relations arm of DMH."[87] Nonetheless, they faithfully attended the advisory committee's public meetings and used the question-and-answer periods to express their opposition to the center. In order for the advisors to genuinely serve as women's advocates, coalition representatives contended, they would need the institutional power to ensure that "all other alternatives have been exhausted"; to guarantee that civil liberties were safeguarded, including access to a grievance process; and to participate in the hiring and firing of staff. CSIV demanded that the advisory group undertake a holistic examination of the sources and causes of imprisonment: "financial pressures, lack of a job, lack of education . . . and the many socio-economic and racial influences on who a person is. . . . The woman's whole situation has got to be looked at if

"Stop the Unit for Violent Women!" poster, 1977. From the
Coalition to Stop Institutional Violence Records, Northeastern
University Archives and Special Collections.

she is to be truly assisted. Real help has to support her 'personhood,' not just
reshape her to DMH's version of a 'good woman.'"[88]

In addition to their tenacious presence at advisory committee meetings,
activists served the governor with a petition bearing 1,500 signatures in June
1977, and in October they staged the mass demonstration at the Boston
Common to denounce the "violent unit." Several hundred of the nearly 1,000
protestors joined CSIV the following day on the University of Massachusetts
Boston campus for a series of educational workshops and strategy conver-

sations.[89] The latter included discussions about the prospect of building a national network of groups around the country working to challenge similar units and a gathering of "organizers working . . . in the areas of battered women, rape, media violence, and sexual harassment in the workplace, and violence against institutionalized women."[90] In December, CSIV held another demonstration on the State House steps opposing a planned appropriation of nearly a half-million dollars for renovation of the maximum-security cells at Framingham and construction of twenty new cells. Activists sardonically pointed out that if the expansion proposal were approved there would "be no need for the Worcester Unit."[91]

Officials acknowledged that the delay in the construction of the center, which was originally scheduled to open in March 1977, was due in part to the growing grassroots opposition.[92] While direct action, petition drives, disrupting public meetings, and gaining media attention forced public debate on the Worcester center's validity and future, the coalition's most effective point of leverage proved to be Massachusetts' Ten Taxpayer Group mechanism. This tool guaranteed self-organized groups of ten taxpaying citizens the right to a public hearing with officials at the Department of Public Health (DPH) who oversaw the state's Determination of Need (DoN) process. Like all proposed government-sponsored health-related projects, the Worcester center required a DoN certification before it could be built. CSIV seized on this opening in the public policy making process and benefited from the left-leaning orientation of the DPH. The coalition facilitated the organization of several taxpayer groups, and each was granted a hearing.

These public hearings collected the testimonies of former prisoners, advocates, and activists and produced a significant body of evidence for denying the DMH its certification. For example, DeCourcy Squire, a member of the Boston Bail Project who had formerly been incarcerated in Ohio for her antiwar activism, carefully detailed her "own experiences and observations" to substantiate her claim that "psychiatric labeling and transfers can be used . . . to cover up institutional abuses."[93] In addition to her own story, Squire recounted that of a seventeen-year-old pregnant woman who refused to undress for the guards conducting her admissions examination and was subsequently transferred to Bridgewater. This nonviolent act of resistance to the treatment of her body as state property was enough to get her labeled dangerous. Squire went on: "The women DOC and DMH are talking about are women who are anxious and women who are angry—because the conditions of our lives have caused anxiety and anger. The Worcester unit is not in any way a solution for this."[94] Former prisoner Lillian Clarke's testimony confirmed the persistence of the mid-century narrative of the aggressive prison lesbian and its severe consequences for masculine women, explaining that she was sent to a maximum-security cell on the grounds that she was "dangerous to innocent young girls" and "unfit for the prison population." In her own words, "the only rule I had ever broken was that . . . I was masculine looking."[95] A taxpayer group of feminist antiviolence activists from western Massachusetts challenged the conflation of all forms of resistance and self-defense with violence by suggesting that "asking a woman to stop being violent when she is constantly the focus of daily violence, within and outside of existing institutions is the same as asking her to commit suicide."[96] MPLF members pointed out the potential for nonconsensual drug experimentation on the unit's prospective prisoner-patients. Among the central themes of this testimony were the need for alternatives to institutional settings and the provocative statement that "not only is there not a need for a center for violent women, there is a very real danger in creating one."[97] The DPH sent multiple pages of questions to the center's proponents in November 1978, but DMH officials failed to respond. Shortly thereafter, the Worcester center was removed from the state budget.[98]

CSIV's campaign against the proposed Worcester center not only achieved a tangible victory, but also generated a counter-narrative of gender, violence, and incarceration. Members of the core group communicated their ideas in a variety of media sources, including opinion editorials in the *Boston Globe* and *Boston Herald* and interviews and feature pieces in activist periodicals such as *Sister Courage, Aegis: Magazine on Ending Violence Against Women,* and *Science for the People.* Pieces published in the alternative media often spoke beyond the pragmatics of opposing the Worcester center to argue for a critical rethinking of the social constructions of criminality and mental illness through the lenses of capitalism, racism, patriarchy, and heterosexism. Taken together, this collection of writings and propaganda traced the convergence of the medicalization and criminalization of sexual and gender deviance, the racial and economic politics of imprisonment, and intimate violence against women in the material realities of women's lives.

The coalition understood initiatives like the Worcester center as part of a long historical alliance between medicalization and criminalization.[99] A leaflet explained, for instance, that "our opposition to this unit is part of our opposition to prisons and mental hospitals in general. . . . They are extreme and brutal manifestations of the racism and classism of our society, and . . . inevitably reflect and serve the interests of the patriarchal, capitalist organization of society, which is, most basically, what we are fighting."[100] In a signature piece titled "The Truth Behind the Bars," the group posited that "there have never been clear lines between who can become labeled a 'criminal' and who can become labeled a 'crazy'"; both "correctional and psychiatric prisons" share an objective of "individual adjustment or pacification" to the existing social order.[101] In the case of the Worcester center, CSIV saw these parallels transfigured into powerful intersections: by importing the "medical model" into the prison setting, corrections authorities would be granted the mechanism to indefinitely extend the sentences of so-called violent women under the auspices of professional medical opinion, thereby bolstering the indeterminate sentence that many prisoners and their allies were fighting to destroy. Indeed, during the 1970s, a wide range of political actors—from those on the left who sought more transparency and less coercion to those on the right who sought harsher penalties—helped to produce a sea change away from the indeterminate sentence, and the therapeutic rehabilitative ideal upon which it rested, and toward determinate sentencing.[102]

The very behaviors that correctional and mental hospital authorities sought to curtail were conceptualized in CSIV's analysis as legitimate responses to institutional harm. Moreover, subjection to biomedical abuse might, in turn, actually "increase disruption" and make for a "self-fulfilling prophecy."[103] Coalition writers suggested that the act of labeling worked to detach an individual's behavior from her social, political, and institutional context, including her prescribed treatment. "Crazy" behaviors were strategies for navigating and surviving the conditions of confinement in prisons and mental institutions. "Any crazy behavior," wrote Arlene Sen of MPLF and CSIV, "is really connected in some way to the issues of power and powerlessness— sexism, racism, class, heterosexism, ageism, etc."[104] CSIV drew upon Phyllis Chesler's nationally acclaimed trade book, *Women and Madness* (1972), which had lent empirical credibility to feminist critiques of psychiatry in the early 1970s. Chesler's research confirmed that women comprised the majority of the institutionalized psychiatric population in the United States, and that diagnosis and treatment were shaped by race, class, gender presentation, and sexuality. The "especially narrow definitions of appropriate behavior for women" that mental hospitals and prisons enforced rendered any expressions of independence or autonomy as nonnormative and dangerous: "For example, inappropriate behavior for an inmate may include political activism or organizing activity, refusal to accept medication, refusal to accept arbitrary orders, or refusal to do prison work."[105] Protest was constructed as a masculine activity and thus doubly circumscribed.

News of CSIV's campaign traveled through the alternative press to reach imprisoned activists at Bedford Hills, prompting three black women to write a statement of solidarity with CSIV that was published in the widely circulated feminist periodical *off our backs*: "We feel that a [behavior modification program, or BMP] is not to help the women but to tear down the resistance. It's a mind destroying program that the administration puts sisters in who resist the oppression of the system. Anyone who resists is unbalanced and in mental disarray to them. . . . Our main purpose for writing this letter is because all of the sisters involved in this letter was in a BMP. We feel that if the unit for Violent Women in Massachusetts goes through . . . we most definitely will suffer."[106]

Outside the walls, CSIV observed, "it is not insignificant that the perpetrators of the proposed Worcester unit try to dismiss the vocal opposition . . . by labeling us 'a bunch of dykes.' . . . As women begin to organize and chip away at the system which oppresses us, those with a vested interest in maintaining that system will continue to throw out the labels: 'dyke,' 'crazy,' 'wild,' 'violent.'"[107] Notably, CSIV had emerged in the wake of the success of a multiyear gay liberation campaign to remove homosexuality from the American Psychiatric Association's (APA) *Diagnostic and Statistical Manual*'s list of mental disorders.[108] As Regina Kunzel has argued, although this historic victory helped to dislodge the dominant understanding of homosexuality as pathology by recasting it as "healthy" and "normal," it also reproduced binary conceptions of healthy/sick and able-minded/disabled that underwrote other forms of social exclusion and hierarchy.[109] CSIV was part of a radical queer strand of antipsychiatry that sought to destabilize the profession's power altogether and to rethink concepts of health and mental illness given their capacity to facilitate carceral power.[110]

The ubiquitous use of tranquilizers and psychotropic drugs as a frontline strategy of control and punishment came under fire in CSIV's and Framingham prisoners' writings. As one contributor to *Turning Point* wrote in 1977: "If you have a deep rooted problem, real or imaginary, and attempt to convey these feelings to the powers that be, you are shuttled off to that pseudo psychiatrist in residence. . . . His remedy for everything is 200 mg of thorazine, Mellarill, or any one of the latest 'untried' mind deadenizers. You can't go thru life in here or society doing the 'Thorazine Shuffle,' but any overt attempt to deal with your anger and that's what you'll be doing. . . . As a matter of course, any outbursts will be dealt with accordingly. Not the reasons but the deeds. So what recourse do you have left except to hold back the dam and wait til you are 'released' back to society to unleash the torrent. This is of their own making, they pay the piper."[111]

The oft-heard slogan, "Free Our Sisters, Free Ourselves," aptly epitomizes the group's contention that the Worcester center could be construed as an attack on "*all* women." Activists argued that the center was an especially violent "response to all women who are angry and fighting back against the power of the patriarchal system to define our roles and control our lives."[112] It ensconced narrow definitions of acceptable women and simultaneously created opaque and broad definitions of violent ones. As Breece recalls, "We could see from the vagaries that it was a big wide fishing net and that anybody at any given time could fit their criteria."[113] CSIV writers, however, routinely emphasized the ways in which race, class, sexuality, and gender expression mediated women's relationships to policing and incarceration, and the coalition they represented embodied these differences of social location to a meaningful extent. Those most likely to end up in a Worcester center, activists speculated, would be "poor women, Black women, Hispanic women, Lesbians—any woman who lacks sufficient money and privilege to escape incarceration by the State."[114]

Centers such as this one, activists reasoned, could have particularly severe consequences for women who used physical violence to defend themselves from sexual attackers and batterers. The self-defense cases of Joan Little, Inez García, Yvonne Wanrow, and Dessie Woods that are discussed in the previous chapter illuminated the interconnectedness of issues of rape, institutionalized racism, and violence by law enforcement and custodial officers. In an interview with *FAAR News*, CSIV member Lee Austin conjectured that women in similar circumstances to García, who at the time was fighting her murder conviction in California, might "inappropriately end up at Worcester."[115] Indeed, the impossibility of self-defense in the prison setting was among the factors that led the coalition to publicly denounce incarceration itself as a form of "violence against women."[116] By the mid-1970s this term often functioned in local and national feminist networks as an umbrella for various forms of male violence against women. The implications of including incarceration within this rhetorical frame exceeded basic addition. As it reconfigured *violent women* as victims of institutional violence and foregrounded *imprisoned women* as subjects of feminist discourse, CSIV challenged the liberal legal imaginary in which *criminals* and *victims* were discrete populations and called for alternatives to criminal justice.

Prefigurative Politics and the Uses of Community

Upon their victory in the Worcester center struggle, CSIV activists declared that they "must hold the line and move on to create the real alternatives we need."[117] Although they understood that preventing the expansion of behavior-modification units was vital, their larger vision of abolishing "the whole violent system" led them to propose a "strategy that includes four aspects: anti-institutional work, support work for women already incarcerated, support for genuine alternatives for people in crisis or distress, and, finally, personal practice to overcome the violence that pervades our daily lives."[118] Throughout its roughly five-year existence, CSIV straddled a familiar tension for social justice radicals between fighting to reform existing institutions and creating alternative forms of social and political life.[119] Reform campaigns and support work could, and often did, eclipse the goal of "prefiguring" their vision of community-based programs in their daily practice, but CSIV activists found ways to advocate alternative notions of health, safety, justice, and belonging through their writings and educational activities.[120] Their epistemology of violence impelled them to call for "transformative justice" approaches to interpersonal violence and conflict that are in line with the goal of fundamental social transformation.[121]

The idea of *community* was used in at least three ways in CSIV's writings: it was a result of an intentional and possibly arduous process of social organization; an antithetical counterpart to the state; and a staging ground for imagining otherwise.[122] CSIV activists envisioned that the various social movements in which it was anchored would together build a "broad network . . . of communities, families and friends of prisoners and psychiatric inmates, cultural workers, and advocates of alternatives" to the prison/psychiatric state with what they described as a "freedom/struggle culture." This counterculture would be premised on self-determination, "self-love and other-love," and social accountability, and cultivated through slow and extensive development of small mutual-aid collectives.[123] In this sense, community was crucially different from the state: "We cannot and must not expect that the state will work to make us strong, healthy, and clear, or teach us how to work collectively on meeting our needs. The state needs to keep us divided, wary of our neighbors, scared of deep feelings, and distanced from anyone in crisis."[124] Reflecting the rhetoric and practices of Black Power activists, CSIV argued that "real alternatives" were *community-controlled* structures. The group envisioned community-determined mechanisms for supporting people in emotional crisis, for holding accountable those who harm others, and for freely and safely expressing grief and anger without punitive or pathologizing reprisals. A criminal legal approach to rape and battery, they posited, both usurped women's self-determination and promised more institutional violence.[125] Moreover, social movements themselves might promote healing: "Several years after getting out of the hospital," wrote MPLF and CSIV member Arlene Sen, "I became involved in [the mental patients' liberation movement] and in the women's movement. My participation has been instrumental in my finally feeling better, in my understanding of why I was feeling so badly, and of how and why I was oppressed by Psychiatry."[126]

Although they regularly acknowledged that some women may, in fact, "need intensive emotional support," CSIV members unequivocally maintained that locked and coercive institutions were not the solution for emotional distress. Nor were the new community mental health centers, which were envisioned as replacements for the large, locked state mental hospitals that gradually (though unevenly and incompletely) were being closed during the 1970s and 1980s.[127] Instead, CSIV contended, "the administrators and psychiatrists of these centers . . . are not from the working-class communities in which they are often placed, but are generally from white and privileged communities. . . . They focus on individual 'sickness' rather than, for example, unemployment and lack of childcare."[128] While the group conceded the necessity of social services in the short term, it argued that "to the extent possible, participation in any service must be voluntary, and show respect for the individual's need for self-direction and growth."[129] Self- and peer-directed services, based in values of interdependency, autonomy, and egalitarianism, would safeguard against forms of professionalism and hierarchy that fostered dependency and exploitation. This ethos coalesced the self-help politics and practices of CSIV's multiple political allies and influences: the radical health, prisoners' rights, antirape, battered women's, and mental patients' liberation movements.

Although CSIV activists challenged the notion that "communities are organic, natural, spontaneous occurrences,"[130] the concept of community control nevertheless remained abstract. When it came to identifying community-controlled alternatives in action, the coalition lifted up many of the organizations in its wider network, particularly feminist-run battered women's shelters and the Elizabeth Stone House, while also pointing to batterers' counseling programs, rape crisis services, food cooperatives, and other community-based initiatives that demonstrated the potential "to survive without the intervention of the state."[131] The key element of a viable alternative to institutionalization was an understanding "that emotional crisis happens within a political, social, and economic context."[132] Although CSIV members knew firsthand the potential for such projects to reproduce their own forms of social normativity, exclusion, and hierarchy along axes of race, sexuality, language, class, or gender, these concerns were not discussed in their published materials, which were primarily propaganda tools. Along similar lines, activists also advocated "women having control over what happens to rapists and batterers within their communities . . . and offenders learning to live as neighbors in caring communities."[133] Yet they did not acknowledge that a vision of "women having control" potentially subsumed other modes of difference, such as that between women with and without personal experiences of rape and battering, nor did they elaborate what roles men might play in creating a culture of nonviolence. That *community* remained an imprecise concept in their political writings illustrates the complex and difficult ideas it could be burdened to capture, or wind up bracketing.

Feminist Solidarity in Difference

The group's organizational structure and process became an important site for applying aspects of its radical egalitarian and abolitionist vision. CSIV's organizational structure was comprised of two concentric circles: a broad, mixed-gender network of individuals and groups, and a much smaller core group whose membership was limited to women. CSIV members sought to establish a visible feminist presence in the larger, mixed-gender anti-incarceration movement, as well as to cultivate "the best possible atmosphere [for their] continued political education and growth."[134] This atmosphere was a conscious project rather than assumed to exist automatically among women: each member had to be "dedicated to the work of creating a reality that is more self-determining and mutually responsible than the dominant culture."[135]

Steeped in feminist principles of participatory democracy, the organization adopted a number of protocols designed to encourage equitable participation in dialogue and decision making. Each meeting began with a "check-in," followed by the group working together to develop the agenda. Facilitators and notetakers rotated weekly, decisions were largely made by consensus, and publicity materials were written collaboratively. While these practices were certainly time-intensive and likely limited the participation of women for whom a several-hour weekly meeting was not feasible, they were designed to counter possible dynamics of entitlement and marginalization between those who had been labeled "crazy," "violent," "sick," or "dangerous" by dominant cultural authorities and those who were experienced in navigating public bureaucracies as nonprofit, social service, or health care workers.[136]

The diversity of social locations and lived experiences represented in the group was identified as "a strength, not a liability."[137] Foregrounded in CSIV's "Principles of Unity" was a declaration that members should proactively confront and negotiate differences of "race, class, sex, sexual preference, religion, age, ethnic background, and other life experiences such as incarceration."[138] I interpret these statements as more prescriptive than descriptive, signaling the kinds of conflicts and negotiations that likely emerged in the process of coalescing a diverse activist network within "social geographies already structured around gender, race, class, and sexual exclusions."[139]

In a period when many feminists in Boston and beyond contentiously debated the theories and practices of gender separatism and the boundaries of women-only spaces, CSIV treated "women" as a category of identification rather than of medical and legal ascription. Trans women activists in Boston issued public challenges to exclusionary feminists at least as early as 1974. Writing for *Gay Community News*, Margo Schulter admonished local gay and lesbian and feminist movements for their complicity in trans oppression: "It appears that this pastime of supporting liberation for some but not for others is still going strong right here in our own progressive community of Boston. . . . No one is suggesting that anyone has a responsibility to devote all of her/his time to fighting transsexual oppression. However, I do mean to say that as a transsexual, a woman, and a lesbian, I feel that everyone has a responsibility to cooperate with the transsexual cause to the extent of not denying space for meetings and not disavowing transsexual rights."[140]

Initially, as Sunny Robinson recollects the situation, CSIV had no formal political "line" on trans inclusivity. Rather, embracing inclusion was more like an organic orientation for a group whose business was challenging the social construction and criminalization of gender deviance. The question of trans inclusion did, however, crystallize as an organizational conflict in 1978 when a newcomer to the coalition accused the core group of deceiving her and the "Greater Boston Women's Community" by failing to advertise that its members included a "male-to-female transsexual."[141] The newcomer was soon asked to leave CSIV on the grounds that her demand for biology-based gender regulation was "anti-feminist" and "divisive."[142] Shortly thereafter, a small ad hoc group of local women issued a request in the feminist newspaper *Sojourner* that all "organizations, businesses, and spaces identifying themselves as 'women-only'" send a representative to an upcoming community forum on the issue of "male-to-constructed female transsexualism within the women's movement." The same letter outlined the group's ideal policies: that all trans persons identify themselves as such when seeking to join a women's organization; that all women's organizations inform local feminist communities of their respective analyses of transsexualism; and finally, that organizations should "make known to the women's community their position on transsexuals as potential members and whether transsexuals exist in their organization."[143] Intended to surveil and exclude trans women, these policy proposals manifested a transphobic narrative that trans women were "really men" and that as such they posed a threat to feminist women's right to autonomous space and even their safety. These policies implicitly reproduced a crude assumption that "women-only" spaces were free from harm and hierarchy. Among those organizations expressly requested to attend the forum were CSIV, the Cambridge Women's Center, and Ja Shin Do, a feminist martial arts studio. Trans women, on the other hand, were expressly disinvited.[144] Writing in *Sojourner* soon after, two of the cofounders of Ja Shin Do pointed to internal dissention and miscommunication about whether trans women were welcome as one of several key breaking points that led to the short-lived studio's closure.[145] The Women's Center, on the other hand, had a clear policy "of nonexclusion for all women, which includes women with a transsexual history."[146] The ad hoc group would not prevail. *Sojourner* printed several condemnatory responses to the "Statement on Transsexualism," characterizing it as aggressive and discriminatory, as well as a diplomatically worded statement from the Cambridge Women's Center announcing its decision to leave its current policy of inclusion untouched.[147]

These events prompted CSIV core members to hash out and commit to their stance on trans inclusivity:

> We, as a Coalition, stand firmly against the oppression of all people. For this reason we will not tolerate the oppression of any person for any part of their being. . . . What is to prevent other women coming to the Coalition with their own personal definitions of what constitutes a woman, and requiring us to reject those that the definition excludes? We must denounce such a personal definition as unsisterly, and not, in our rush to comply with it, become unsisterly ourselves. Instead, we must learn to recognize divisive attacks, even when they are couched in the language of feminism.[148]

At the crux of CSIV's campaign against the Worcester center was a politics of gender self-determination; former prisoners and ex-mental patients, those involved in the sex trade, and others stigmatized or policed for nonconforming gender performances and sexual desires that joined either CSIV's core group or the wider network helped carve out the coalition's more expansive conception of *all-women space*. As literature scholar Emma Heaney suggests, recovering "trans-feminist solidarities of the 1970s" helps to "restore trans women's claims to feminism and women's autonomy to historical memory."[149] In CSIV's conception, prison abolition included an end to the surveillance, policing, and punishment of gender nonconformity.

* * *

CSIV's activity waned considerably after the successful campaign against the proposed centers for "violent women" who were imprisoned. It played a part in several efforts to challenge the construction of similar "secure care units" for youth confined in the state's juvenile justice system before it fully dissolved back into the movements from which it emerged.[150] Although the coalition developed and sustained a "larger vision of trying to create a real healing system," the advent of the Reagan administration pushed this experimental dimension of its work even further out of reach.[151] Under Reagan's policies of austerity, organizations in the coalition that provided direct services faced funding cuts, as did other social and legal service organizations where some individual members of the core group had found employment.

Yet CSIV's antiviolence politics continued to reverberate through local activist milieus after the coalition disbanded. Core members sustained their ongoing work with the Boston Bail Project, Elizabeth Stone House, and Families and Friends of Prisoners, among other organizations. They also participated in a number of emerging efforts, including the Free Willie Sanders campaign and the Coalition for Women's Safety, as well as a mobilization to abolish the death penalty in the state. Connie Breece and others with the Framingham Prison Project were instrumental in the early years of Aid to Incarcerated Mothers, a project initiated by two MCI-Framingham prisoners in 1979 that developed legal advocacy, support group, and transportation programs to help imprisoned parents preserve their relationships with their children.[152]

Mobilizations to defeat behavior modification programs and special units for so-called violent women were a key node in the development of an anticarceral feminist politics in the 1970s. CSIV's efforts to challenge the consolidation of a prison-to-mental-hospital pipeline in Massachusetts involved building relationships across multiple identities and places, and analyzing the interconnections of multiple systems of confinement—what disability studies scholar Liat Ben-Moshe calls the "incarceration matrix"—and capitalism, racism, patriarchy, and compulsory heterosexuality.[153] In the hands of CSIV, the slogan "Stop Violence Against Women" drew lines of connection among MCI-Framingham and Massachusetts' state mental hospitals; prisoners' rights, psychiatric survivors,' and sex workers' rights groups; and women's shelters and rape crisis and feminist health centers.

This local story of alliances demonstrates how carceral violence functioned as a "cross-cutting issue" that could link multiple (and multiply) marginalized constituencies in Greater Boston.[154] These linkages not only allowed CSIV to meet its most concrete objective of preventing the center, but also turned the organization's campaigns into coalitional spaces through which social movement ideologies were cross-fertilized. As mental patients' rights, prisoners' rights, and feminist groups coalesced, they developed an analysis of violence that connected the politics of mental health, the politics of state repression, and the expansion of medicalized imprisonment to hierarchies of race, gender, class, and sexuality. This culminated in a vision of abolishing all forms of incarceration. As the following chapter discusses, the anticarceral feminism practiced by organizations such as CSIV took shape not only in relation to local contexts but through the translocal print culture of women's prison newsletters.

3. Printing Abolition

The Transformative Power of Women's Prison Newsletters

And, if I know anything at all,
It's that a wall is just a wall
and nothing more at all.
It can be broken down.
—Assata Shakur, "Affirmation" (1987)

Queerness is essentially about the rejection of a here
and now and an insistence on potentiality or concrete
possibility for another world.
—José Esteban Muñoz (2009)

The first issue of the Seattle-based grassroots publication *Through the Looking Glass: A Women and Children Prison Newsletter* hit activist bookstores, feminist mailboxes, and prisons and jails in the spring of 1976. The dozen mimeographed tabloid-size pages featured stories about conditions in Washington State's women's prison and the use of grand juries to harass local leftist activists. Readers also learned the latest news about Yvonne Wanrow's protracted legal battle, and some heard, perhaps for the first time, about Gloria Timmons, a local African American woman recently imprisoned for killing her violently abusive husband. The Through the Looking Glass (TTLG) collective, which published the newsletter, declared its multifaceted and ambitious feminist mission on the inside cover: "to remind people that women and children are locked up . . . to encourage analysis of different forms of incarceration . . . to communicate ideas on how to improve conditions, reduce the numbers of us in jails, and shorten sentences while believing that society needs to be radically changed so that prisons of any kind will no longer exist, to communicate across the barriers that have been put up to keep us in, or out," and to create a place where women incarcerated in various prisons "can communicate to each other."[1]

Two years later, on the other side of the country, a feminist collective based in Brooklyn, New York, launched a women's prison newsletter of its own. As was also true of TTLG, Women Free Women in Prison (WFWP) was a primarily white, working-class, and lesbian group; a few members of these groups described themselves as survivors of psychiatric institutions or former prisoners. Both TTLG and WFWP engaged in various forms of "prisoner support work," such as transporting children to see their incarcerated parents and coordinating letter-writing campaigns, as well as political education and direct-action organizing. After three years, WFWP decided that a newsletter could play a key role in publicizing incarcerated women's political thought and activism and facilitating communication across prison walls within and beyond the Northeast. *No More Cages: A Bi-monthly Women's Prison Newsletter* would also analyze "the parallels between prisons and other institutions used to lock people up" and promote interchange between "the prison movement and the anti-psychiatry movement."[2]

In 1980, the two groups struck a mutually supportive agreement to publish on alternate months and encourage their respective readers to subscribe to the other's newsletter.[3] Although they depended entirely on volunteer labor and grassroots fund-raising, WFWP managed to keep *No More Cages* in print for five years, and TTLG sustained its newsletter for more than a decade.

Part of a "revolution in ephemera" that took place in the long 1970s, *No More Cages* and *Through the Looking Glass* emerged at the intersection between the print culture of antiprison activism and what came to be called the Women in Print movement.[4] They resembled many other grassroots and underground periodicals, "juxtaposing typed and handwritten text, photographs and hand-drawn graphics, signed and unsigned articles, and layout that appears professionally done alongside typos, misnumbered pages, and crooked lines of text."[5] Several feminist periodicals, including such titles as *Big Mama Rag*, *off our backs*, and *Lesbian Tide*, regularly included a page or more on happenings in and around women's prisons, as did antiprison periodicals such as *Midnight Special*, *Bar None*, and the gay liberation publication *Join Hands*. TTLG and WFWP often reprinted and remixed material from these and other left-wing publications. What set their newsletters apart, however, was their central focus on women's prisons and imprisoned women's writings.

This chapter explores the "world-making project" of women's prison newsletters. Queer studies scholars Lauren Berlant and Michael Warner explain that "'world,' like 'public,' differs from community or group because it necessarily includes more people than can be identified, more spaces than can be mapped beyond a few reference points, modes of feeling that can be learned rather than experienced as a birthright."[6] Bringing together disparate voices and places, these publications helped to build a highly decentralized, cross-regional women's prison movement in the 1970s and early 1980s. They functioned as a critical forum through which a racially, economically, and geographically diverse cross section of incarcerated activists and their allies forged "unsystematized lines of acquaintance" and exchanged ideas, strategies, and updates, enabling information to traverse institutional and local boundaries.[7] The newsletters also constituted an imagined community, as they allowed an unknowable number of people, many of whom would never meet directly, to conceive of themselves as part of a shared culture—or *world*—of opposition.[8]

The chapter examines how this outlaw counterpublic incubated a politics of prison abolition that centered carceral violence against women. Grassroots print cultures, as feminist scholar Maylei Blackwell has suggested, are important sites for "helping us to understand the development of . . . ideology, discourse, and political praxis in a way that accounts for how ideas traveled through local formations as well as larger cross-regional circulations."[9] As rare archives of numerous imprisoned women's activist writings, *No More Cages* and *Through the Looking Glass* shed light on the ways in which these missives influenced social movement discourses beyond bars and shaped the trajectory of antiracist and queer feminist politics. Contributors, both captive and free, used these platforms to amplify their organizing efforts by appealing to readers to lend support to and spread the word about campaigns to improve prison conditions, oppose behavior modification regimes, halt new prison construction, and defend women who had killed their batterers and sexual assailants. In the process, this counterpublic culture circulated trenchant critiques of the institutional violence of incarceration and of the chasm between a prisoners' rights movement focused on men's institutions and feminist antirape and battered women's activism increasingly enmeshed with the criminal justice state. Moreover, the world constituted by these publications fostered life-supporting relationships and alternatives to the dominant political culture that systematically devalued and excluded those deemed criminally other. Additionally, by tracing the trajectories of the collectives behind *Through the Looking Glass* and *No More Cages*, the chapter explores their efforts to build alliances with imprisoned women, both in print and in person.

This Newsletter Is an Action

Prisons rely on isolation. Visiting, phone, and mail regulations limit prisoners' access to their loved ones and others concerned about their well-being. Geography plays a key role in generating isolation, since many institutions are located far from prisoners' communities of origin. Inside the walls, security classification schemes, policies limiting physical and verbal interactions, and the well-founded fear of reprisal all work to isolate prisoners from one other. These practices help to make prisons inaccessible, even invisible, to much of the public, shielding institutional authorities from scrutiny and accountability. In the 1970s, prison activists on both sides of the bars employed what historian Dan Berger calls a "strategy of visibility" to counteract this problem.[10] They turned to alternative media to challenge dominant ideologies of crime and punishment and to bring greater attention to prisoner organizing in leftist and feminist milieus. By circulating information and facilitating relationships that enabled incarcerated people to resist their conditions, newsletters and newspapers such as *No More Cages* and *Through the Looking Glass* represented a palpable threat to the prison as a "total institution."[11] It is precisely for this reason that prison authorities regularly attempted to thwart the circulation of these publications and that prisoners repeatedly listed mail censorship as a major grievance.

Prison newspapers and newsletters represented one strand of a multifaceted and widespread radical print revolution in the 1960s and 1970s that involved new leftists, antiracist radicals, gay liberationists, feminists, and antipsychiatry activists. The radical feminist Robin Morgan opened her 1970 anthology, *Sisterhood Is Powerful*, by announcing: "This book is an action." The editors of alternative newspapers shared that conviction.[12] Across the country, hundreds of activist groups made and distributed their own news media, and together these antiestablishment journalists created an "underground press" that reached millions of readers. Among the conditions of possibility for this revolution was the development of the inexpensive and easy-to-use technology of photo-offset printing.[13] Many papers, including *No More Cages* and *Through the Looking Glass*, relied on the Liberation News Service (1967–1981) for graphics, bulletins, and photographs to supplement locally generated content.[14] Embracing advocacy in their reporting and addressing their readers as comrades in struggle, activist newspapers "educated, politicized, and built communities."[15] They fomented cross-local, cross-regional, and cross-wall communications and alliances.

In the context of prison newspapers and newsletters, it is important to distinguish between antiprison publications and those sanctioned by prison authorities. Some one hundred institutions had prisoner-produced news organs in the 1970s and early 1980s that were sponsored by the administration. By and large, the editors of these publications failed to obtain approval from censors to publish anything that criticized prison conditions or policy. From the vantage point of officials, a prison newsletter was a vocational opportunity with rehabilitative potential, not a forum for dissent.[16] These stood in dramatic contrast to several clandestinely produced prisoner publications and more than a dozen radical inside-outside publications that circulated during the period.[17] Among the latter were black nationalist newspapers, such as *Arm the Spirit* and *Midnight Special*, and newsletters produced by local and regional organizations, such as the New England Prisoner Association and the San Francisco gay liberation group Join Hands.[18] Most of these publications included at least some coverage of cycles of rebellion and repression in women's prisons, as well as letters and communiqués from women prisoners.

No More Cages and *Through the Looking Glass* were part of the Women in Print movement, a distinctly feminist strand of the radical print revolution. By the early 1970s, more than 500 grassroots feminist newsletters and newspapers were in circulation.[19] From advertising local events to explaining how to start your own consciousness-raising group or rape crisis center, these publications became a primary way in which women learned about, located, joined, and helped to grow feminist movements. The proliferation of feminist news media was complemented and facilitated by the emergence of feminist bookstores, printing presses, and publishers in urban centers across the country, within which lesbian women often played central roles.[20]

At least a dozen feminist periodicals, almost all of which were written and produced by lesbians and women of color, saw imprisoned women as prospective readers and offered them free subscriptions.[21] A smaller number of these publications, particularly those based in places where women's prison activism burgeoned in the 1970s, regularly covered prison happenings as well as the cases of women facing incarceration for their political activism or their acts of self-defense against rape and battering. The Third World Women's Alliance's emphasis on incarceration in its quarterly newspaper, *Triple Jeopardy* (1971–1975), reflected and extended the organization's commitment to working on issues felt most acutely by multiply marginalized women of color and its involvement in defense campaigns for black and Puerto Rican women political prisoners. Others that made conditions in women's prisons and jails a journalistic priority, such as Denver's *Big Mama Rag*, New Orleans' *Distaff*, Los Angeles' *The Lesbian Tide*, and Washington, D.C.'s *off our backs*, did not reflect a particular organizational agenda but mirrored the concerns of local and regional activist networks.

Drawing on their experiences as readers and writers of the alternative press, members of the Through the Looking Glass and Women Free Women in Prison collectives envisioned and created prison newsletters that linked women in prison to one another and to those outside. They aimed to bring "the issues of the Prison Movement and the Anti-Psychiatry Movement . . . together with the Anti-Racist, Women's and Lesbian and Gay Movements."[22]

Dykes Organizing between the Bars

The Through the Looking Glass Collective

The TTLG collective emerged out of a Seattle-based feminist organization called the Women Out Now Prison Project (WON), a support and organizing group formed in 1973. One of the key founders of the collective, a white, working-class, self-described dyke from rural Oregon named Rita "Bo" Brown, had recently returned to Seattle after serving a year in a federal prison in the Los Angeles area for mail theft. She had begun developing an antiracist consciousness and cut her activist teeth while incarcerated, thanks in part to a friend who was involved in an "underground black women's reading group."[23] Upon returning to Seattle, Brown enrolled in courses at Seattle Central Community College, where she joined an activist group that visited prisoners at a nearby men's institution. She also formed a connection with a program at the University of Washington (UW) for men being released on parole from Walla Walla State Penitentiary, Washington's oldest and largest prison, located in the southeastern corner of the state. Through these and other local activist circles, Brown met Therese Coupez, a white working-class UW student, and several others who shared her interest in creating an organization dedicated to supporting women prisoners. The group decided to concentrate its energies on Washington's new women's prison located in Pierce County, roughly an hour southwest of Seattle.[24]

Prior to establishing the Purdy Treatment Center for Women, Washington State had incarcerated women with felony convictions in a separate structure on the grounds of the men's prison in Walla Walla. The women's annex was severely crowded, and recreation, job training, and education programs were nearly nonexistent. Purdy Treatment Center promised to become "one of the nation's most enlightened correctional institutions," according to officials. The prison's name, along with its physical resemblance to a "community college campus," was meant to communicate its ostensible anticustodial approach. Purdy's program of "progressive freedom" meant that compliant prisoners were rewarded with increasing degrees of mobility and privacy, graduating from locked units to self-locking rooms and finally to two-person, two-bedroom apartments for those participating in work and education release programs.[25] Moreover, the prison's first superintendent advertised her "hope that hundreds of citizens will be coming to the center from the community . . . providing encouragement and guidance to the residents, and letting the people who support our institutions with their tax dollars see that the program is working."[26] WON leveraged the prison's commitment to citizen engagement, cloaking its own prison abolitionist and anticapitalist politics in the institution's vocabulary of training, personal development, and productive citizenship after release.

The new organization of "ex-convicts and friends" quickly drew women students who had been volunteering with the men's prison programs, as well as other leftist feminist lesbians.[27] Within its first year, the organization brought women from more than thirty Seattle-area organizations into the prison under the rubric of vocational training and skill development, including self-defense instructors, a band of "queer puppeteers," and representatives of the Lesbian Resource Center and the local chapter of COYOTE (Call Off Your Old Tired Ethics), a sex workers' rights organization.[28] "So we were women outside trying to help women inside transition back into the community and get involved," as one former member explains it.[29] WON responded to prisoners' desires to see their loved ones more often by organizing a weekend carpool program between Seattle's predominantly African American Central District and Rainier Valley neighborhoods and the prison. Additionally, the group fund-raised to provide what monetary support they could to women just released on parole, participated in defense campaigns for women imprisoned for defending themselves from male violence, and helped to link prisoners with progressive women attorneys willing to do pro bono work. An informational letter described the underlying aim of these activities as to "try to help convicts recognize their power to demand change as a united body."[30] This support work, the group suggested, was in service of their long-range vision of "the abolishment of prisons and the full restoration of all human and civil rights."[31]

Several events precipitated the end of WON and the formation of TTLG in its stead. In the fall of 1975, two of WON's principal cofounders, Brown and Coupez, left the group to join the George Jackson Brigade, a clandestine armed group named in honor of the famed prisoner activist and Black Panther who was killed by guards at California's San Quentin State Prison in 1971. The small mixed-gender and predominately white group advocated and engaged in armed resistance against capitalism and the state; it claimed responsibility for several bank robberies and more than a dozen pipe bombings of various government and corporate targets.[32] By 1978, Brown and Coupez (along with the rest of the Brigade) were behind bars for their participation in these actions. Both became readers and occasional contributors to *Through the Looking Glass* and *No More Cages*.[33]

Around the same time that Brown and Coupez joined the political underground, a small group of women who had worked together on *Moonstorm*, a lesbian feminist newsletter in St. Louis, Missouri, moved to Seattle. The remaining WON membership, together with these newcomers, decided to form a collective that would continue the carpool program and other forms of direct support for women imprisoned at Purdy, as well as create a women's prison newsletter.[34]

TTLG's membership fluctuated over the organization's eleven-year run, but the group generally hovered around fifteen. Publishing a monthly (and later quarterly) newsletter on a shoestring budget with an entirely volunteer staff of working people required frequent meetings that went long and late. The collective made decisions by consensus, and individual members were encouraged to have a hand in the substantive work of corresponding with imprisoned writers, generating content, and working on layout, as well as expected to take part in the routine tasks such as mimeographing, folding, stapling, stamping, and mailing. In addition to the several hundred copies mailed to prisoners each month, stacks of *Through the Looking Glass* were delivered to feminist bookwomen at Mad Woman and It's About Time, as well as two anarchist bookshops, Red and Black Books and Left Bank Books.[35] Some TTLG members belonged to Seattle's Lesbian Feminist Radio Collective, which produced a regular show for the noncommercial station KRAB-FM; occasionally, they would "just read *Through the Looking Glass*" on the air.[36] Alongside the constant grind of newsletter production, TTLG members sustained their concrete support work for prisoners and their families and engaged in various educational, advocacy, and direct action organizing activities.[37]

The Women Free Women in Prison Collective

WFWP's beginnings can be traced to a series of prisoner uprisings in 1974 at Bedford Hills Correctional Facility, located roughly an hour north of Manhattan, New York City, in an affluent, overwhelmingly white section of Westchester County. Though Bedford Hills was not proclaimed a beacon of rehabilitation like Purdy Treatment Center, Attica-inspired reforms helped to open up the prison's gates to artists, educators, and legal volunteers in the early 1970s. When a black prisoner activist named Carol Crooks was severely beaten by a group of guards and placed in segregation in February 1974, news of this incident traveled swiftly to prisoner advocates on the outside. Afeni Shakur, one of the Panther 21, was working at the time as a paralegal at South Bronx Legal Services. She and several other women formed a defense committee for Crooks and helped her to retain an attorney.[38] In August, the court ruled that Crooks's rights to due process had been violated by the prison, and she was sent back to general population. Not even a month passed before she was once again brutalized by a group of guards and thrown back in segregation. This abuse catalyzed roughly seventy women prisoners, the majority of whom were African American and Latina, to stage a major demonstration.

When Crooks and nearly two dozen women involved in the "August Rebellion" were transferred to the Matteawan Complex for the Criminally Insane in Dutchess County, a small group in New York City calling itself Women Against Prison made frequent trips up the Hudson River Valley to the notorious institution and funneled information to and from the prisoners' loved ones and advocates at South Bronx Legal Services.[39] Crooks's 1974 lawsuit became the first of many brought by her and other prisoners over the course of the decade. According to sociologist Juanita Díaz-Cotto, the more that prisoners and their advocates turned to the courts for redress for institutional injustices, the more prison administrators obstructed their path: "Tactics included labeling prisoners who sought reforms as 'disruptive,' 'violent,' and 'troublemakers,' threatening prisoners with reprisals if they challenged institutional rules and regulations or participated as plaintiffs in the lawsuits, and promising additional 'privileges' to prisoners who informed on their peers."[40] Moreover, officials continued to use the pipeline from the prison to the state hospital that had been in place at least since the mid-1960s.[41] In blatant violation of their due process rights, seven African American women were transferred to the facility's segregation unit in 1976 and subjected to a behavior modification program called Steps toward Eventual Acceptance of a Disciplined You, or "STEADY."[42] Women Against Prison continued to make weekly trips to visit the "Matteawan sisters" until a federal judge ordered that they be returned to Bedford Hills.[43] Around this same time, the group decided on a new name. As a former member recalls, "While we were against *all* prisons, we felt it was important to make clear that we were women working to free *women* in prison."[44] Notably, the group rejected biologically deterministic conceptions of gender; at least one of the prisoners WFWP regularly visited at Matteawan was a transgender woman.[45]

As Díaz-Cotto has documented, black, Latina, and white prisoners, especially so-called long-termers, forged unprecedented cross-racial solidarities in the face of persistent repression, refusing to allow correctional officers or administrators to exploit racial distinctions. An underground multiracial coalition collected stories of abuse and discrimination, drafted and circulated petitions, and liaised with outside activists.[46] In the summer of 1978, more than three-quarters of Bedford Hills' 450 prisoners, "after many months of filing grievances," waged a nonviolent, daylong strike against "increased beatings and harassment by guards" and excessive use of segregation, as well as mail tampering, limited phone access, little "gym and yard time," and egregiously low wages.[47] When the administration refused to negotiate with the strikers, prisoner leaders called upon New York City activists for a loud and visible display of solidarity. Together with a group called Solidarity with Sisters Inside, WFWP organized a "Coalition to Defend Women at Bedford" that rallied at the prison gates in August and helped to disseminate the prisoners' list of demands through alternative media.[48]

After several years of visiting prisoners, packing courtrooms, and organizing protests and educational programs about prison conditions, WFWP members resolved to concentrate on publishing a bimonthly newsletter in an effort to nurture the fledgling women's prison movement. Members argued that bourgeois bias within the women's movement and male supremacy within the antiprison movement conspired to render imprisoned women invisible. By channeling a portion of their energy into a newsletter, WFWP members sought to increase the level of support for women prisoners within an assemblage of radical and progressive movements. *No More Cages* was designed to be a forum for exchanging information, creating knowledge, and documenting resistance.[49] An essay by a WFWP member in the 1980 activist anthology *Top Ranking: Essays on Racism and Classism in the Lesbian Community* described the newsletter's aims as alleviating "the isolation of women in prison" by facilitating communication "between women in different prisons, but also between 'them' inside and 'us' outside, so that we can learn to understand each other and each other's struggles and work together to change the system."[50]

Although the collective remained quite small—at times having as few as four members—comrades, friends, and lovers pitched in to help with everything from addressing and stamping copies to designing covers. Among this wider network of helpers were several affiliates of the Liberation News Service and members of the Brooklyn-based collective, Dykes Against Racism Everywhere (DARE).[51] Fund-raising for the newsletter also created opportunities for other antiracist feminist organizations in New York City, such as DARE, Asian Lesbians of the East Coast, and Salsa Soul Sisters, to lend their support by cosponsoring and organizing benefit events.[52] Like TTLG, WFWP continued its prisoner support work alongside its alternative media

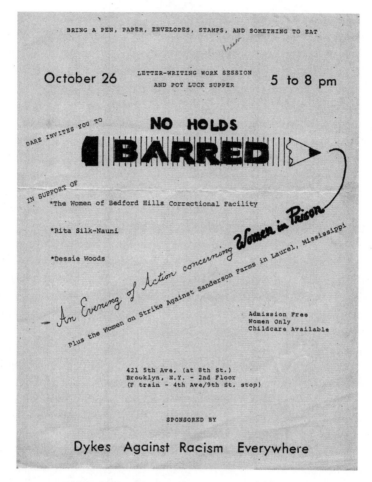

Dykes Against Racism Everywhere flier. Courtesy of the Lesbian
Herstory Archives.

production and treated its newsletter as an outreach tool to help expand local
feminist opposition to women's imprisonment. By dedicating themselves to
putting their abolitionist politics in print, these small collectives had a reach
and impact that far exceeded their numbers.

Creating a Counterpublic
against Incarceration

A letter published in *No More Cages* in January of 1982 attests to the connections generated by the newsletter. An imprisoned woman wrote:

Hello Sisters, How's it going? I'm still in the struggle. A few months ago I sent a letter, Poem, and Picture and asked for correspondence to my dismay alot of the letters I received from sisters inside I cannot answer because of the corresponding rules at this institution. I'm sending a poem I wrote this morning along with this letter please Publish this letter and the poem. To all the womyn who wrote me thank you very much. I only wish I could return the feeling you sent my way. Thank you. . . . Keep the newsletter going I love it! It's the best thing that's happened to me since arriving in this hellhole called Prison.

This missive illustrates the power of antiprison newsletters and the counterpublic they created. Contributors used these publications to circumvent administrative roadblocks and address an imagined community of imprisoned resisters, survivors of incarceration, advocates, and allies belonging to "incommensurate geographies."[53] For some, participating in this print culture was a vital means of countering the demoralizing effects of institutionalization. As one Bedford Hills prisoner put it in her request for a subscription to *No More Cages*: "For all it's worth, I'm a Black lesbian interested in one day becoming a writer. Who knows maybe your newsletter will help keep me inspired. Prison has a way of breaking a woman down. I don't want it to happen to me."[54] Imprisoned writers found in these newsletters a sense of companionship and camaraderie with one another, an audience for their creative and political expression, and evidence of the existence of people and groups urgently concerned about the injustices of incarceration.

The January 1982 issue of *No More Cages* included letters, poetry, manifestos, and statements of demands by writers imprisoned in more than a dozen different institutions in the Midwest, Northeast, and Pacific Northwest. Readers learned, for example, about a hunger strike at Muncy state prison in Pennsylvania led by several members of Philadelphia's MOVE, a black liberation organization that was subjected to a massive, military-style attack and bombing by the police. The strikers were protesting severe overcrowding and a lack of institutional protocols for preventing the spread of communicable diseases.[55] Acts of advocacy, expressions of solidarity, and requests for information and support flowed in multiple directions. A "jailhouse lawyer" at Menard Correctional Center in Illinois wrote to request a subscription so that he might "become more familiar with the plight of my sister prisoners" and offered his self-taught legal skills; a feminist attorney replied to a prisoner's request for legal advice in a previous issue; a deaf prisoner suggested strategies her "hearing sisters" might use to better communicate with deaf women at their own institutions. Interspersed throughout the issue were journalistic pieces, reprinted from leftist or feminist periodicals or penned by collective members, on such topics as the disproportionate incarceration of people with

Cover of *No More Cages*, June–July 1983. From the Bromfield
Street Educational Foundation Prison Newsletter Collection,
Northeastern University Archives and Special Collections.

cognitive and psychological disabilities; a fire that took more than two dozen
lives at a Mississippi women's prison; the impunity of corporate crime as juxtaposed to a sharp spike in prostitution-related arrests; and recent prisoner
advocacy and organizing efforts in Oregon and Washington. On the short list
of "books free to women inside" recommended by WFWP were the renowned
anthologies, *All the Women Are White, All the Blacks Are Men, But Some of
Us Are Brave: Black Women's Studies* (1982) and *This Bridge Called My Back:
Writings by Radical Women of Color* (1981).[56] *Through the Looking Glass* was
characterized by a similar heterogeneity of subjectivity, genre, and purpose.

The two newsletters' subscription lists grew to include several hundred people incarcerated in more than 150 different jails and prisons in the years around 1980. Imprisoned readers of these publications likely numbered more than a thousand, since a single copy might change hands multiple times within a cell block or dormitory. Both newsletters regularly included writings by and news about incarcerated women activists who were generally well-known among feminists and leftists and viewed as political prisoners, such as Assata Shakur and Puerto Rican independistas Lolita Lebrón and Alejandrina Torres. Most contributors' imprisonment, however, resulted not from social movement activity but from getting caught in the carceral dragnet for committing survival crimes or "because they offended this society's moral standards."[57] These contributors opted for varying levels of anonymity and self-identification to mitigate the tangible threat of institutional retribution. Most shared where they were incarcerated, some also provided a first name, and some gave a full name and prison mailing address and requested direct replies. Many identified themselves in letters as African American or black, Native American, and lesbians or dykes as they elucidated the ways in which racism, settler colonialism, and heteropatriarchy structured both the prison as an institution and the conditions of their criminalization. A number of politically active prisoners in men's institutions, including at least one transgender woman, subscribed and occasionally contributed to these newsletters as well.[58] (Throughout the chapter, I have included any racial, ethnic, tribal, sexual, and gender identifications that imprisoned contributors chose to make known in their writings.) Although both publishing collectives regularly expressed a desire to reach women institutionalized in psychiatric hospitals and made their publications "free to prisoners and psychiatric inmates," institutional barriers proved intractable. Another factor limiting participation in these print communities was fluency and literacy in English. Neither editorial collective developed bilingual materials, despite the growing number of incarcerated monolingual Spanish-speaking immigrants in the early to mid-1980s.[59]

Prison authorities actively sought to block prisoners' participation in these print communities as both contributors and readers.[60] Mykki, a white, lesbian-identified woman imprisoned at Purdy, wrote to WFWP to inform the group that she had "not been receiving your newsletter every 2 months. Sometimes I receive a slip in its place that says I can't have it because it contains plans of escape, etc, in it. They do this more frequently with the newsletter 'TTLG' especially if any newsletter contains anything I've written."[61] Writing for a radical periodical could easily result in disciplinary action. In an Arkansas prison in 1976, for example, a woman who had recently

Cover of *Through the Looking Glass*, February 1979. From the Atlanta Lesbian Feminist Alliance Periodicals Collection, Sallie Bingham Center for Women's History and Culture, Rubenstein Library, Duke University.

published a letter in a feminist newspaper produced in Eugene, Oregon, was accused of "mutiny," beaten by guards, and placed in maximum security.[62] A person imprisoned at the California Institution for Women in the early 1980s stated that she chose "not to include my name in this letter, because one of the women here is locked down for calling the news."[63] Others made the same decision as Sharron Wallace, an African American woman who suffered years of solitary confinement in a Midwest prison. She was well aware that writing to these publications would "cause a great deal of retaliation" toward her, yet she "had come to the conclusion that to be forced to live in such confinement and under such wretched conditions was itself a kind of death" and therefore chose to take the personal and political risks of circulating her name and story as broadly as possible.[64]

In December 1976, the U.S. Bureau of Prisons issued an official ban on "gay" publications in the federal prison system. Officials rationalized that gay and lesbian prisoners would be "outed" by receiving such literature and would, in turn, face greater risk of social isolation along with harassment and violence from other prisoners.[65] At least some state departments of corrections banned gay publications on the grounds that they endorsed and promoted deviant sexual behavior.[66] In 1977, TTLG began to receive return mail from several federal prisons.[67] The newsletter may very well have been flagged for its queer content, but it also bore the return address of its fiscal sponsor, Seattle Gay Community Services. Rather than end or conceal this organizational affiliation, TTLG reaffirmed "the hated word gay," declaring that it conveys "love and unity among women, and enables us to reach across prison walls to each other. We will not deny who we are and what we work for, even though . . . [that would] make prison officials a little more comfortable, more likely to decide that we are harmless and helpless enough for 'their' prisoners to read."[68] The group appealed to allies to write to their legislators and galvanize community groups to take action on this issue, and encouraged those inside to continue sharing their "direct knowledge of discriminatory practices."[69] Prisoner and gay and lesbian rights organizations in collaboration with several affected publishers successfully toppled the ban by bringing a legal suit in 1980, but censorship of antiracist, feminist, and gay liberation literature remained pervasive in county, state, and federal institutions.[70] In turn, imprisoned activists often named mail tampering and censorship as among their key grievances. In one instance, three prisoners at the Ohio Reformatory in Marysville took steps to file a class action lawsuit when they became aware that prison officials had banned *No More Cages*. As a result, the superintendent relaxed the ban, but the group reported to WFWP that they still endured harassment from guards and administrators in retaliation for their collective action.[71]

Despite these institutional barriers, a multitude of people on both sides of the bars utilized *No More Cages* and *Through the Looking Glass* to myriad ends. Contributors expressed themselves creatively; circulated news of strikes, campaigns, and other prison happenings; recruited allies and sympathizers; and countered the isolation of incarceration. Readers could compare conditions of confinement in dozens of prisons and jails throughout the country while imagining themselves as part of broader political communities that traversed the walls of these institutions.

Cover of *No More Cages*, September–October 1979. From the Coalition to Stop Institutional Violence Records, Northeastern University Archives and Special Collections.

Outlaw Knowledges of Violence and Antiviolence

No More Cages and *Through the Looking Glass* served as sites of convergence and exchange, as well as archives of subjugated knowledge. Conversations in the pages of these newsletters produced understandings of violence against women that implicitly, and sometimes directly, critiqued the mainstream feminist movement both for embracing a law-and-order approach to rape and

battering and for marginalizing women prisoners, including those incarcerated for fighting back against their abusers. Contributors, both captive and
free, analyzed the political economy of punishment; racial, gender, sexual,
and economic hierarchies shaped who would (and would not) be sent to
prison and for how long and in what conditions they would be confined.
Letters and essays from prisoners testified to sexual harassment, abuse, and
coercion and identified practices that were part of the "normal functioning of
the prison"[72] as forms of violence, including body cavity searches, inadequate
or absent medical care, rules limiting verbal and physical interactions, and
behavior modification regimes. At the same time, these publications illuminate what the anthropologist James C. Scott has called "hidden transcripts"
of everyday resistance to imprisonment. As sociologist Avery Gordon has
argued, the "body of subjugated knowledge" found in insurgent prison literature contains a "radical methodology of imprisonment, a pedagogy of
finding and making life where death and destruction dominate."[73] Serving
as repositories for the critical thought of women prisoners and their allies,
these publications offered a powerful counter-narrative of violence against
women that elucidated the violence of the carceral state and contended that
prison abolition should be a feminist demand.

The Criminalization of Survivors

Nearly every issue of *No More Cages* and *Through the Looking Glass* contained
news of the legal battles of women facing criminal charges or appealing
convictions related to defending themselves against rape and battering. Although they were founded after Joan Little's and Inez García's court victories,
these newsletters kept their names and stories in circulation. They followed
Little's continued legal troubles by providing coverage of her incarceration
until she was paroled in 1979 and provided consistent updates on Yvonne
Wanrow's and Dessie X. Woods's legal struggles, which culminated in 1979
and 1981, respectively. The Little, García, Wanrow, and Woods cases inspired
significant cross-movement organizing in part because these fight-back stories coalesced into an allegory of gendered racial power and resistance. But
these newsletters also covered dozens of cases that never achieved the same
national-level visibility, including those of women of color who killed their
intimate partners, rather than an acquaintance, stranger, or state agent. *No
More Cages* and *Through the Looking Glass* provide a crucial window onto
a world of local defense organizing that otherwise left few archival traces.

Readers learned of the case of Edna Louise Pipkins, a twenty-seven-year-
old working-class African American woman living in Hartford, Connecticut,

who killed her live-in boyfriend after enduring two years of abuse. Pipkins had called the police on twenty-three separate occasions. The combined efforts of women from her housing project and the Hartford Interval House, a battered women's shelter where she had sought support, were instrumental in securing a dismissal of her charge of manslaughter. The Edna Louise Pipkins Defense Committee educated the Hartford community about the facts of her case and collected more than 1,000 signatures to deliver to the court on her behalf. WFWP remarked: "In legal terms it is said that Edna Louise Pipkin [sic] won her case. It would be more accurate to say that she escaped the usual punishment of imprisonment faced by most poor women of color who fight back against their batterers."[74]

Both newsletters covered the case of Paula Three Stars, an Oglala Sioux woman living near Seattle who shot and killed her abusive partner of more than six years in 1983. The previous year, Three Stars had called the police for help. As her pan-indigenous, women-led defense committee chronicled in No More Cages, she was told there was "nothing they could do. Realizing the police would not respond to a domestic dispute, Paula called again and reported a robbery. The police responded, but rather than take her to a shelter, they took her to jail for making a false report."[75] Three Stars was originally given ten years for first-degree manslaughter, but thanks to the efforts of her defense committee she successfully appealed for a sentence of three years of probation.[76] On the other side of the country, supporters of Bulesa Gibbs declared victory when a New Jersey judge decided to sentence Gibbs to probation rather than prison after an all-white jury found the African American abuse survivor guilty of "atrocious assault and battery" against her husband. According to a story produced by the Liberation News Service and published in both newsletters, Gibbs's supporters had packed the courtroom for the duration of the trial and delivered hundreds of letters and a petition to the court. "There was consensus among everyone in the courtroom that [the judge's] leniency was directly attributable to this wide response."[77]

Readers learned about a successful community mobilization in Cincinnati to defend an African American woman named Anna Small. Small shot her neighbor, rumored to be a Ku Klux Klansman, when he threatened her life and broke into her home in January 1980. The man had verbally and physically harassed her for years: "Anna was insulted daily, rocks were thrown at her house, gasoline was spread on her lawn in an apparent attempt at arson . . . police provided little or no protection during this time."[78] When she was charged with involuntary manslaughter, a handful of labor, church, and women's groups forged an alliance to politicize her case.[79] The dissemination of numerous stories of success affirmed the grassroots strategy of participatory defense and its potential to mitigate judicial racism and sexism.

Yet most abuse survivors who killed in self-defense in the 1970s and early 1980s were convicted rather than acquitted, and incarcerated rather than sentenced to probation. For imprisoned self-defenders such as Juanita Thomas and Robin Anderson, women's prison newsletters served as forums for sustaining communication with supporters, soliciting legal aid, and finding resonance in others' accounts of intimate and state violence.[80] In 1979, Thomas, an African American mother of five who worked as a janitor in Lansing, Michigan, killed her live-in boyfriend when he sexually attacked her at knifepoint one night after she had suffered more than a decade of his physical, emotional, and sexual violence. Thomas was convicted by a jury of ten white women and two white men of first-degree murder and sentenced to life without parole. She recalled that advocates at the local battered women's shelter initially lent their support, but "once I went to prison they soon forgot about me real quick."[81] A small group of women activists calling themselves Support Group for Women in Prison made Thomas's case their central focus in the early 1980s. This group utilized *No More Cages* to find and learn from other activists engaged in similar advocacy work around the country.[82]

Similarly, the Committee to Free Robin Anderson used the newsletter to circulate information and build a wider base of support for the Bedford Hills prisoner. Anderson, a low-income, African American woman living on Long Island, had "called the police on twenty separate occasions" over the course of two years "and yet the police, if they came at all, only drove [her husband] around the block and released him." When he attacked her with an iron in late December 1976, she stabbed him with a kitchen knife. Following the advice of her court-appointed lawyer, Anderson pleaded guilty to manslaughter and received a sentence of five to ten years at Bedford Hills, which separated her from her young son. In her letter, which was published in *No More Cages*, Anderson described her sentence as punishment for "refusing to remain a 'battered-wife.'" Just after she became eligible for clemency in 1979, she was charged with second-degree assault for hitting a guard. Anderson, who maintained her innocence, was summarily convicted by an all-white jury and faced an additional sentence of three to seven years. Anderson appealed to readers to help her secure reliable legal aid, write letters on her behalf, and visit the prison to "see for yourself." She concluded by pointing out the parallels between her home and the prison: "I am not a danger to society, I have never been, I am a woman that just 'got tired' of having my ass kicked three times a day, I left him and begged the courts for protection, their reply was 'that is a domestic problem!' Here I am now in prison, and the new male guards are talking about kicking us in the 'but[t]'! What are we to do as women?"[83]

Both *No More Cages* and *Through the Looking Glass* regularly provided coverage of the protracted case of Rita Silk Nauni, a Lakota Sioux woman imprisoned for killing one airport security officer and wounding another in 1979. Thirty-year-old Nauni fled Los Angeles for Oklahoma with her ten-year-old son to escape her husband's violent abuse. Upon landing in Oklahoma City, Nauni learned that bus service to her destination was suspended because of a labor strike. She removed some clothing from her son's bag so he could manage the weight as they set out on foot with plans to hitchhike. Shortly thereafter, they were detained on the side of the road by airport police for littering. Nauni maintained that one of the two officers "manhandled and attempted to force" her son into a security car, making her fear for the child's physical safety. As the second officer attempted to restrain her, she gained control of his gun: "A scuffle resulted and one officer was killed, the other wounded." Nauni and her son then fled in the airport security vehicle. In an interview with TTLG, local Native American activist Frances Wise (Wichita-Caddo), coordinator of Nauni's defense committee, recounted what happened next:

> When the police officer rammed his cruiser into hers that forced her off the highway, the other police cruisers from Oklahoma City and from the airport security force, they all just converged on the scene. They jerked her from the police car, handcuffed her with her hands behind her back, and took her around to the back of the police car, and it was at that point that six to eight police officers knocked her to the ground and kicked her and stomped her. . . . There were witnesses at a restaurant across the highway from where she was stopped who filed complaints with the Internal Affairs Division of the Oklahoma City Police Department for the way she was treated once she was apprehended and placed under arrest. . . . She was taken to Intensive Care at University Hospital and she had broken fingers, a black eye, and a concussion.[84]

Wise, who had been a central leader in the Oklahoma chapter of the American Indian Movement, and a handful of other Native American women activists swiftly formed a defense committee. According to *No More Cages*, the local Native American Center had received numerous reports that "these same two officers . . . had abused their authority many times."[85] Although the committee's efforts produced a groundswell of community support for Nauni and provided crucial funds for her legal expenses, she was ultimately convicted by an all-white jury of first-degree manslaughter and assault with a deadly weapon and egregiously sentenced to 150 years in prison. Updates on Nauni's case in the two newsletters stressed its connection to Yvonne Wanrow's and situated these and other examples of Native American women fighting to maintain custody of their children, resist police violence, and defend themselves from intimate violence in the context of "escalating attacks on Native American people as well as on women throughout the country."[86] Nauni's claim that fear for her son's life caused her to shoot the two police officers was likely controversial in some activist circles, yet these newsletters endorsed the indigenous feminist analysis put forth by the defense committee that her actions could not be evaluated apart from her experiences of intimate and colonial state violence.

As they circulated and juxtaposed news and analyses of numerous cases of women who had fought back against their assailants, *No More Cages* and *Through the Looking Glass* made a searing critique of the criminalization of women's survival strategies in the context of gendered racism, economic oppression, rape, and battering, illuminating the complicities of the "racist, sexist court" system, law enforcement, and the prison in sanctioning and perpetuating intimate violence.[87]

The Institutional Violence of Imprisonment

In April 1981, Carol Ann Wilds filed a suit against the Indiana Department of Corrections for creating "an environment . . . that is ripe for coercion and extreme influence over female prisoners concerning sexual harassment and exploitation by male guards and supervisory personnel." In a piece published in both *No More Cages* and *Through the Looking Glass*, Wilds explained that because of "repeated abuse by male personnel of both myself and other female inmates, and out of concern for the future of my recently born child, fathered by a Department of Corrections employee, I am requesting that this matter be tried by jury." Wilds, a white, working-class woman from rural Kentucky, was 22 when she went to prison for shooting her violent husband, who was also her pimp. She argued that for four years her constitutional right to freedom from cruel and unusual punishment had been violated by "corrupt Department of Corrections employees who force indecent liberties upon me and others through intimidation, coercion, fraud, promises of medical treatment, preferential job placements, monetary gain, conduct adjustment board leniency, and guarantees of early release from prison." Her breaking point came the night that a male guard had the depraved audacity to proposition her for sex while she lay shackled to a prison hospital bed after a liver biopsy. Wilds turned to the underground press in her quest "to have sexual

harassment branded cruel and unusual punishment even in a punitive setting. To accomplish this, it is necessary that I have support from my sisters
throughout the nation who are in agreement with me on this issue."[88] With
the help of a "jailhouse lawyer" from the National Prisoners Rights Union,
she filed suit in U.S. District Court. Although the Department of Corrections
roundly condemned the charges, telling the press that this was an isolated
case fabricated for "personal gain," this position grew untenable as dozens
of other prisoners began contacting the press to share their stories of either
witnessing or directly experiencing sexual harassment and coercion, through
which several other women became pregnant. Although the publicity and
investigations her suit provoked led to the dismissal of several guards and
the resignation of the prison's superintendent, Wilds's target was the whole
"program," or culture, of coercion.[89] "The issue is by all means not that of, 'one
bad apple' in the barrel of 'Good Apples' in the Department," she explained.[90]

When we read these newsletters cumulatively, they become evidentiary
archives of the systematic character of state-sponsored sexual violence and
coercion in U.S. prisons. The Free Joan Little movement of 1974–1975 helped
to create a political opening for women prisoners and free world activists
to expose sexual violence throughout the country's prisons.[91] In California,
Florida, Indiana, New York, North Carolina, Ohio, and elsewhere, women
prisoners protested this carceral culture of state-sponsored rape, harassment,
and coercion through writing, reporting, filing suits, and striking.[92] When
a federal prisoner in Lexington, Kentucky, reported that a guard had raped
her, officials refused to take action. She then filed a district court suit against
the guard as well as against the administration for negligence. In response,
she was written up for "engaging in sexual acts" with a correctional officer,
thrown in segregation, and eventually transferred to the federal prison for
women in Alderson, Virginia.[93] June Boyd, a gay-identified, African American woman and a frequent contributor to *off our backs*, *Through the Looking
Glass*, and *No More Cages* found herself in solitary confinement after she
"signed two statements on their staff members, one of whom [she] had sex
with on several occasions." In 1979, Boyd helped to start a prisoner organizing group at Muncy called Sisters of Unity; this group made "unwarranted
verbal and/or physical abuse by guards or matrons or nurses" one of their
five key grievances and areas for action.[94]

In addition to confronting forms of sexual harassment, coercion, and violence that corrections officials denied, concealed, and formally condemned
but actually tolerated or protected, imprisoned contributors politicized several routine custodial practices, including strip searches and body cavity
searches, "frisking" procedures, and policies in some prisons requiring that

those in solitary confinement be stripped of their clothes and denied even a bed sheet.[95] The ostensible objective of refusing clothes and bedding was suicide prevention, but in practice it produced degradation and humiliation. At the Clinton Correctional Facility for Women in New Jersey in 1977, a group of activists submitted a list of grievances and demands to the administration with a brazen pronouncement: "We have exhausted our tolerance as to verbal uniformed pacification. . . . We will no longer remain silent and be continuously exposed to verbatim fruitless promises of remedies to the prevailing problems." Among their chief concerns was the invasiveness of routine "pat frisks" and "strip frisks," and they smuggled a copy of the procedural instructions for these searches to *Through the Looking Glass*.[96] Other imprisoned writers theorized the racialized sexualized violence of solitary confinement in their dispatches. Writing from a segregation cell in the Maryland Correctional Institution for Women in 1979, an African American woman explained to readers that the prison had

> three different areas where you can be held in solitary confinement . . . "degrees" of solitary, if you can believe that a mentality exists that can get "into" refining and intensifying what is already an excruciatingly maddening type of torture. . . . Detention is Step I for everyone getting ready to undergo this "process." . . . You can be kept in Detention cells naked from 3 days to 2 years. . . . The actual physical nudity [the warden] forces on women who are to be placed in Detention reflects, and (he hopes) instigates the psychological stripping that is his real goal. He attempts to render you so much clay to be molded and shaped into his conception of what a woman consists of, or in the case of African women, to eradicate those traits that we as an alleged inferior people have no right possessing.[97]

The introduction of male guards at Bedford Hills prison in 1977 spurred protest. Although this step initially took place under the auspices of ending sex discrimination in employment within corrections institutions in accordance with Title VII of the 1964 Civil Rights Act, many activists linked the shift to an uptick in calls for security, order, and an end to "liberal permissiveness" at the institution.[98] They emphasized that most of the several dozen new employees guarding the predominantly downstate, black and Puerto Rican prison population were white men from rural, upstate communities, some with prior experience working in maximum-security men's facilities. Shortly after men joined the guard force at Bedford that spring, a group of ten black women, including several Muslim women, filed a federal class action suit charging multiple prison officials and the New York State guards' union with invasion of privacy as well as violation of the religious rights of Muslim prisoners.[99] The court's decision in 1978 was considered a "partial victory" for the activists: male guards would no longer work night shifts in the housing units or staff the shower areas, limiting their presence in places where they could gaze at naked women. Carol Crooks, who spearheaded the class action, reported to WFWP that in the wake of the ruling "the administration is intensifying its repression" through such means as restricting time in the yard, one of the only locations for women from different housing units to communicate and strategize, as well as limiting phone calls and delaying mail deliveries. Crooks herself claimed that guards "set up" an altercation between her and another prisoner on the cusp of her parole hearing in 1978, an incident that cost her parole and was punished by another stint in segregation.[100]

In May 1980, the court's decision was reversed on appeal on the grounds that it infringed on men's civil right to equal employment opportunity at the prison. Activists wryly remarked in *No More Cages* that women prisoners at Bedford and elsewhere had yet to secure their own rights, for example, to vocational training opportunities on par with those in men's institutions. Moreover, they situated this lack against the backdrop of increasing overcrowding and its potential to generate both abuse and resistance; by 1980, 400 people lived in an institution built for 250.[101] Despite this blow, prisoners as far away as California took keen interest in the newspaper's coverage of the Bedford Hills prisoners' class action. One woman wrote to WFWP to request a copy of the court records and share her own account of what she understood to be comparable conditions at the California Institution for Women in Frontera.[102]

As historian Regina Kunzel has shown, with the exception of the infamous "Daddy Tank" for gender-nonconforming lesbians at the Los Angeles women's county jail, women's prison officials did not appear to make it a matter of formal policy to segregate those perceived to be lesbians in the mid-to-late twentieth century.[103] Nevertheless, *No More Cages* and *Through the Looking Glass* demonstrate that other institutional forms of policing "homosexuality" and gender nonconformity abounded in the 1970s and early 1980s. Racialized norms of compulsory heterosexuality underwrote projects of social control and rehabilitation in women's prisons. Tactile expressions of affection of any sort could swiftly be labeled as lesbianism. Theresa King, who was incarcerated at a state prison in the Pacific Northwest, recounted: "If somebody's having a problem, I've learned the best thing to do is to go over and give them a hug, give them some support. But here, you can't even touch somebody, let alone hold their hand or put your arm around them. That's homosexual activity."[104] A prisoner at Purdy writing in *Through the Looking Glass* in the early 1980s observed that lesbians "who refuse to hide their sexual desires for each other," and especially those who are not "the same color," could expect to "become targets for frequent harassment attacks." In her case, write-ups for homosexual activity were adduced as relevant transgressions in her parole hearing: "I never thought I would be given a life sentence just because I am a lesbian."[105] Two black lesbian women interviewed by members of TTLG for a piece titled "Racism at Purdy" in 1980 corroborated that "they're just on top of you all the time" when white women and black women display any signs of intimacy, from physical touching to visiting one another's rooms. One interviewee added: "When you go before the [parole] board, you have to dress and act like you're white."[106] Here, acting white and straightening up meld into a single mandate to perform normative femininity—rendered synonymous with "good behavior"—in order to be considered for parole. Historian Evelynn Hammonds argues that since the nineteenth century "black women's sexuality has been constructed in a binary opposition to that of white women: it is rendered simultaneously invisible, visible (exposed), hypervisible, and pathologized in dominant discourses."[107] The intensive policing of interracial intimacy also points to the ways in which prison officials produced and depended upon racial hierarchies for social control.

The newsletters documented the dense interplay of psychiatric power and carcerality in women's prisons in the 1970s and early 1980s. Psychiatric disability functioned as justification for labeling, drugging, segregating, and transferring unruly prisoners, and unruliness was not only a matter of conduct but one of racial, gender, and sexual embodiment. An African American prisoner activist in Kansas commented acerbically in a letter to *No More Cages*, "Whenever I have a question of law I am sent to the psychologist's office."[108] Letters and feature stories documented the institutionalized use of psychotropic drugs—which some activists referred to as "valium violence"—and the increased construction of new specialized units, both on campus and off, for women labeled troublesome, violent, and dangerous to themselves or their peers.[109] Several Bedford Hills prisoners described this common attitude: "Anyone who resists is unbalanced."[110] A contributor to *No More Cages* imprisoned at the California Institution for Women recounted, "Some of my friends have gotten themselves shipped out to Patton, a state hospital, not because they're really crazy; but because they go off due to the staff's actions on them."[111] A diagnosis of "mentally disturbed" facilitated the transfer of the ten black women at Bedford Hills to the Matteawan Complex for the Criminally Insane in 1976. WFWP recounted parts of the class action complaint brought by the "Matteawan Ten" against the New York Department of Corrections with the assistance of the National Prison Project of the American Civil Liberties Union (ACLU): "One of the women

. . . was once removed from her cell, taken to the strip room, and beaten severely. Another one . . . refused her medication, was thrown into the strip cell, and was forcibly injected with Prolixin. A sign was hung outside her door reading: 'This nigger is crazy again.' The food was cold, stale, and, the women believed, drugged. They were often denied medical attention." After three years of litigation, the judge ordered corrections officials to discontinue their practice of shipping women to Matteawan and awarded the plaintiffs $45,000 in damages. Despite the relatively small sum, the settlement was unprecedented. "It is a victory which none of us, the women inside and those of us outside supporting them, thought could be won," WFWP told readers.[112]

The ubiquity of accounts of forced drugging was matched by the ubiquity of prisoners' demands for better health care. These issues converged at the point of medication, where "valium violence" coincided with prison officials' refusals to provide safe and reliable access to life-sustaining medications for conditions not related to mental health, such as epilepsy, diabetes, and high blood pressure. Basic medical care routinely appeared at the top of prisoners' lists of demands published in *No More Cages* and *Through the Looking Glass*. Letters recounted how long delays to see a doctor or get a prescription refill and staff inaction in the face of medical emergencies complicated chronic and terminal illnesses. "There are epileptics, diabetics, and asthmatics who have all had their medication taken away by the doctor . . . with the doctor claiming 'you're not sick, it's all in your head.'"[113] From jails and prisons, incarcerated women told of enduring prolonged waits to see a doctor during their pregnancy and being shackled during childbirth. Some testified to being sterilized either without their consent or under false pretenses. In an interview with Liberation News Service published in *Through the Looking Glass*, Carol Crooks said that in "1977 it was like they had a sale going around here. And I was put in that sale and got my uterus removed. They said I had a fibroid tumor. I went down to a hospital in New York (City) to have the operation. . . . About 40 women were on the list that they needed to have their uterus removed. . . . A lot of Black women won't ever have kids again."[114] On both sides of the bars in the 1970s, black, indigenous, and Latina women were most vulnerable to this pervasive form of reproductive violence.[115]

Activists also argued that systemic medical neglect threatened to turn women's punishments into death sentences. An open letter signed by the "Women of the California Institution for Women" and published in *No More Cages* in 1982 mourned the loss of a prisoner whose death, in their view, could have been prevented and called upon all concerned people to help them to force the California Department of Corrections to uphold its legal obligation to provide adequate medical care: "To sentence a woman to the

California Institution for Women, especially a person with obvious medical problems, is inflicting the death penalty on that inmate without due process of law, because their very life is in danger at the hands and discretion of present Administration and inadequate medical facilities and staff."[116] In these newsletters, prisoners memorialized friends and lovers lost to medical neglect and urged readers to help them demand institutional changes.

Agitating to obtain treatment for their own health emergencies or those of their peers could result in reprisal. In the wake of the June 1975 rebellion at the North Carolina Correctional Center for Women in Raleigh, working conditions in the prison laundry underwent modest reform, but prisoner activists reported that medical care remained abysmal. In 1977, TTLG reported that "disciplinary charges were brought against nine women who attempted to get medical attention for a sick comrade and to rescue another woman from a burning cell."[117] At the California Institution for Women in 1978, more than half of the prisoners participated in a sit-in to protest "atrocious medical conditions, quantity and quality of food, unsanitary conditions in the kitchen and hospital," and more. After holding out for thirty-two hours, the roughly 400 protestors agreed to return to their cells on the warden's guarantee that there would be no disciplinary action. Writing in *Through the Looking Glass*, the San Francisco Bay Area feminist group Women Against Prisons relayed that "200 women have been locked in their cells. . . . They have not been allowed hot food or exercise. They have been charged with serious rule violations which could affect their release date and custody status. . . . The women have added Warden Anderson's removal to their list of demands."[118] Muncy prison in Pennsylvania was the site of a protracted struggle concerning a multitude of health-related grievances, including spoiled food and poor medical treatment for pregnant women. Petitions signed by more than half of the prison population and prisoner-authored letters to the editor published in local newspapers and grassroots prison newsletters brought retaliatory punishments for those identified as the lead organizers, including extended time in the maximum-security unit and confiscation of mail.[119]

Though women's prisons remained the center of gravity for both of these newsletters, they mapped, dissected, and contested a broader carceral landscape of locked institutions and "cages." They published or reprinted pieces penned by activists affiliated with groups such as the Alliance for the Liberation of Mental Patients (Philadelphia), Mental Patients Liberation Front (Boston), and the Network Against Psychiatric Assault (Berkeley), as well as by the Coalition to Stop Institutional Violence. The collectives' own writings probed how various institutions of confinement functioned as containers for social Others deemed disposable, defective, or deviant. As one TTLG member put it, "Lesbians are considered 'crazy' and locked up in psychiatric facilities, elders are called a 'burden' or 'unuseful' and put in nursing homes. . . . Women are locked up for fighting back when men attempt to beat, rape, or kill us."[120]

"The State Is in No Way Our Ally in the Struggle against Rape and Battering"

Prisoner solidarity work profoundly influenced feminist radicals who espoused critical positions on law-and-order approaches to interpersonal violence. Corresponding with and publishing the writings of numerous people imprisoned in women's and men's prisons throughout the country prompted TTLG and WFWP members to regard criminalization-centered approaches to stemming violence against women as a contradiction in terms. Both groups utilized their newsletter to express this view. In a statement of purpose that often appeared in the opening pages of *No More Cages*, WFWP decried the marginalization of imprisoned women in "a movement where violence against women has been a primary target of organizing." The group attributed this situation "to the fact that much of the work in the women's movement has been done from the perspective of white, middle class women, and so it has not focused on issues primary in the lives of women of color and poor women—and it is exactly these women that make up the majority of women in prison."[121] Collective members reserved particular criticism for white, middle-class feminists who championed physical self-defense for women yet failed to dedicate themselves to organizing efforts for those convicted and incarcerated for killing their batterers and sexual attackers.[122] TTLG urged feminists in Seattle who had, in fact, shown support for such women to consider the importance of "visiting and giving support to womyn who are jailed for *other* reasons. . . . We can recognize, learn from, and support different womyn's struggles to survive in this sexist, racist, classist society, without necessarily supporting or advocating the particular choices womyn have made."[123] Similarly, WFWP advocated the view that "ALL prisoners are, in fact, political prisoners."[124]

These activists understood themselves as laboring to grasp "where exactly violence against women lives in the midst of a network of oppressions."[125] As Janet Howard of WFWP put it, feminist activists who saw "male domination" as the principal source of "women's physical oppression . . . miss seeing other bruises and deep scars."[126] These activists appear to have rejected the notion held by some in the "white dominated women's movement" that women prisoners simply endured "magnified and intensified" forms of "male op-

Cover of *Through the Looking Glass*, July 1978. From the Atlanta Lesbian Feminist Alliance Periodicals Collection, Sallie Bingham Center for Women's History and Culture, Rubenstein Library, Duke University.

pression."[127] As the newsletters gathered together a plethora of critiques of the racialized and gendered violence of the carceral state, both TTLG and WFWP argued for strategies to challenge interpersonal violence that aligned with their abolitionist visions. In 1978, TTLG reprinted a series of updates compiled by the recently launched *Aegis: A Magazine on Ending Violence Against Women* on legislative changes in several states that would expand criminal punishment for domestic violence. The collective followed the piece with this critical appraisal:

We support the work of these women in getting these states to finally recognize violence against women as a serious societal problem. However, we don't believe that the long term solution to this problem is putting the abusers in prisons; it is clear, tho, that we have not worked out an alternative to prison. Prison is a violent environment. . . . We too feel rage at the men who abuse women but recognize that the anger must be directed in the long run toward the real enemies. These are the men at the top who profit by keeping the vast majority of the people down and attacking each other. We feel our energies should go to working against this larger enemy instead of working for longer and insured prison terms.[128]

Similarly, WFWP members argued that legal reforms should be evaluated against a commitment to racial justice and abolishing prisons, and only pursued with a critical awareness that "the state is in no way our ally in the struggle against rape and battering."[129] Although they may "bring small concessions to women's safety," enhanced policing, tougher sanctions, and more women in law enforcement would "more likely strengthen the repressive, racist power of the police, the courts, and the prisons" and bolster institutional violence against women multiply marginalized by racial, economic, gender, and sexual oppression. Although these groups had a well-defined understanding of why they opposed the feminist antiviolence movement's "carceral creep," as social movement scholar Mimi Kim describes it, identifying short- and medium-term alternatives to criminalization for imposing social sanctions and holding perpetrators accountable was a more formidable task.[130]

Outlaw Alliances: Identity, Power, and Belonging

A leaflet created and distributed by WFWP during Gay Pride Week in New York City in 1981 posed the following contradiction to its readers: "This weekend, hundreds and thousands of lesbians and gay men will take to the streets in gay pride marches in every major city across the country. But what about those of us who can't march? WHAT ABOUT THOSE OF US WHO ARE LOCKED UP IN PRISONS, JAILS AND PSYCHIATRIC INSTITUTIONS?" WFWP explained to its audience of white, middle-class lesbians and gay men that "heterosexist oppression" pervaded the country's prisons, which were currently "bursting with working class, poor, and Third World peoples." As evidence, the group explained that a prison record of "homosexual activities" could function as a weapon of character assassination in "future court cases." The leaflet detailed the "strict rules about physical contact" and their uneven enforcement, arguing that these, in and of themselves, constituted a dangerous behavior modification strategy. It reminded readers of the historical and contemporary pathologization of homosexuality and the involuntary institutionalization of numerous lesbians and gay men. WFWP concluded: "This week and every week we need to remember all the lesbians and gay men locked up in state institutions. We must remember *all* the people behind bars. And we must do *more* than remember."[131] This piece of ephemera captures the collective's intertwined commitments to educating "the outside" and providing material support to prisoners in the service of a long-term abolitionist vision. As it appeals to a sense of kinship between queers in the streets and "the queer queers" in the prisons (as Boston activist Mike Reigle dubbed lesbian and gay prisoners) while also emphasizing the racial political economy of imprisonment, the leaflet suggests group members' own routes to and investments in antiprison work.[132]

Many of the working-class, queer women who joined these collectives identified as outlaws in a compulsorily heterosexual world dominated by middle-class norms of propriety. Their encounters with imprisonment, police harassment, juvenile detention, psychiatric institutionalization, or expulsion from their families of origin shaped their pathways to feminist prison activism and their relationships—both imagined and interpersonal— with imprisoned women.[133] An outlaw sensibility produced a desire to forge alliances with those caged for participating in criminalized economies, resisting physical abuse, and failing to adequately perform economic productivity, gender conformity, or respectable domesticity. The majority of WFWP's members and at least a portion of TTLG's were Jewish, some from left-wing families directly affected by the 1950s Red Scare. As sociologist Becky Thompson has argued, "Jewish women and lesbians led the way" in white antiracist feminist activism in the 1970s and 1980s, culling insight from their contested belonging in the larger "women's movement that was, nevertheless, still homophobic and Christian biased."[134] Both groups regularly delineated for readers the racial, ethnic, class, and sexual identities of their respective collective bodies.

While declarations of their Jewish, queer, and working-class identities conveyed collective members' personal and familial histories of persecution, exploitation, and marginalization, when these primarily white groups acknowledged their racial composition they were seeking to convey an antiracist consciousness and accountability. As TTLG described in its contribution to *Top Ranking: A Collection of Articles on Racism and Classism in the Lesbian Community*, "racism pervades all the issues we encounter in our prison and jail support work, in the news we get from prisoners and in our group discussions."[135] In this way, the two groups practiced a "politics of relation" that emphasized the asymmetries of oppression and privilege structuring the lives of those gathered under the sign of women but also identified shared political commitments and vision, and a "shared marginal relationship to dominant power," as a basis for coalition building.[136] Activists used the newsletters to point to the unavoidable power differential between imprisoned and "free" activists, encouraging the latter to grasp the crucial importance of not "throwing a letter on the pile and then forgetting it's there" or otherwise "leav[ing] the people inside hanging at the mercy of the state."[137]

While both organizations focused on women's prisons in an effort to re-dress the marginalization of women prisoners on the left in the 1970s, they also reflected their founders' desires to work collectively and autonomously with other feminist women. Hence, while they conceived of themselves as "part of a mass movement of oppressed people"[138] and to varying degrees participated in other mixed-gender organizations and activist spaces, TTLG and WFWP members do not appear to have ever entertained the possibility of men as members. Whereas WFWP's core group consistently remained lesbian-identified, a few straight-identified women filtered in and out of TTLG over its eleven-year existence. Despite clearly valuing autonomous space for women and lesbians, both organizations ultimately endorsed an intersectional ideology, theorizing racism, capitalism, imperialism, and het-eropatriarchy as interlocking. Lesbian separatism was a central and contested politics in the social geographies of these activists. As a world-making project, separatism emphasized that women's primary relationships should be with other women and, in turn, idealized the "women's community" as one free of harm and hierarchy. These ideas were heavily criticized by radical women of color activists in the 1970s as a "dangerous and reactionary" political platform invested in a biologically deterministic definition of "women" and woefully inadequate for addressing the multiple "sources of women's oppression."[139]

Although WFWP's work was indeed women-centered, collective members found themselves in the position of having to defend their prison activism to some white women in "the NYC lesbian community." Writing in *Top Rank-ing*, WFWP cofounder Charoula Dontopoulos recounted: "I have been often asked by other lesbians . . . why I, a lesbian, found it necessary to work with/for women in prison. . . . It is to say that women of color, and poor women, who are in prison cannot possibly be lesbians. It is to say that to do work which is not directly related to lesbian issues is taking away from the lesbian move-ment, is divisive, and weakening, and not important enough for lesbians to be involved in. It is to say that the problems of every day survival which women of color and poor women are plagued with have nothing to do with our women's movement. What then *is* our women's movement? To be for women, and to ignore the special plight of women in prison is a contradiction."[140] Like its close ally, Dykes Against Racism Everywhere (DARE), antiracism led WFWP to differentiate between an investment in autonomous lesbian organizing and an embrace of lesbian separatism. Coeditors and DARE members Sara Bennett and Joan Gibbs wrote in their introduction to *Top Ranking*: "We can not liberate ourselves in a vacuum and/or by assuming that the solution to all of the oppressions that lesbians face, particularly those of Third World lesbians, lies in the liberation of our heads and spaces [from] men."[141]

By the mid-1980s, these collectives increasingly contended with attrition as founding members cycled out. This form of volunteer labor had always been time-consuming and emotionally intense, but it became more arduous as the broader social movement milieu that incubated these groups waned. Prison authorities' various means of limiting as well as overtly sabotaging communication between prisoners and their supporters made the rhythms of support work irregular and unpredictable. All these conditions contributed to activist burnout. The fact that these organizations remained entirely grassroots-funded and unincorporated constrained their ability to recruit new members beyond the predominantly white lesbian feminist activist communities from which they emerged. Each collective drew staying power by blurring the boundaries between hours devoted to political work and time spent with friends, lovers, and chosen family.[142] WFWP, for example, was cofounded by two couples. A former TTLG member recalls "pulling all-nighters" to lay out issues of the newsletter in members' living rooms and the intensity of the weekly prison visiting schedule. Many members lived collectively with one another, and very few, if any, had young children.[143] The small scale and severely limited finances of these organizations prohibited them from developing any form of "reentry" support to recently formerly incarcerated women aside from a small amount of "gate money" or a place to sleep for a few nights. TTLG's unrealized aspiration to develop a transitional living program would have certainly helped to create the conditions of possibility for more women released or paroled to Seattle to become involved. Although TTLG's weekend ride-sharing program brought them in direct contact with prisoners' family members, the collective's cultural and political specificity curtailed the prospect of these primarily African American families becoming more active in the organization. By the mid-1980s, both *No More Cages* and *Through the Looking Glass* had ceased publication.[144]

* * *

During the early years of the prison buildup, *No More Cages* and *Through the Looking Glass* played a crucial role in the making of an abolitionist feminism.

These newsletters served as switchboards, helping to generate communication and collaboration across disparate and uneven locations. They now provide us with archives of a translocal culture of opposition to gendered, racialized, and sexualized carceral violence. Moreover, print media not only documented activism; it helped to produce it. As this chapter has shown, imprisoned and free activists used these publications to compare conditions, exchange strategies, overcome isolation, recruit allies, and collectively generate theoretical insight. As Robin D. G. Kelley reminds us, "collective social movements are incubators of new knowledge."[145] The counterpublic created by *No More Cages* and *Through the Looking Glass* put imprisoned women at the center of feminist antiviolence discourse, criticized the criminalization of survival and the institutional violence of incarceration, and affirmed an outlaw politics of affiliation and belonging. Moreover, it advocated alternatives to a criminal justice–centered approach to preventing sexual and domestic violence.

The next chapter moves us from women's prison activism to street-level organizing. As activists confronted the role of police in sanctioning and committing violence against women of color, they called for and experimented with nonstatist strategies of emergency response and prevention that flowed from their intersectional understanding of power and oppression.

4. Intersecting Indictments

Coalitions for Women's Safety, Racial Justice, and the Right to the City

> As Black women who are feminists we are struggling against all racist, sexist, heterosexist and class oppression. We know that we have no hopes of ending this particular crisis and violence against women in our community until we identify all its causes, including sexual oppression.
> —Combahee River Collective (1979)

> Black feminism has always sought to connect the dots. . . . In many ways, we really politicized the Rape Crisis Center . . . in terms of taking on the state, taking on the antiapartheid movement, taking on housing, taking on a whole lot of other issues that the gender lens didn't necessarily see as women's issues that we did.
> —Loretta Ross (2005)

In August 1980 more than a hundred activists gathered in Washington, D.C., for the First National Conference on Third World Women and Violence. Organized by the black feminist–led D.C. Rape Crisis Center, the conference marked the first time that black, Latina, Asian, and Native American women working in rape crisis centers (RCCs) and battered women's shelters in the United States convened both nationally and autonomously.[1] Over the course of the three-day event, conference attendees culled lessons from their experiences as antiviolence organizers in communities of color and as people of color working in majority-white RCCs and battered women's shelters. Conference coordinators Loretta Ross, Nkenge Touré, and Deirdre Wright named "isolation, alienation, and racism" within feminist antiviolence organizations as a key rationale for the gathering and their larger goal of cultivating a new national network of women and men of color engaged in antiviolence activism.[2] A significant catalyst was pervasive concern about these organizations' increasing involvement with the criminal justice state.

The conference organizers acknowledged the "intense mistrust" fostered by "racism/insensitivity on the part of the police" as a basis for solidarity among U.S. Third World antiviolence activists. Short-term reforms, they argued, must be gauged against the long-term goal of the "elimination of this society as it presently stands, with its promotion of racism, classism, sexism, capitalism, and imperialism." Attendees debated the merits of chan- neling energy toward improving criminal justice sanctions and questioned what "more prisons, longer sentences, and increased convictions" accomplish aside from "penaliz[ing] the most disadvantaged of offenders" and bolster- ing the legitimacy of an expanding prison system.[3] In an array of workshops ranging from alternatives to police intervention to international solidarity movements to ending sterilization abuse, participants grappled with the formidable challenges of crafting an analysis of violence against women of color that accounted for multiple colonial and racial histories, global contexts, and overlapping patriarchies, as well as a praxis of *antiviolence* that disrupted rather than reinscribed the forces of racial criminalization and inequality.[4]

The D.C. Rape Crisis Center was well positioned to initiate and coordinate this meeting. It often fielded inquiries about its approaches from women of color advocates in other cities "because of its unique position as an established center ran by a Third World staff, with a significant number of Third World volunteers giving services to as many Third World as white victims."[5] The organization's independence and autonomy from criminal justice funding made it a suitable host for a conference that sought to escape the fog of law- and-order feminism. The organizers' nationwide call drew participants from Boston, New York, the San Francisco Bay Area, Miami, Minneapolis–Saint Paul, and Philadelphia, as well as many from the Washington metropolitan area.[6] Among those who traveled from Boston were several members of the Coalition for Women's Safety, a black feminist–led alliance of feminist, antiracist, and economic justice organizations based in Boston's majority people-of-color neighborhoods. This coalition was propelled into being by a harrowing spate of killings of black women and girls in the winter and spring of 1979 and the troubling responses of both the Boston Police Department and city's mainstream news media. More than a year later, it continued to function as a clearinghouse and coordinating body for antiviolence organiz- ing in the city's neighborhoods of Dorchester, Roxbury, the South End, and Jamaica Plain. Attendees shared their reflections on this unprecedented local coalition and its nonstatist, community-based approach to violence against women, in the process corroborating the conference's critique of the inter-twined racism, sexism, and classism of law enforcement.

This chapter looks closely at black feminist–led antiviolence organizing efforts in Boston and Washington, D.C., in the years around 1980, exploring their conceptualizations of violence against women and their theories and practices of violence prevention.[7] In both of these highly segregated and stratified cities, black feminist organizations played leading roles in forging coalitions that crossed lines of race, class, gender, sexuality, and neighbor-hood and advancing an antiviolence politics that insisted on the interconnec-tions among policing and imprisonment, rape and battering, and racial, eco-nomic, and gender oppression. These coalitions reoriented local discourses of violence against women around a critique of state harm and a mandate for alternatives to criminalization and incarceration. I begin in Boston, tracing the origins of the Coalition for Women's Safety in the murder crisis of 1979 and examining the formation's ideology, structure, and strategy. I highlight the intellectual and organizational leadership of the Combahee River Col-lective in the coalition, demonstrating the pivotal influence of this group of self-described black lesbian feminist socialists on the alliance's intersectional analysis of power and violence. The chapter then turns to Washington, D.C., providing a history of the development of black feminist leadership at the city's Rape Crisis Center and an examination of a series of "coalitional mo-ments" in which the RCC served as a force of interconnection between white feminists and black nationalists; antigentrification, antiprison, and antirape activists; and black, Latina, Asian, and Native American activists working on issues of rape and battering both within and beyond the capital.[8]

"Twelve Black Women: Why Did They Die?"

Between late January and May of 1979 twelve black women and girls, rang-ing in age from fifteen to fifty-one, were slain within a three-mile radius that cut across Boston's adjacent neighborhoods of Dorchester, Roxbury, Jamaica Plain, and the South End. Strangled, stabbed, or beaten to death, their bod-ies were found in parks and vacant lots, in trash bags and on sidewalks, or in their apartments, some dismembered or burned.[9] The quick succession and brutality of these killings generated widespread terror in the city's black community. As the death toll continued to rise throughout the winter and spring, it became painfully clear to neighborhood residents, the victims' families, and community leaders that they could not count on the Boston police or the local newspapers to see these killings as a crisis demanding urgent attention. Police officials appeared apathetic and slow to marshal adequate resources for the investigation, deepening the existing fault line between black Bostonians and the city's overwhelmingly white police force. Reporters covering the cases of the first several murders in the *Boston Globe*, the city's largest and most respected paper, described the women and girls as "runaways" and "ladies of the night," insinuating that the victims were involved in the sex trade and therefore culpable for their own demise, and downplaying their family and neighborhood ties.[10]

Some of the victims' family members and other neighborhood residents took special offense at police officials' and the media's starkly contrasting response to a nearly coterminous series of eight rapes in the predominantly white and middle-class Brighton section of Boston that same winter. On February 1, just four days after the bodies of two black girls were found in garbage bags on a street in Roxbury and three days after a third body was found in a vacant lot, the police called a town hall meeting in Brighton to discuss the status of the rape investigation that drew more than 700 local residents, the District Attorney, and numerous reporters. Several weeks later, when Roxbury residents convened the first of many community meetings in response to the series of murders, no mainstream press attended and, according to an independent feminist journalist, only "one police deputy superintendent showed up—and he was late."[11] Some pointed out that the number of reported rapes in Roxbury in 1978 was triple that of Brighton.[12]

Yet the connection between the "Brighton rapes" and the "Roxbury murders" was more than comparative. As activists came to argue in the months ahead, in both cases "violence against women and racism" intersected. The seven rape victims in Brighton between November 1978 and February 1979 all identified their assailant as a thin, bearded, black man, in his twenties or early thirties, with a pockmarked complexion and a Caribbean accent. At the February 1 community meeting, police officials announced that they had just arrested a suspect by the name of Willie Sanders, providing the crowd with an eight-year-old photograph of the thirty-nine-year-old African American man from a traffic arrest file (his only police record).[13] With a smooth complexion and a slight southern accent, Sanders hardly matched the descriptions provided by the victims; the Roxbury resident came to the attention of the police only because he worked as a painter in one of the apartment buildings where several of the rapes occurred. Following a series of suggestive and faulty lineups, he was charged with four of the assaults and jailed with a bond of $50,000.[14] While he was detained, another rape by a perpetrator fitting the description occurred, yet Sanders continued to be deemed the "Brighton rapist" by the press.[15]

At this moment of crisis, the Combahee River Collective emerged as a key bridge builder among the many individuals and organizations activated by the murders, and as an ideological beacon for an intersectional, coalitional mobilization. As Combahee member Barbara Smith later reflected, the collective was "ideally positioned to link the coalitions that grew among black and white people, feminists and nonfeminists."[16] The group was first established in 1974 as the Boston chapter of the National Black Feminist Organization (NBFO).[17] Early members included Smith and her twin sister Beverly Smith, Demita Frazier, Sharon Bourke, and Margo Okazawa-Rey, who together brought to the table years of participation in antiwar, civil rights, black liberation, feminist, and gay and lesbian liberation movements. In 1975, the group cut formal ties with the NBFO after deciding that the national organization was "headed in a reformist direction" at odds with its own socialist, anti-imperialist, and queer politics.[18] Combahee was initially a consciousness-raising group and a political "home base" for its members, who participated in a variety of other feminist and black community–based organizations, campaigns, and projects focused on abortion and sterilization abuse, rape and battering (including the defense campaigns for Joan Little and Inez García), health care, and lesbian rights.[19] Through this variegated political work, Combahee members had formed connections with many of the individuals and organizations that eventually converged in the Coalition for Women's Safety. Between 1976 and 1980, when it folded, the collective organized a series of working retreats that brought together a larger collection of black feminist radicals in the Northeast—the Black Women's Network—to engage in political study and theory development.[20] As the group declared in its now-canonical 1977 manifesto, "A Black Feminist Statement," it took as its "particular task the development of integrated analysis and practice based upon the fact that the major systems of oppression are interlocking."[21]

On April 1, after the sixth body had been found, 1,500 people, most of them black, walked together in the rainy streets of the South End to collectively express their grief and outrage. One of the co-organizers of the demonstration, Marlene Stevens, later reflected: "We didn't want to walk down to City Hall or to the Commons, we wanted to walk in our own neighborhoods. It was the most moving situation that I've ever been involved in in my life."[22] In February, Stevens and several other seasoned women community activists had banded together to launch a new grassroots organization, aptly called Crisis, and the idea of the memorial walk grew out of the organization's weekly meetings. Despite the organization's female leadership, the overwhelming majority of those who spoke at the demonstration were men and, much to the frustration of Barbara Smith, who was in the crowd, "they were saying things like, 'we need to protect our women; women need to stay inside the house.' Nothing about sexual politics or sexual violence. It was all about racial crimes."[23] That evening, she set to work drafting a pamphlet titled *6 Black Women: Why Did They Die?* that offered an "integrated analysis" of the racism and sexism underpinning the murder crisis and its treatment by the police and press, as well as putting forward an alternative set of recommendations for ensuring the safety of black women and girls in Boston.

Written for "Third World women," *Why Did They Die?* argued that "sexual oppression," which is inextricable from racial oppression, was one of the root causes of the killings, pointing out that all of the victims were women and girls. Calls for male protection rooted in interpretations of the murders as "solely racial or racist crimes" or calls for women to remain in their homes denied the realities of sexual and domestic violence. This counterargument only became more poignant over the course of the spring and summer as two additional women's bodies were discovered in their apartments, and police arrested the boyfriends or lovers of several of the victims. "WE HAVE TO LEARN TO PROTECT OURSELVES," the pamphlet urged, capitalizing for emphasis. It affirmed black women's capacity to defend themselves and one another, while at the same time participating in organizing efforts to address the conditions that underlay violence against women. To these ends, it included a long list of "self-protection" tips, followed by a three-tiered community resource list. At the top was information about regular meetings in Roxbury and the South End related to the murders, including those hosted by Crisis, and just below this was contact information for a handful of self-help organizations in Dorchester, Roxbury, and the South End that were "providing services in connection with the recent violence." Lastly, there was a list of other organizations "working against and providing services for violence against women," some in the affected neighborhoods and others across the river in Cambridge.[24] By May, this resource list was a close match for the roster of the newly created Coalition for Women's Safety, and the black feminist analysis put forth in the pamphlet became an ideological touchstone, even an informal manifesto, for the new alliance. Members of Combahee, Crisis, and several other organizations based in the affected neighborhoods saw the need for greater coordination and consolidation of their efforts, envisioning a "city-wide network of people committed to solving the problems of racism, sexism and violence."[25]

In a letter written in late April to past participants in Combahee's Northeast regional retreats, Demita Frazier enclosed a copy of *Why Did They Die?* and attempted to convey the intensity and urgency of Combahee's organizing in the crisis atmosphere: "If we ever felt any question about the importance

Combahee River Collective pamphlet. Courtesy of the
Lesbian Herstory Archives.

of the work/actual existence of our retreat group, the destruction of these women's lives has made it vividly clear, at least to me, that our purpose has been painfully delineated. As Barbara [Smith] has always said, they are intent upon killing us and ours is a voice of clarity in the patriarchal wilderness."[26] By the end of the year, roughly 30,000 copies of the pamphlet had been distributed, and specific portions republished in a range of publications in-cluding *Aegis*, *Radical America*, and the 1981 anthology *Fight Back! Feminist Resistance to Male Violence*.

An Intersectional Coalition for Women's Safety

Over its nearly two-year lifespan, the Coalition for Women's Safety (CWS) promoted cooperative interchange in a city in which activists typically found it "very hard to really cross neighborhoods."[27] The initial meetings took place at Women, Inc., a community-based organization in Dorchester that provided substance addiction treatment and housing to poor women.[28] Representatives of roughly twenty different groups attended, including projects that grew expressly out of the murder crisis, particularly the Dorchester Green Light Program and Crisis; service organizations such as Women, Inc., Community Programs Against Sexual Assault (CPASA), and the Roxbury Multi-Service Center; and multi-issue social justice organizations such as the Dorchester Youth Alliance, Jamaica Plain City Life, and Combahee River Collective. In Jamaica Plain, a group of feminist activists formed a CWS caucus that sent a liaison to the biweekly coalition meetings. These groups and individuals coalesced around a "bottom line commitment to work towards ending vio-lence against women in our neighborhoods."[29]

Those who regularly attended CWS meetings and coordinated work on behalf of its organizational and individual members comprised a diverse array of seasoned community activists—black, Latina, and white women, lesbian and straight, feminist and nonfeminist, low-income, working-class, and middle-class. They included Kattie Portis, founder of Women, Inc.; Mar-lene Stevens and Novlette White, both with Crisis; Lili Piñero of CPASA; Barbara Smith; and Margo Okazawa-Rey and Sondra Stein, both with the Campaign for Anti-Racist Education, a project of the multi-issue, multiracial Boston People's Organization.[30] Many in the coalition understood its social, political, and neighborhood diversity to be a tremendous achievement in "a city that is notorious for its racial and class divisions," as Smith observed. Solidarity between members was premised on a recognition, rather than eli-sion, of differences of location and power. This stance took two main forms.

Members of the Combahee River Collective and Crisis protesting the murders of black women and girls in Boston in the winter/spring of 1979. Left to right: unknown, Demita Frazier, Marlene Stevens, Barbara Smith. Photograph © Ellen Shub 2018.

Organizationally, in a rejection of a one-strategy-fits-every-neighborhood approach, member organizations decided how and on what terms they would participate in the CWS's citywide initiatives and which organizing ideas and tools they wanted to borrow from other groups. In terms of consciousness, recognizing and leveraging differences of *social* location meant explicitly acknowledging and engaging in dialogue about race, class, sexuality, and other lines of difference.[31] Sondra Stein, one of the few white women at the coalition table, served as liaison to the Support Group for Women's Safety, the only predominantly white group affiliated with the coalition. As its name implied, the Support Group bolstered rather than guided the coalition's work. More than fifty "concerned feminists," largely from Cambridge, Fenway, Jamaica Plain, and Somerville, self-organized in April 1979 to make themselves available to the coalition or its member organizations for a range of tasks, such as typing, child care, phone-banking, leafleting, and fund-raising.[32] This structure enabled white feminists to contribute their energies to the coalition under the advisement of its black feminist leadership, and, at the same time, it helped to fortify an existing mandate that white feminists interrogate their own racism as it manifested in both ideology and conduct.[33]

Rejecting police and media depictions of the killings as "crimes of passion," members worked together to develop and publicize a counter-narrative that politicized the slayings as violence against women, aided and abetted by the conjoined racism and sexism of elected officials, the Boston police department, and the establishment media. Activists saw the police department's indifference and unresponsiveness to the safety concerns of black residents not only as abusive to the victims' families and to all black women and girls in these neighborhoods, but also as a threat to procedural fairness in the criminal justice system. They closely monitored the investigation and publicly pressed the authorities for updates on its status with an eye toward the due process rights of the suspects, all of whom were black.[34] Following the lead of Crisis, the coalition raised money for the children of the murdered women. Its overarching purpose, however, was to connect and fortify neighborhood-based violence education, prevention, and intervention efforts. CWS members understood this work as a life-or-death imperative and the only means of assessing and attacking the root causes of both the initial crisis that brought them together and the persisting, pervasive reality of lethal and nonlethal violence against women.[35]

Advocating a program of collective self-protection in lieu of calling for increased police protection, several of the coalition's member groups worked to create grassroots emergency services for their neighborhoods. In Dorchester, for example, feminists launched an all-volunteer Green Light Program, training neighborhood residents in self-defense and providing them with a green lightbulb for their front porch to signal that theirs was a "safe home" for anyone under threat of violence on the street. Along similar lines, Roxbury's Crisis established a system of "street reps" responsible for coordinating telephone trees and block watches, as well as offering weekly self-defense classes.[36]

One of the CWS's principal antiviolence strategies was to "raise mass consciousness" about "racist and sexist violence," most often through street-level education. The group organized several multiday leafleting drives in which activists blanketed their neighborhoods with brochures, fliers, and other informational materials.[37] A few member organizations, such as the Dorchester Youth Alliance, developed workshop curricula aimed at high school youth. The coalition's largest undertaking was Women's Safety Month, a five-week community education program in the summer of 1980. In addition to their pedagogical aim, activists sought to drum up support and new recruits for member organizations, and, in turn, to expand the coalition's base. Activities varied from neighborhood to neighborhood, including a firearms workshop in Roxbury, self-defense classes in Jamaica Plain, and a leafleting drive at Betances Festival, an annual Latina/o cultural celebration in the South End. Most members also organized local screenings of a rough cut of a documentary by filmmaker Alonzo Rico Speight about the overlapping activist mobilizations inspired by the cases of Willie Sanders, the twelve murders, and recent police brutality against black women and men, helping to keep issues of racism in law enforcement central.[38]

The coalition's grassroots fund-raising efforts were forms of community education, and even direct action. In July 1979, Audre Lorde and Barbara Smith participated in two poetry readings to benefit the coalition, one at the Solomon Carter Fuller Center in the South End that also included local poets Fahamisha Shariat Brown, Beverly Smith, Kate Rushin, and Dianna Christmas, and one on the Harvard University campus, where Adrienne Rich joined them.[39] In August 1979, with the integral help of the Support Group, the CWS sponsored its first Freedom Stride, a run-a-thon named to echo the 1961 Freedom Rides that challenged Jim Crow segregation in the South's interstate bus system: "Like the Freedom Rides of the Civil Rights movement, it is a coming together of black and white, a crossing of neighborhood lines and color lines; it is putting our bodies on the line against the unfreedom of this society."[40] Five hundred women and men walked and ran the six-mile route that began and ended in Franklin Park, where one of the twelve women had been found, helping to raise several thousand dollars for the coalition and its member organizations. But runners and walkers who spoke to reporters emphasized that the event was "more than just a fund-raiser." Beverly Smith of Combahee saw the race as direct political education about violence against women as well as a demonstration of women's "right to be in the world. . . . Women who run are making a commitment to develop their strength and endurance, and to me, it feels like a feminist commitment."[41] Although the Stride best symbolized women's right to public space and "safe streets," promotional materials also emphasized the CWS's dedication to stemming violence in the home.[42]

Another key aspect of the coalition's work was its displays of solidarity with both Willie Sanders and Bellana Borde. A black undergraduate student at Northeastern University, Borde was badly beaten by a police officer on the morning of December 13, 1979. She had taken shelter in the vestibule of an apartment building while waiting for her bus in the winter weather when a white police officer accosted her, threw her to the ground and handcuffed her, and then kneeled on her chest, all while verbally abusing her. At the police station, when the same officer entered her cell and threw her against the wall, she bit his hand to try and make him cease, at which point he pepper-sprayed her at close range. Borde was charged with trespassing and assault and battery of a police officer. With the help of the National Black Students Association, to which she belonged, and numerous allied organizations, Borde successfully fought the charges. Her countersuit for police brutality, however, did not prevail.[43] By joining demonstrations for both Sanders and Borde and integrating these cases into its propaganda efforts, the coalition asserted the inseparability of these coterminous antiviolence struggles. Borde's case, in particular, was a stark reminder of black women's particular vulnerability to violence at the hands of state agents.

"A Common Enemy Is the Racist and Sexist Criminal Justice System"

"We are totally opposed to male violence against women and we are also totally opposed to racism and racist violence against all black people," Barbara Smith told the audience that had gathered at the Jamaica Plain City Life office. At the evening forum in late August 1979, she was representing both the Combahee River Collective and the CWS. Organizers billed the event as an evening of presentations and discussion about the interconnections between the struggle for "women's safety" in the wake of the killings of black women in southwest Boston and the campaign to drop the rape charges against Willie Sanders, who faced the prospect of life in prison (Massachusetts had no death penalty at that time).[44] Smith shared the mike with representatives of the Willie Sanders Defense Committee, of which she was also a member, and with organizers from City Life, a neighborhood-based economic justice organization and another CWS affiliate.[45] She explained to the attendees that linking the two mobilizations ideologically and practically "is what black feminism is all about."[46] The response of Boston's "white-male establishment" to the murder crisis as well as its framing of Sanders for the series of rapes in Brighton represented instances of terrorism against the black community, Smith argued, and together they demonstrated a fundamental disregard for the citizenship rights and bodily safety of black women and men and of all women. Transforming these conditions would require coalition building, Smith attested, which in turn required "confronting sexism in the black community" and racism in the white feminist community.

The Sanders defense campaign and the campaign for women's safety unfolded alongside and in relation to each other. The Willie Sanders Defense Committee brought together Sanders's wife, sister, and friends in Roxbury; his activist attorneys, who were affiliated with the National Conference of Black Lawyers; and activists in a range of racial justice, prisoner rights, and feminist groups such as Crisis, the Combahee River Collective, the Boston chapter of the Alliance Against Racist and Political Repression, and the Coalition to Stop Institutional Violence. Numerous area churches also endorsed the committee's effort.[47] In addition to fund-raising to defray the excessive

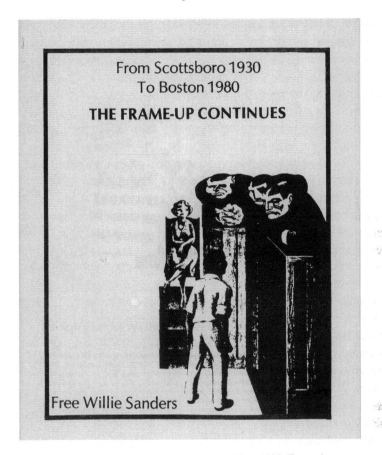

From Scottsboro 1930
To Boston 1980
THE FRAME-UP CONTINUES

Free Willie Sanders

Willie Sanders Defense Committee pamphlet, 1980. From the
Sondra Gayle Stein papers, Northeastern University Archives and
Special Collections.

legal costs—the courts refused to combine the four cases, burdening the
Sanders family with the financial and emotional costs of multiple trials—the
committee worked to publicize a counter-narrative that placed the case in
the context of a long and unfinished struggle against racism in the criminal justice system. In leaflets, fund-raising appeals, interviews, workshops,
and demonstrations, committee members pointed to empirical studies that
documented persistent patterns of antiblack racism in the Massachusetts
courts and in capital rape cases nationally.[48] They insisted that the framing of Sanders belonged to a constellation of recent attacks against Boston's
black community that included rollbacks of affirmative action, welfare rights,
and school desegregation; a spike in police violence; and persistent double

standards of justice for people of color who defended themselves from racist and sexist violence, as well as for those who had not survived such attacks, including the twelve black women killed in the first five months of 1979.[49] Facing an utter lack of what one committee member called "reliable institutions of redress for black people," activists saw a participatory defense for Sanders as the only viable way forward.[50]

In the tradition of people's defense campaigns, a form of organizing that critiques the promise of a fair and impartial criminal justice system, the Free Willie Sanders mobilization was simultaneously concerned with saving Sanders from lifelong incarceration and with struggling for the collective rights of Boston's black residents.[51] As if to corroborate their charges of state racism, committee members themselves came under direct attack from the district attorney, who attempted to subpoena the group's records as well as several of its members, including Willie Sanders's sister Magnolia Sanders.[52]

The defense committee deliberately underlined its opposition to violence against women and its support for the rape survivors in Brighton in all of its outreach materials. Leaflets and fact sheets lamented that the wrongful prosecution of Sanders meant that the police abandoned the effort to apprehend the actual perpetrators.[53] Black and white antiracist feminist leaders of the defense campaign argued that Sanders's case represented a key political opportunity for coalition building:

> The State has historically tried to pit those who fight to end racism against those who fight to stop violence against women. But increasing numbers of women understand that the police are not acting to protect them in the way they handle rape cases. Women have nothing to gain by allowing the State to prosecute Willie Sanders in their name. White women in increasing numbers are coming to understand how racism affects the issue of rape charges. Violence against women and the systematic oppression of people of color are the issues of this case. A common enemy is the racist and sexist criminal justice system which arrested an innocent Black man and used the women who had been raped to build a "case" against him.[54]

Indicting an abusive state, the committee refused a zero-sum game of victimization and encouraged the many white feminists who remained ambivalent about supporting Sanders to grasp the indivisibility of racism and sexism in this instance.[55] Some white women could not fathom "supporting a man in a rape case," seeing it as at odds with supporting women rape survivors.[56] Feminist members of the defense committee urged these women to recognize the hollowness of this stance. As one member wrote in the feminist newspaper *off our backs*, "People who understand that the struggle is one for justice and against oppression understand that you cannot be selective about who you seek justice for. It is achieved for all. Or it is not achieved. That is the role of feminist leadership . . . to have the insight to lead the full struggle."[57]

The overlapping, black feminist–led campaigns for Sanders and women's safety had a pivotal influence on the city's Take Back the Night coalition (TBTN). The first annual nighttime march in August 1978, from the Fenway neighborhood to Copley Square, was organized by representatives from a broad range of feminist organizations, including the Prostitutes Union of Massachusetts, Coalition to Stop Institutional Violence, Combahee River Collective, Transition House, Elizabeth Stone House, Women Against Violence Against Women, and the Alliance Against Sexual Coercion. Reflecting the breadth of the group's concerns, a lengthy manifesto of principles, demands, and solidarity resolutions outlined the group's opposition to violence against women on the street, on the job, in the family home, in locked institutions, in health care, and in the popular media. TBTN's variegated demands included more street lighting, stronger rape shield laws, the decriminalization of prostitution, and public funding for feminist self-defense classes, shelters, rape crisis centers, and a nighttime women's taxi service. As a mark of CSIV's participation, the coalition proposed that Massachusetts use the $600,000 earmarked for the Worcester center for so-called violent women to fund shelters for women in crisis that embraced a feminist philosophy of radical self-help and mutual aid. The most significant topic of debate and dissensus among the 1978 TBTN organizers proved to be "the criminal justice system and its relation to violence against women." While some felt that criminal justice reforms should be prioritized, others believed that "working with a system that continually acts in a racist, sexist manner, and continually channels only poor people through its doors" represented a "dead end." The group had difficulty reconciling its understanding of the criminal legal system as a "perpetual abuser of poor and Third World men and women alike" with its desire to support women survivors—both white and of color—who wanted redress from this very system.[58]

In contrast to the 1978 TBTN march, the rallying point in 1979 was the South End's Blackstone Park, chosen by the core organizers in consultation with the CWS.[59] Organizers endorsed the Sanders defense committee and adopted its message that "scapegoating an innocent Black man is no protection against rape."[60] Brochures and leaflets distributed before and during the 1979 demonstration included Combahee's list of self-protection tips.[61] During the rally, TBTN organizers addressed the 5,000-strong crowd, reading a collectively authored statement that condemned the racism of the Boston Police

Department and the prosecution of Willie Sanders as well as acknowledging the need for white women to continue to "learn from Third World women and to organize against the violence particularly affecting women of color." The key lesson from the year's devastating events, the organizers declared, was that "the state cannot be relied upon to provide women's safety." Coalition building, political education, community censure, and community-based support systems were the building blocks of a strategy for ending interpersonal and institutional violence against women.[62] Despite these messages of solidarity, however, women of color from Combahee, CPASA, and other member organizations of the CWS later expressed concerns about the net effect of a predominantly white, women-only march that snaked through Boston's black neighborhoods with a principal rallying cry of "Stop Rape."[63] Barbara Smith recalls that it was Combahee members who made the suggestion the following year to have "feeder marches that started in the people of color communities that eventually got connected," as a means of striving for more robust, autonomous, and equitable participation of black and other women of color.[64] Smith and other CWS members, which now included the Willie Sanders Defense Committee, encouraged the majority-white core group of TBTN organizers to double down on support of Sanders as part of a larger effort to foreground racial justice in the 1980 demonstration; the lead organizers agreed that "all the women involved in TBTN need to educate themselves about this issue" and be prepared to field questions about the case when promoting the march.[65]

That October, after an eighteen-month battle, and in large part because of the indispensable efforts of the Willie Sanders Defense Committee, Sanders was acquitted of all charges.

Black Feminism at the Center

During the same years that black feminist radicals in Boston helped to forge an unprecedented black feminist–led multiracial and multigendered antiviolence movement, their counterparts in Washington were similarly engaged in the political and intellectual work of linking the violences of policing and imprisonment, rape and battering, and racial, economic, and gender oppression.[66] But, in contrast to Boston where a small, all-volunteer collective performed much of this "bridge leadership,"[67] the black feminist cohort in the capital city that served as a force of interconnection between local black liberation and feminist antiviolence movements was based in the city's rape crisis center. Black women community activists who worked at the D.C. Rape Crisis Center in this period, such as Michelle Hudson, Loretta Ross, Nkenge

Touré, Yulanda Ward, and Deirdre Wright, transected local movements, bringing theoretical and strategic insights from one arena to bear on another. For Loretta Ross, this bridging work resulted in a political life that resembled a "tangled skein of yarn"; "it was a place, it was a time, it was a spirit, it was a particular set of people" that cinched her black feminist consciousness.[68]

The D.C. Rape Crisis Center (RCC) was originally established in the spring of 1972, making it one of the first of its kind in the United States. The founding collective consisted primarily of young, white, working-class and middle-class women who were involved in the women's liberation movement, and many were rape survivors themselves.[69] The cofounders devised a two-pronged strategy: provide peer-to-peer advocacy while working to stem sexual violence through political education. The antiestablishment ethos of women's liberation informed the group's original blueprint for an independently funded, nonhierarchical, all-volunteer organization. The aim to keep overhead low was facilitated by the decision to base the Center in a collective house in Northwest Washington in which several members lived. Their first decisive step was to set up a twenty-four-hour emergency phone service (later reduced to 9:00 a.m. to 9:00 p.m.), which swiftly became the heart of the organization's culture and activity.[70] Within months the collective had successfully recruited more than two dozen new volunteers to work the crisis line and participate in the organization's budding community education program.[71]

From the RCC's inception, the group struggled with the fraught question of whether and how to work with the city's police department. On the one hand, many survivors' anguishing stories of being demeaned, harassed, and dismissed by law enforcement—experiences that activists would come to call "second rape"—convinced members that police policy and conduct were urgently in need of reform.[72] On the other hand, they suspected that the "police bureaucracy" would prove intractable and that perhaps the RCC's most effective role in reform would be that of indirect antagonist.[73] The group debated whether or not to encourage a woman to report a rape, weighing the risk of mistreatment against the concern that underreporting corroborated the apathy and abuse of the police and made it all the more likely that men who rape would face no social sanction. Collective members ultimately reached consensus on a policy that reflected the fundamental feminist principle that every woman is entitled to personal autonomy: they would neither dissuade nor encourage reporting a rape to the police. Volunteer counselors would provide information and validation, offer a compassionate ear, and invite them to become involved in the political life of the RCC. But, they resolved, "if a woman does wish to report the rape a Center member will accompany her to the police."[74] This stance soon became hegemonic in feminist anti-violence institutions.

Within its first year of operation, the RCC's survivor-centered approach compelled the staff to rethink its initial circumspection about venturing onto the terrain of law enforcement reform.[75] In 1973, a representative of the organization joined the city council's public safety task force as it undertook a review of Washington's municipal-level response to rape. The public hearings convened by the task force provided RCC activists with an opportunity to indict "a legal system with low prosecutions and convictions rates" as a key barrier to preventing rape, and to directly influence the council's recommendations for policy changes.[76] Among the reforms the RCC successfully championed were recruitment of more women to the district's police force and training police on how to interact with rape survivors. Conspicuously absent from the center's public rhetoric during its first two years—both in the task force hearings and in its trailblazing publication, *How to Start a Rape Crisis Center*—was any acknowledgment or analysis of the racial and class politics of criminal justice. The center's participation in the task force opened it up to questions and criticisms from black women community activists who urged both the RCC and city officials to consider the intertwined histories of rape and racism and the reality of racial disproportionality in arrest, prosecution, conviction, and sentencing rates.[77]

The RCC's initial "single-axis analysis" of the criminal justice system's handling of rape cases was, in part, a reflection of the racial uniformity of its members.[78] Despite the founders' stated intention to build an organization that represented a "broad cross-section of backgrounds and experience," they recognized that their volunteer pool largely reflected their own social locations and political orientations—an especially problematic and glaring reality in a majority black city.[79] Grappling with the dilemma of how to diversify the predominantly white organization led the collective to create salaried positions and intentionally recruit working-class women of color activists for these jobs. Several core members were working-class women themselves, and their own class consciousness likely informed this process.[80] In 1974, the Center received a contract from the Department of Health, Education, and Welfare (HEW) to expand its educational work into the district's public school system and hired a young African American woman named Michelle Hudson for the new HEW-funded position of community education coordinator. Then the staff learned of and contacted Nkenge Touré, cofounder of a local revolutionary black nationalist self-help organization called Save the People, who had recently started a women's discussion group about rape in Northeast Washington.[81] Touré worked with the hotline and community education programs before she became the RCC's general administrator in 1975. She and Hudson both saw the potential for the center to become a fulcrum for linking the city's black liberation and women's movements, provided that they could expand its emerging black feminist leadership.[82] As Touré remembered her first months at the RCC, "I was very passionate about the issue of rape . . . and very disturbed by what seemed to me to be the lack of a presence of black women and women of color in the movement. But certainly many of our clients were black women. So what was going on in my mind was, one, how to serve women and, two, how to get more women of color involved in the Rape Crisis Center and get the Rape Crisis Center more connected with the community"—by which she meant the black community.[83] Support from white feminist members for these goals was bolstered by the emerging stories of Joan Little and Inez García, which poignantly illustrated the intersection of rape, resistance, and racism in the criminal justice system.

The number and proportion of women of color affiliated with the center climbed over the next several years. One strategy that brought an influx of black and Latina staff between 1976 and 1978 was contracting with the Comprehensive Employment and Training Act (CETA) and Volunteers in Service to America (VISTA) programs. Roughly ten women of color worked at the RCC through these minimum-wage, civil service and job-training programs before the organization canceled these contracts.[84] During this period, the RCC began offering support groups for Latina-identified survivors and translating its publications into Spanish.[85] Aside from the temporary staff surge through CETA and VISTA, the number of paid workers was generally small and grew slowly. Black women continued to hold the majority of salaried positions, including Deirdre Wright, who coordinated the counseling program for several years, and Loretta Ross, who served as general administrator from 1979 to 1982. Ross began volunteering at the center in 1978, recruited by her comrade and friend Touré. The two had met through the City Wide Housing Coalition, a federation of tenant associations fighting the displacement of poor and working-class people of color from central city neighborhoods, and they had made another political home together in a small Marxist-Leninist study group of local black activists. The late 1970s also saw an uptick in the number of black women volunteers, and by 1980 a few black women had joined the board of directors, including Howard University student and City Wide activist Yulanda Ward.[86]

By the late 1970s, through the collaborative effort of black and white radical women on the staff, the RCC had become what Loretta Ross has described as a "space for black feminism to grow and flourish."[87] Hudson, Touré, Wright,

Ross, Ward, and other black women radicals brought issues of racism, poverty, and criminalization to bear on the organization's analysis of sexual violence and methods for its prevention, and at the same time they helped to infuse a consciousness of violence against women into local organizing efforts for racial and economic justice.[88]

An example of this coalitional approach was Washington's first-ever March to Stop Violence Against Women in 1978 (later "Take Back the Night"). The RCC joined with the Task Force on Abused Women of the Women's Legal Defense Fund and the recently launched D.C. Area Feminist Alliance (DCAFA) to organize the citywide demonstration that was the culmination of Anti-Rape Week, the RCC's community education project. Though it represented a rigorously coalitional effort between the three sponsoring organizations, the march was principally coordinated by the Violence Against Women Task Force of the DCAFA.[89] "Rather than rely on the criminal justice system as the only way to deal with violence against women, solutions involving empowerment of women, education of men, and community action are being promoted instead," the organizers explained in the DCAFA newsletter.[90] The majority of the eight hundred demonstrators were women, but some, mostly black, men joined the nighttime march. The route wound through the predominantly black and Latina/o low-income neighborhood of Adams-Morgan to the adjacent DuPont Circle, a predominantly white and middle-class neighborhood that had recently been dubbed Washington's "gay ghetto."[91] As Anne Valk suggests in her history of feminist activism in Washington, the organizers' controversial decision to allow men to participate in the march was a testament to the RCC's black feminist politics and leadership in the coalition. While some white radical feminists affiliated with DCAFA felt that including endorsements and participants from mixed-gender community organizations would confuse the march's focus on *women's* right to the public space of the street, RCC members argued that a "women-only" march would deter women of color from participating as well as miss an opportunity to strengthen alliances with black community organizations. Although the RCC's position prevailed, minutes from a DCAFA meeting in May reveal that the issue remained contentious, compelling leaders of the Violence Against Women Task Force to recommend "workshops around race and class issues" for its membership.[92]

The organizers' emphasis on self-defense led them to invite Linda Leaks of the African People's Socialist Party and the National Committee to Defend Dessie Woods to address the postmarch rally. Leaks recounted Dessie Woods's and Cheryl Todd's harrowing encounter with an armed white man who attempted to rape the two black women. According to a reporter from *off our*

March to Stop Violence Against Women in Washington, D.C., in April 1978.
Photograph © 2018 JEB (Joan E. Biren).

backs, Leaks pinpointed "the primary issue in Woods's case as the illegitimacy of the state apparatus" that convicted and incarcerated her, and "the sexual oppression of black women by white men as one of the instruments for maintaining the 'colonial terror' which oppresses all black people in America."[93] Touré and Wright had only recently returned from the women's prison in Milledgeville, Georgia, where they visited Woods and interviewed her for *Aegis* magazine.[94] The defense campaign's formulation of white men's rape of black women as a form of colonial violence was not immediately understood or embraced by all of the demonstration's organizers; Leaks's remarks compelled some white DCAFA members to suggest that the group should continue learning more about the theory of internal colonialism adopted by the African People's Socialist Party and expressed in the defense campaign.[95]

Through intense negotiation over the course of several months, organizers hashed out an extensive list of principles, positions, and demands that was subsequently endorsed by sixty-nine progressive and radical organizations. In it, they outlined their reasons for emphasizing community accountability and censure over "criminal justice solutions," declaring that "the majority of men who rape or batter are not arrested," those who do get "convicted serve time in prison where violence is constantly reinforced," and those who serve time are eventually released back into a "society which condones and even fosters violence against women." In the final analysis, they argued, the criminal justice system manifests the racial, economic, and gender inequality of society as a whole, making an investment in criminal justice remedies misguided and dangerous. Marshaling examples such as uneven access to quality legal representation and racial disproportionality in capital punishment, the group argued that criminal-justice racism could not be separated from sexual and domestic violence. Rejecting a carceral approach to male violence, the document proclaimed: "We seek to increase women's mobility and freedom of movement without relying on the criminal justice system to restrict men's freedom of movement." Only through genuine "re-education" could men's violent behavior be transformed. Despite the group's centrally stated desire for the march to "take emphasis away from the police and criminal justice systems," however, when it came to formulating immediate demands on the city, the focus and onus boomeranged back to criminal legal approaches. Calls for sensitivity training of criminal justice officials, crime victim compensation, more police foot patrols, and more women and people of color on the police force sat awkwardly alongside the organizers' anticarceral stance.[96] The document thus betrays the difficulty activists faced in identifying tangible methods of violence intervention and prevention that did not inadvertently reproduce an ideology that preventing violence against women was principally a matter of crime control.

"The Vastness of Our Task"

At the end of the decade, the RCC was convinced that women and men of color organizing around issues of rape and battering throughout the country needed "to build and consolidate a network" that could not only identify strategies for upending racism in the predominantly white feminist antiviolence movement but also craft an ideology of "Third World women and violence" that attended to the interconnections of white supremacy, patriarchy, capitalism, and colonialism.[97] A national conference seemed a logical first step, and the center was well positioned to call such a meeting. Many women of color advocates around the country knew of the center's black feminist leadership through the nationally circulating activist periodical *Feminist Alliance Against Rape Newsletter* (*FAAR News*), the predecessor of *Aegis*, as well as through the center's popular and regularly reprinted publication, *How to Start a Rape Crisis Center*.[98] Some advocates had contacted the center directly in recent years, seeking advice or camaraderie and reporting stories of institutional racism and feelings of isolation and estrangement at their own agencies. Conferences sponsored by the Law Enforcement Assistance Administration and the National Center for the Control and Prevention of Rape in the late 1970s afforded some opportunity for "minority women" working in feminist institutions increasingly enmeshed with criminal justice agencies to begin a discussion of their organizations' philosophies and practices; but more than anything, these circumscribed meetings pointed to the need for autonomous spaces for networking, theorizing, and strategizing.[99] The founding in 1978 of the National Coalition Against Domestic Violence, an unprecedented alliance of local feminist shelters and other programs, and the establishment shortly thereafter of its Women of Color Task Force, may also have encouraged the RCC staff to take the leap to invite their far-flung counterparts to Washington. Additionally, Loretta Ross, Nkenge Touré, and Yulanda Ward—three of the primary conference coordinators—were all actively involved in the founding of the National Black United Front—a leftist, nationalist formation—and its first annual convention in August 1980.[100]

The organizers' nationwide call for "Third World activists in women's issues, service providers and community participants" drew attendees from a range of organizations and places outside of Washington, including CPASA and the Coalition for Women's Safety in Boston, New York Women Against Rape, and the Bay Area Defense Committee for Battered Women, as well as women from Miami, Minneapolis–Saint Paul, and Philadelphia.[101] The conference was the apex of the center's annual Anti-Rape Week. The event kicked off with an evening program of film, poetry, music, and food at the Unitarian Universalist All Souls Church in Northwest Washington, the center's current headquarters.[102] The following two days of workshops took place around the corner at the National Memorial Baptist and Calvary United Methodist churches.[103] A registration fee of $25 (roughly $70 in today's dollars) was the primary source of funding, but the center secured some money from the Office of Domestic Violence in the Department of Health, Education, and Welfare, provided that the organizers write a series of position papers based on the conference proceedings. As gestures of solidarity, women at All Souls donated money, white women RCC volunteers donated child care labor and coordinated local transportation for out-of-town attendees, and Black Panther artist Malik Edwards designed the conference logo.[104]

In one sense, the Third World Women and Violence conference could be construed as a meeting of the proverbial margins of the feminist antiviolence movement. Yet the organizers' and attendees' manifold political affiliations meant that the conference represented a distinctive position and perspective emerging at the interface of multiple social movements. Taken together, participants brought organizing experience on a myriad of issues including rape and battering, indigenous sovereignty rights, gentrification, health and welfare rights, prison conditions, police brutality, state repression of activists, nuclear militarism, reproductive freedom, and Pan-African solidarity. The slate of workshops and panel discussions manifested the coordinators' desire to "connect the dots" between multiple forms of violence, scaling from the interpersonal to the imperial. These ranged from "Medical Abuses (sterilization)" and "Feminism and Third World Women" to "Working with Men Committing Violence" and "Lesbianism: Third World Perspective."[105] Members of the "International Panel" provided a discussion of state-sponsored violence against women in Angola, South Africa, Chile, and Nicaragua and inspired passage of a formal, conferencewide resolution to demonstrate support for the South African Anti-Apartheid movement.[106] A month earlier, Ross had attended the second UN-sponsored World Conference on Women, fueling her interest in transnational organizing.[107]

Indeed, the name chosen for the conference signaled the organizers' desire to reconfigure "minority women" in the United States as part of a global "Third World majority" whose lived experiences required an intersectional analysis of patriarchy and gender violence. While many U.S. radicals of color adopted the umbrella term "Third World" as early as the 1960s to signify and enact an "affiliation with an international anticolonial community,"[108] the conference coordinators made a point of elucidating and opening up for discussion their own usage: "The definition of 'Third World' proposed for the Conference is those nations of people struggling to break the shackles of colonialism and neocolonialism. Principally, this includes those nations of Asia, Africa, the Pacific, South and Latin America, and Native and Black Americans who suffer under a form of domestic colonialism here in this country. While Third World was originally a phrase coined primarily to describe a state of economic dependency and the lack of technological advances, these same characteristics of underdevelopment tragically describe the condition of Black, Asian, Hispanic, and Native American women worldwide."[109] Seen through this anticolonial, internationalist lens, an "alarming consistency" of labor exploitation, reproductive control, and sexual violence pervaded histories of genocidal acts against indigenous peoples, racial slavery and Jim Crow, the making and policing of U.S. national borders, and U.S. imperial wars in Asia, forming a foundation for an interwoven analysis of violence against those facing "the triple oppression of race, class, and sex."[110] In their overview of the proceedings, Ross, Touré, and Kathy Powell, another African American RCC staff member, contended that rape and abuse in contemporary society must be analyzed in the context of this transnational genealogy of violent subjection.[111]

The summary papers by the conference organizers provide partial insight into the discussions that occurred about the place of the criminal legal system in analyses of, and solutions to, violence against women of color. They report a consensus that antiviolence movements must earnestly contend with the record of police violence against women and men of color and racially disproportionate rates of incarceration. The intertwined forces of racial, gender, and economic oppression conspired to lock up the "most disadvantaged of offenders," most reliably when their victims were white women and less often when their victims were women of color. Moreover, as recent legal cases had shown, the most marginalized women survivors of violence were also unjustly incarcerated. Although a few attendees saw the question of what role men might play in the antiviolence movement as "either premature or diversionary," there was a fairly broad consensus behind a formal resolution that uprooting violence against women of color would require "re-educating," rather than incarcerating, individual men who perpetrate rape and battering; in addition, greater numbers of progressive men of color (around ten of whom had attended the conference) should be engaged in advocating community-based sanctions against interpersonal violence. The absence of heated controversy about this resolution reflected the fact that the majority of the women in attendance were participating in mixed-gender political organizations alongside organizations focused on sexual and domestic violence. On the other hand, and relatedly, the "Third World Women and Feminism" workshop surfaced a more divergent range of viewpoints. Whereas some participants were concerned that an "analysis of power and its distribution within the feminist ranks" was not yet "dominant within the majority white movement," others explained that their reluctance to identify with feminism stemmed primarily from their understanding of feminism as a separatist, "anti-male" project that disregarded the "political realities of Third World people."[112]

Implicit in the argument for reeducation was an understanding of rape and battering as fundamentally social problems, rather than the results of individual pathology. During the workshop entitled "Working with Men Committing Violence," center staff discussed their long-standing relationship with Prisoners Against Rape (PAR), a black prisoner–led organization inside Lorton Reformatory, which was operated by the Washington, D.C., Department of Corrections in nearby Fairfax County, Virginia. William Fuller and Larry Cannon, both self-described former rapists, founded the group in 1973. In an essay published in *FAAR News* that year, the men declared that their "project was fundamentally concerned with attacking the historical, political, social, and economic ingredients" of a culture of rape that is "ingrained into the masses from the cradle."[113] Fuller participated in the workshop by proxy, sending a short essay to be read by his colleagues. In it, he explained that his involvement in prisoner organizing in the early 1970s led him to recognize the "anti-social" nature of the violence he had committed "both in the street and prison." A "reformed violent and aggressive individual," Fuller and other members of PAR sought to produce their own model of rehabilitation, based on "liberating and educating counseling" led by people who are "politically conscious of the oppressive practices of our society and how it influences the behavior of its people." He urged the workshop attendees to recognize the possibilities of men's expanded participation in antirape organizing, with the caveat that "women be in the majority of any decision-making process."[114] This view had led him to contact the RCC several years earlier to request collaboration. Center staff made regular trips to Lorton to participate in a study group with PAR, packing in copies of feminist reading material. Although Ross remembers that her organization was initially ambivalent about working directly with men who had been convicted of rape, unsure whether the prisoners were sincere in their motives or if time spent with PAR would be a misuse of their finite organizational capacity to serve survivors, the RCC-PAR alliance became a point of pride as well as an influential dimension of the center's activity. Ironically formed inside of, and in spite of, a prison environment, the study group represented the potential of radical political education-based interventions. Discussions with PAR about the prevalence of rape perpetrated by both guards and prisoners inside the men's facility at Lorton informed the RCC activists' critique of the prison system as an inherently violent institution that only extends the use of rape as a weapon of domination.[115]

The conference organizers' reports pointed to sexism in racial justice and black nationalist movements as a key barrier to enacting community accountability and censure. Noting that most sexual assaults are intraracial, the RCC authors postulated that men of color who commit such violence have internalized white hegemonic gender norms of male dominance and aggression. Racial oppression shapes "the lifestyle, values, and culture of Third World people, and the effects trickle down to impact the relationships among men and women of color."[116] Given these conditions, they argued, resistance to sexual and domestic violence should be reconceived as an antiracist political priority: "Racism, economics, employment, housing, and education or the lack of them are the reality of Third World existence under oppression. This has made survival the number one priority for Black and other Third World people. In line with this, many progressive people active in organizations (particularly men) felt it was inappropriate or incorrect to work around the issue of violence against women, which they considered a white woman's issue. . . . Our community must be educated to understand that ending such violence is another form of survival. This violence must be ended to ensure collective unity."[117] While the call for community accountability and censure echoed the principles and demands of the 1978 March to Stop Violence Against Women, it more squarely addressed the predicament of women of color affected by intraracial gender violence. Touré formulated the situation in her speech: "Historically, we don't call the police. If our communities work together, we can find alternatives. If I'm not going to call the police, I want you all to get out there and kick his ass. It's a copout for our brothers to use the issue of racism to make us feel bad."[118]

The disproportionate number of women of color imprisoned for injuring or killing their attackers and batterers corroborated the argument for community-based sanctions. Over the course of the two days, presenters pointed to the cases of Joan Little, Inez García, Yvonne Wanrow, and Dessie Woods as exemplars par excellence of "the injustices of the criminal justice system as it related to Third World Women." Their cases demonstrated that black, brown, and indigenous women faced similar racialized punishments in response to their acts of self-defense. For some women of color in attendance, their participation in the freedom campaigns for the four women had helped convince them to get involved with the predominantly white feminist antiviolence movement.[119]

At the same time, the event illuminated issues of difference, social distance, and uneven representational power among black, Latina, Asian American, and Native American women. The small number of Asian American and Native American women at the predominantly African American conference prompted a collective acknowledgment that competing national and international activist events may have prevented some women from attending. In late July, thousands of indigenous people and other concerned activists attended a ten-day gathering in South Dakota focused on defending the Sacred Black Hills of the Lakota nation from uranium mining and nuclear power development, and the first-ever National Asian/Pacific American Women's Conference took place in Washington the previous weekend.[120] At one point during the convening, a group of Latina attendees "seized the mike" to criticize the organizers for over-representing black women on the program and neglecting to offer language translation services, and called for the creation of a Latina caucus.[121] The confrontation elucidated the contingent and constructed nature of the political identity category of "Third World women" and directly inspired passage of a resolution that "transcultural workshops" be required at future conferences. In their postconference report, the organizers emphasized the importance of building bridges "between Black and Latino women in terms of culture, resources, and participation"; "arriving at a comfortable unity" would require "self-criticism and criticism."[122] As conference participant Cherríe Moraga wrote a month later in her preface to *This Bridge Called My Back*, "It is not a given between us—Chicana and Black—to come to see each other as sisters. . . . I keep wanting to repeat over and over again, the pain and shock of difference, the joy of commonness, the exhilaration of meeting through incredible odds against it."[123]

By its conclusion, the conference had invited its one hundred participants to see themselves as active subjects of an emergent political discourse on violence against women of color. As one of the organizers reported in the next issue of *Aegis*, "the greatest points of unity seemed to be an understanding of the vastness of our task as third world women to develop ideology, direction, programs and community support toward the elimination of violence against third world women. . . . We accept the challenge to struggle with our own inner differences, face all outside contradictions and arrive at a strong ideology."[124] Although the D.C. center staff's goal of organizing a second national conference in 1981 did not come to fruition, some of the attendees were involved in helping to create other opportunities for women of color antiviolence activists to convene nationally in the following years. Sandra Camacho and Cherríe Moraga cocoordinated "A Movement of New World Women," a 1985 gathering "by and about women of color and the violence against us" sponsored by the Women of Color Caucus of New York Women Against Rape.[125] Another key site of ongoing conversation was the Women of Color Task Force of the National Coalition Against Domestic Violence (NCADV). "Building a Colorful Coalition," a daylong institute for women of color organized by the task force, took place in conjunction with NCADV's 1982 conference. As the task force's founding chairperson P. Catlin Fullwood recalls, participants had a shared "understanding that economic justice, and sexual health, and reproductive justice, and freedom from violence, and racial justice were all connected—that all of these things were interrelated."[126]

"It Is Not Enough to Expose Those Who Pulled the Trigger"

Less than three months after the Third World Women and Violence conference, on the night of November 1, RCC board member and conference co-organizer Yulanda Ward was shot and killed in Southeast Washington. Earlier that day, Ward had chaired the first-ever meeting of the student section of the National Black United Front. She and three young men from New Jersey who attended the meeting drove to the black, working-class neighborhood of Buena Vista after midnight to attend a Halloween party. According to her companions, four armed men approached them on the street, threatening to shoot at any sign of resistance. Three of the assailants proceeded to frisk and rob the three men, while the fourth refrained from searching Ward and instead put a high-caliber pistol to her head and shot her. The police swiftly arrested two men in the neighborhood and relayed to the press that this was a straightforward case of a "robbery gone wrong" in a crime-ridden area.[127]

Although she had only lived in Washington for four years, Yulanda Ward was a highly visible and respected community organizer at the time of her death, described by her closest colleagues as a "rising leader" and a "warehouse of information" who was imaginative and disciplined, brilliant, and "always on the move."[128] The twenty-two-year-old had relocated from her home city of Houston, Texas, to attend Howard University. On campus, Ward joined organizations whose activities ranged from advocating affirmative action to defending political prisoners. She also immersed herself in grassroots politics, serving as cochair of the City Wide Housing Coalition, vice president of the RCC's board, informal coordinator of the D.C. Study Group, and catalyst for both the youth section of the National Black United Front and a new national alliance of black tenant organizers fighting displacement, the Grassroots Unity Conference. She shared most of these political affiliations with both Loretta Ross and Nkenge Touré.

Ross, Touré, and others to whom Ward was a cherished comrade issued a swift and resounding public rejection of police officials' assessment of the murder as a random crime committed by ordinary perpetrators. They pointed to the assailants' singling out of Ward as well as their expensive weapons, and informed police and reporters that Ward and several of her housing activist colleagues had received harassing phone calls and had their homes and offices broken into in the months leading up to the attack. Another member of the Grassroots Unity Conference in Philadelphia was arrested the same weekend. They also claimed that a local Department of Housing and Urban Development (HUD) official had warned Ward the previous winter that she would be hurt unless she abandoned her research and organizing.[129] She had become a vocal opponent of HUD's Section 8 housing program, arguing that its underlying goals were to displace and disperse poor and predominately black residents from the central city, isolating them in suburban areas in order to regentrify the urban core and quell dissent.[130]

To RCC and City Wide activists, the killing was a clear and concrete example of the state's propensity to engage in violence against those who posed a threat to the racial, economic, and gender order. The group launched the Yulanda Ward Memorial Fund, vowing to sustain public pressure on the authorities to conduct a rigorous investigation while also pursuing its own private inquiry, and pledging to extend Ward's legacy of student, housing, and antiviolence organizing.[131] In January, after hearing that police would be releasing the initial suspects due to lack of evidence, they presented evidence of the "failures of the police and U.S. Attorney's office" to investigate the murder. Their list of allegations, based on their own sleuthing, included that police failed to obtain or act on information provided by Ward's companions, rushed to arrest suspects whose appearance did not conform to the eyewitnesses' descriptions, neglected to canvass for or interview potential witnesses, and delayed searching the suspects' homes for more than a month yet "sealed and searched Yulanda's apartment only hours after her death." Moreover, they expressed concern for the welfare and due process rights of the initial suspects, who had been held for two months.[132] Within days of the press conference, Touré, cochairperson of City Wide Jimmy Garrett, and a third member of the Memorial Fund were subpoenaed by the grand jury appointed to investigate the case and instructed to hand over the files of the fund, RCC, and City Wide.[133] Now under direct duress, the leaders decided to establish a formal Support Committee, open to all "who wish to contribute their time, skills, and/or other resources" to the fund's objectives. This body drew together a wide array of local activists, including members of the African People's Socialist Party, DCAFA, Feminist Alliance Against Rape, Feminist Law Collective, and the National Black United Front, as well as representatives from the RCC and City Wide.[134]

Through press releases and conferences, public events, demonstrations, and writings, the Fund and Support Committee crafted a counter-narrative of the murder as a "deliberately planned execution" of a young, revolutionary black woman leader whose activism challenged the racist capitalist state: "We can see how Malcolm was killed . . . King was killed . . . George Jackson was killed . . . Assata Shakur is running for her life . . . and now Yulanda Ward was killed, in an equally brutal and efficient fashion."[135] The choice to assassinate a "rising" leader rather than a nationally recognized, charismatic figurehead represented an evolution in the FBI's COINTELPRO (counter intelligence program) strategy meant to destabilize and immobilize local progressive movements, they postulated. Ward's role as an interconnector of local and national movements and the "pivot around whom much community work revolved" made her a valuable target.[136] "Most of our basis for this assassination theory is observation and political experience of the way things work in this country," Touré told reporters.[137] In April 1981, when the grand jury indicted four young black men for Ward's murder and the robbery of her companions, Fund representatives stated publicly that it was "not enough

Why Was Yulanda Ward
ASSASSINATED ?

Political Background

THE DEATH OF YULANDA WARD MUST BE EXAMINED IN THE CONTEXT OF THE STRUGGLE AGAINST OPPRESSION INTERNATIONALLY, IN THE US, AND HERE IN WASHINGTON, WHY DID HER ASSASSINATION HAPPEN AT THIS TIME, IN THIS WAY?

INTERNATIONAL

In Africa, South America, the Carribean and Asia people are demanding control of their land, resources and labor. To gain control--and hold it--the people have risen in armed revolt. As a result, US corporate and banking interests have lost billions of dollars in superprofits--and stand to lose billions more. In reaction, the US Government is stepping up its programs of massive destabilization, resettlement, pacification and selected assassination of revolutionary organizers and leaders.

NATIONAL

In the US there is a resurgence of fascism. Under the banner of the KKK, the Nazis, and the "Moral" majority front, racist and fascist organization has today, with the election of Ronald Reagan, reached the <u>highest</u> levels of sophistication, effectiveness and power. The murders of Black Atlanta children, of Blacks in Buffalo and New York, the Greensboro Massacre, the release of murdering cops in Miami--all signal an atmosphere in which it is acceptable to maim, rape and murder Blacks.

But where there is repression, there is resistance. In Miami, Philadelphia, Brooklyn, Cleveland, Wrightsville...in countless towns and cities...it is growing.

The response of the government is quick and ruthless. A war has been declared on Blacks and other poor people. The tactics are familiar: massive destabilization, resettlement, pacification and selected assassination of revolutionary organizers and leaders.

D.C.

In Washington, as in many other cities, the tactic of resettlement is called "spatial deconcentration." How does it work? First, drive all the poor people out of a neighborhood. How? Eliminate all housing by giving landlords incentives to abandon their buildings; close down public housing; increase property taxes; and cut all housing, health, education and transportation services; and eliminate jobs.

When people have been forced to move, direct them to a housing program called Section 8, which subsidizes rental payments that are above 1/4th of a tenant's income.

But there is a catch to Section 8. When you apply for the money, they tell you no money is available for D.C. If you move to certain suburban counties, you can have the money. In this way, thousands of people are being resettled away from their culture, public transportation and jobs--and each other. Meanwhile, upper class people flock back to the inner city.

MEMORIAL SERVICES

Thursday, November 6
Rankin Chapel
Howard University Campus
5 p.m.

Sunday, November 9
Calvary Methodist Church
1459 Columbia Road NW
3 p.m.

CONDITIONS OF WOMEN

The economic conditions of women gets worse, as the crisis of capitalism deepens. More than ever, women are being forced out of jobs, prevented from getting them, or being

Profile Of A Revolutionary

"She was always helping people.
She was always worried about what was fair and right."

-Emeola Kirby (Yulanda Ward's mother)

Yulanda became politically active in grade school in Houston, Texas, participating in public speaking and oratory contests. She helped organize a Black Student Union in high school and was a National Merit Scholar finalist. Tall, thin and agile, she excelled in every sport. She particularly loved basketball, tennis and biking.

"Yulanda left home for Howard full of hopes."

-Emeola Kirby

In her first three years at Howard, she worked with Student Aid to Political Prisoners and the Academic Freedom Fighters. She also worked with the National Committee to Overturn the Bakke Decision and the Southern Africa News Collective.

"Everytime you met with Yulanda,
you learned something."

-Loretta Ross
(Yulanda's friend)

Before her senior year (she planned to return to school next January to finish her B.A. in Political Science), Yulanda took a year off. She went on the Board of the D.C. Rape Crisis Center and assumed major responsibilites, including fund-raising. She also coordinated the Third World Women's Conference this year.

"The more visible she became,
the more harrassment she got."

-Jimmy Garrett
(Yulanda's friend)

She was Co-chairperson of the City-Wide Housing Coalition and worked closely with tenants' organizations throughout the City, becoming deeply involved in the fight against spatial deconcentration. She met with tenants in other cities who were fighting the same resettlement strategy, and helped organize the Grass Roots Unity Conference.

Recently Yulanda became active in the new National Black United Front. She helped form a student League of the Front, and was acting Chairperson at a meeting of the students at Howard the afternoon before her assassination.

Money is urgently needed. Yulanda's body must be sent back to Houston, and funds are needed to bring her

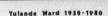

Yulanda Ward 1958-1980

"Why Was Yulanda Ward ASSASSINATED?" broadside by the City Wide Housing Coalition, November 1980. From the Loretta J. Ross Papers, Sophia Smith Collection, Smith College.

to expose those who pulled the trigger in Yulanda Ward's murder. We must expose those who employ the assassins. It is only then that we can get at the real truth of this heinous act and prevent its reoccurrence."[138]

The Memorial Fund's most ambitious and creative political demonstration was intended to accomplish exactly this. The "People's Grand Jury Hearing" was held in Southeast Washington in June 1981, a daylong program designed to continue to bring attention to Yulanda Ward's unsolved murder while situating it in relation to "the repression/suppression of dissenters in general," and to place the fund's recent experience of grand jury abuse in this context.[139] Among those "indicted" for genocide, "violation of human rights and dignity," treason, obstruction of justice, harassment, grand jury harassment, murder, assassination, "undermining the morale of the people," or conspiracy were editors and writers at the *Washington Post*; top administrators at Howard University; several city council members; the District's mayor, Marion Barry; several HUD officials; much of the U.S. Attorney's office; and members of the police department and judiciary.[140] According to a subsequent press release, a multiracial "jury" of local activists heard testimony from nearly a dozen organizations, including those fighting displacement, rape, apartheid, and state repression, that "added to the mountain of evidence indicting a U.S. foreign and domestic policy that denies human rights and thwarts people's struggles for self-determination abroad and implements racist and misogynist programs at home."[141]

Testifying on behalf of the RCC, Arleen Rogan told those assembled that she believed Ward chose to dedicate her time and energy to the center because she grasped that "rape is a survival issue for Third World women" and that relying on the criminal justice system for protection or redress is "a very cruel joke." She continued: "It is not yet clear whether Yulanda's murder was the result of a specific conspiracy of state and capital or whether it was part of the routine violence generated in third world communities in the United States. The state knows what it is doing when it relies on its victims to keep each other in line and to kill each other off if necessary. . . . If it can provoke an individual to murder 12 Black women in six months as it did in Boston in 1979, it can claim that the source of violence is the third world community and not the Department of Defense which demands billions of dollars to make war, and it can justify the local police's occupation of third world communities and the terrorization of its citizens." Identifying a racist, capitalist state as the facilitator, sponsor, and source of interpersonal violence in economically oppressed, people-of-color neighborhoods, Rogan and others affiliated with the fund refused a singular answer to the question of who killed Yulanda Ward, and why.[142] Indeed, when in November 1981 one of the four defendants agreed to turn state's evidence, and the other three accepted plea deals for lesser charges, the fund doubled down on its position that convicting the four gunmen hardly constituted accountability and justice for Yulanda Ward. Rather, preventing the case from coming before a jury was "the state's latest play."[143]

The Yulanda Ward Memorial Fund dissolved roughly six months later, although some level of activity continued through the D.C. chapter of the National Black United Front.[144] The impact of Ward's death on the local housing movement only fueled the political assassination theory. The City Wide Housing Coalition crumbled under the weight of her murder: "People stopped coming to meetings, were afraid to come to meetings. A lot of people just melted back into their lives, whether they were schoolteachers or bus drivers or hospital workers."[145]

The Yulanda Ward mobilization also rocked the RCC, crystallizing a latent conflict between select staff and board members over the center's political analysis and strategy. Although the Memorial Fund and Support Committee had been peopled with RCC founders and current staff and board members, this closely interwoven relationship—Ross remembered the center as "ground central" for the fund—deepened a fault line between the staff and a faction of the board over the breadth of the organization's mission and vision. Two years earlier, a segment of primarily white, middle-class women board members had pressed Ross to justify how a forum organized by the staff on the gender politics of black nationalist movements constituted antirape work. Board members contended that the center's leadership in the Yulanda Ward mobilization was a distraction from the work of supporting survivors of sexual assault and threatened the center's reputation with the police department. As Ross recalled: "It was our offices that the press was coming to . . . and in many ways it just hardened a small minority, but a vocal minority of the board, who felt that we had strayed away from the central mission of only working on sexual assault. Not even violence against women—no one could tell us that what happened to Yulanda was not violence against a woman—but sexual assault." Unlike their counterparts, center staff saw a through-line connecting local authorities' negligent response to Ward's murder and the political, economic, and social conditions that facilitate sexual and domestic violence against black women.[146] In other words, whereas black feminist radicals on staff understood their work with the Memorial Fund as a logical extension of their intersectional analysis of gender violence, some board members interpreted this activity as mission creep. This divide resonates with a nationwide conversation among antiviolence activists at the turn of the 1980s about social movement professionalization and its effect on antiviolence organizations' politics, missions, and values. Debates about professionalization, which were inextricably linked to debates about criminalization, intensified as the national political climate veered abruptly to the right.

Members of the RCC's first cohort of black feminist leaders moved on in the early 1980s; in 1987, Touré was the last to leave. Like most feminist-founded rape crisis centers that persisted through the Reagan era, the D.C. center increasingly relied on state money to stay afloat. Its anticarceral rhetoric and politics subsequently dimmed, yet the center remained (and remains) a key hub for women of color-led antiviolence services and organizing.

* * *

In the spring of 1979, black women in Boston demanded to know, "Who is killing us?"[147] The following year, activists in Washington vigilantly pressed the question, "Who Killed Yulanda Ward?" In both cases, coalitional organizing produced answers that were multiple and layered, defining the women's killings as manifestations of the interlocking relationship between racism and sexism and insisting that neither culpability nor redress were reducible to the arrest and incarceration of individual perpetrators. These antiviolence mobilizations asserted black residents' collective "right to the city," refusing police and media narratives that depicted the women's deaths as the natural consequences of living in "crime-ridden" neighborhoods, and understanding the fight against the displacement and dispersal of people of color from the central city as intrinsically linked to the fight to end rape, abuse, and other forms of interpersonal violence against women in these same communities.[148] As the City Wide Housing Coalition argued, displacing black people to Washington's suburbs meant isolating black people from one another and diminishing their collective power to enact change at the neighborhood level. In Boston, the Coalition for Women's Safety tested this theory of neighborhood-based organizing, as its member organizations wove discussion and action about violence against women into the everyday social geography of Dorchester, Roxbury, Jamaica Plain, and the South End.

The alliance between the Coalition for Women's Safety and the Willie Sanders Defense Committee, and the alliance between the D.C. Rape Crisis Center and Prisoners Against Rape, reflected a black feminist politics of "connecting the dots" between race and gender, rape and racism, and interpersonal and state violence.[149] Drawing black women's and black men's experiences of police, judicial, and carceral violence into the same frame, these alliances pointed squarely to the limitations and harms of a law-and-order feminism. Sanders's supporters urged white feminists to grasp that the Free Willie Sanders campaign was, ultimately, an antirape campaign. Black women radicals at the RCC engaged progressive black men—including those with a history of perpetrating sexual violence—as necessary allies in the work to end rape and battering, which they understood to be a matter of black community survival. The Third World Women and Violence conference provided a space for these and other activists to converge, compare and reflect upon their local struggles, and outline an antiviolence praxis rooted in an intersectional analysis of oppression.

Epilogue

Twenty years after the D.C. Rape Crisis Center convened the First Third World Women and Violence Conference, activists working in sexual and domestic violence agencies, social justice organizations, and universities converged in Santa Cruz, California, for "The Color of Violence: Conference on Violence Against Women of Color." The event was a referendum on mainstream antiviolence feminism and its support from and for the carceral state in an era of increasing racialized criminalization, imprisonment, and austerity. Participants appraised the ways in which interpersonal violence and state violence compound each other in the lives of racialized and marginalized women. The gathering called for antiviolence strategies that fought rather than corroborated the growth of the United States' *prison-industrial complex*—a term that a reemerging prison abolition movement was helping to popularize.[1] With nearly 2,000 attending and the same number turned away for lack of capacity, the coordinating committee decided to launch a new national network of local organizations and working groups to sustain the conversations held that weekend: INCITE! Women of Color Against Violence.[2] In her keynote address, Angela Davis prophesied "this conference will be remembered as a milestone for feminist scholars and activists, marking a new moment in the history of anti-violence scholarship and organizing."[3] Davis's forecast proved accurate. Between INCITE!'s first and fifteenth anniversary conferences, there was a groundswell of organizing and writing that critiqued the dangers and contradictions of what were increasingly called "carceral feminist" policies and explored more socially transformative methods of addressing gender violence.[4]

INCITE!'s 2015 conference in Chicago, themed "Beyond the State: Inciting Transformative Possibilities," also drew upward of 2,000 people to strategize about how to "end colonial, racial, and gender-based violence . . . without relying on policing, mass incarceration, restrictive legislation, and other systems of violence and control."[5] A main plenary session entitled "The Fight for Our Lives: The Criminalization of Self-Defense," moderated by longtime antiviolence activist Mariame Kaba, featured Yvonne Swan (formerly Wanrow) in conversation with Marissa Alexander, CeCe McDonald, and Renata Hill, three black women who had recently been incarcerated for fighting back against intimate partners or strangers and around which activists had organized. The conference organizers' choice to link Swan to Alexander, McDonald, and Hill helped to illuminate a longer history of collective fights against the criminalization of black and indigenous women's self-defense.[6]

Alexander joined the plenary by videoconference from her home in Jacksonville, Florida, where she was under house arrest. She was convicted in 2012 of aggravated assault for firing a single shot from her legally registered gun into the ceiling of her home. The gunshot was a desperate attempt to scare off her estranged husband, who had beaten and strangled her only moments earlier, and who had a documented history of violence against both Alexander and a previous intimate partner. By the time an appellate court judge heard her appeal and overturned her guilty verdict in 2013, she had already spent two-and-a-half years behind bars. Facing a retrial and the possibility of serving sixty years in prison, the mother of three agreed to a plea deal in 2014 that required her to spend 65 more days incarcerated and two additional years detained in her home under electronic surveillance.[7]

CeCe McDonald also took a plea deal for second-degree manslaughter out of fear of spending two decades, rather than two years, in prison. The young trans woman and several of her friends encountered a group of white people on a summer night in Minneapolis in 2011. The strangers hurled racist, homophobic, and transphobic epithets at them before one woman smashed a glass into McDonald's face. A brawl broke out, and when a man charged at her, the fashion school student reached for a pair of fabric scissors in her purse and stabbed him. The wound was fatal. Only McDonald was arrested that night; she was charged with second-degree murder.[8]

Renata Hill and six of her friends, all black, lesbian-identified women in their late teens and early twenties from Newark, New Jersey, were out walking in Greenwich Village on a summer night in 2006 when a man threatened to "turn them straight" by raping them. He then physically attacked two of the women. Fearing for her friends' lives, another one of the women used a knife she carried in her purse to inflict a minor stab wound on the attacker. All seven were hit with charges of gang assault, assault, and attempted murder. Three women pleaded guilty to avoid the unknowns of a trial; the other four, including Hill, fought the charges and went to prison; they have all subsequently been released.[9]

The plenary demonstrated the web of interpersonal and state violences as well as the transformative potential of participatory defense organizing. The campaign to "Free the New Jersey 4" drew attention to the interworkings of racism, misogyny, and homophobia in the case, challenging the legal charges and media narratives that framed it as a "gang assault" by a "lesbian wolf pack."[10] The larger scope of the later "Free Marissa Now" and "Free CeCe" mobilizations in part reflects their emergence alongside the Black Lives Matter movement. Activists frequently paired Alexander's and McDonald's cases of self-defense in contrast to the acquittal of George Zimmerman, the neighborhood watch volunteer who claimed he acted in self-defense when he stalked and killed the unarmed, black, seventeen-year-old Trayvon Martin in 2012 in Sanford, Florida.[11] Alexander and McDonald's family members (both of origin and chosen) and numerous other activists formed ad hoc groups as well as utilized the resources of existing organizations to raise money and educate various publics about these cases. Their efforts helped produce the demands that #blackwomenslivesmatter and #blacktranslivesmatter, situating the two cases in relation to growing movements against racialized police violence and incarceration.

At the 2015 INCITE! conference in Chicago, the seeds were planted for a new national organizing formation, Survived and Punished, that would coalesce existing defense campaigns in order "to build a larger movement to support survivors and abolish gender violence, policing, prisons, and deportations."[12] Since its inception, the coalition has used its website as well as the hashtag #SurvivedAndPunished to amplify and archive numerous freedom campaigns anchored by local social justice organizations and ad hoc groups in various parts of the country. Like the Say Her Name campaign (#sayhername) created by the African American Policy Forum that demands attention to police violence against black women and girls, also launched in 2015, this upsurge in grassroots mobilizations for domestic and sexual violence survivors has played a key role in expanding social movement dialogues about gender-based violence and mass incarceration.[13] As importantly, these mobilizations have engendered forms of material solidarity that have altered the course of the legal cases of survivor-defendants.

* * *

My initial interest in the topic of this book began in 2000 when I joined an emerging organization in Seattle called Communities Against Rape and Abuse (CARA). CARA was founded by former crisis-line volunteers and program staff at Seattle Rape Relief after the nearly thirty-year-old agency shuttered its doors in the face of financial strain. The new member-led organization prioritized marginalized groups that were least likely to access Seattle's sexual assault services embedded in local hospitals, the sheriff's department, and the prosecuting attorney's office and experimented with creative prevention and intervention strategies.[14] CARA became an affiliate of INCITE! as well as engaged in collaborations with another recently established national organization, Critical Resistance, whose mission was—and remains—to abolish the prison-industrial complex.

It was in this context that I became interested in the historical interconnections between feminist social movements and the carceral state. I was eager to learn how racial criminalization and state violence were addressed by feminist antiviolence activists on the *front end* of mass incarceration. Why and how had a carceral feminist agenda won out over other alternatives? What kinds of ideas and practices had taken shape beyond the purview of state incorporation and feminist mainstreaming? What kinds of work directly opposed both state and feminist carceral turns? A few years later, when I began digging in various archives for records of this earlier moment, these questions continued to grow: How did prison activists, on both sides of the bars, engage the language of "violence against women" as well as the rape crisis center and battered women's shelter movements? In what ways did these same activists shape the larger radical prison movement of the era? And ultimately, how was this work part of an *ongoing* feminist antiviolence movement centering criminalized, incarcerated, and other marginalized women and trans people?

As this book has shown, during the 1970s a loosely linked collection of ad hoc groups, organizations, and coalitions helped forge a feminist politics that indicted the carceral state for racialized and gendered violence. This activist current influenced social movement debates about the parameters and sources of violence against women, the politics of self-defense, the policing of gender and sexual expression, the significance of multi-issue and coalition-based organizing, and the possibilities of prison abolition. The freedom campaigns for Joan Little, Inez García, Yvonne Wanrow (Swan), and Dessie Woods—like the campaigns for Marissa Alexander, CeCe McDonald, and the New Jersey 4—fueled critiques of a crime-control approach to gender violence and brought a new level of activist attention to conditions facing incarcerated women. These defense campaigns exceeded the individual survivors by shining a light on systematic injustices, while also insisting that their individual fights to stay alive or out of prison demanded unrelenting collective mobilization.

Defense organizing informed and catalyzed activist efforts that confronted the institutional violence of imprisonment. Organizing inside and outside of women's prisons, along with the radical print culture that cut through the walls, revealed how gender and sexual regulation and racial control intersected in carceral settings. Activists staked the claim that incarceration itself constituted violence against women. The Coalition for Women's Safety, the alliances cultivated by the D.C. Rape Crisis Center, and the Coalition to Stop Institutional Violence all critiqued law enforcement–based solutions and imagined alternative modes of violence prevention and intervention that did not hinge on the confinement and further subjugation of racialized men, presaging twenty-first-century initiatives for transformative justice. Campaigns against the expansion of invasive behavior modification programs in women's prisons critiqued the coercion of treatment and the politics of psychiatric diagnosis, resonating with recent activist calls for "care, not cages" and their attendant critiques of authorities' proposals to revamp or build new prisons and jails under the auspices of improving mental health care.[15]

This book has offered a history of feminism and the carceral state in the late twentieth century as a contribution to the larger collective project of upending today's hegemonic story that incarceration is necessary to end gender violence. The anticarceral current of the 1970s and early 1980s and the feminist prison abolitionism of the twenty-first century share a genealogy, one that reminds us of the interdependence of struggles, the multiplicity of feminisms, and the power of coalition.

Notes

Abbreviations

SBC   Sallie Bingham Center, Rubenstein Library, Duke University, Durham

SCLSSR   Southern California Library for Social Studies and Research, Los Angeles

SGS   Sondra Gayle Stein Papers, Snell Library, Archives and Special Collections Department, Northeastern University, Boston

SL-HU   Schlesinger Library, Harvard University, Cambridge

SL-NU   Snell Library, Archives and Special Collections Department, Northeastern University, Boston

SSC   Sophia Smith Collection, Smith College, Northampton

TL   Tamiment Library, New York University, New York

VOFOHP   Voices of Feminism Oral History Project, Sophia Smith Collection, Smith College, Northampton

WHCC   Women's History and Culture Collection, Special Collections, Shields Library, University of California-Davis, Davis

WSL   Washington State Library, Olympia

Introduction

1. Marcy Rein and Carol Anne Douglas, "Women Unite: Reclaim the Night," *off our backs* 8, no. 6 (June 1978): 9; D.C. Area Feminist Alliance newsletter 1, no. 2 (Apr 1978), Julie LaValle Jones Papers, SBC.

2. DCAFA newsletter (Apr 1978).

3. Rein and Douglas, "Women Unite," 9.

4. Nkenge Touré and Deirde Wright, "Dialogue with Dessie," edited by Nancy McDonald and Julie Alibrando, *Aegis* (July/Aug 1978): 9–13.

5. Some of the formations examined in this book were comprised of a majority of black women; others were multiracial and included black, Latina, Asian American, indigenous, and white women; and still others were predominantly white and devoted to antiracist solidarity. Most had many lesbian participants, and some were predominantly lesbian. All could be described as advancing a left politics. As Cathy Cohen defines the term, a "left framework makes central the interdependency among multiple systems of domination. Such a perspective also ensures that while activists should rightly be concerned with forms of discursive and cultural coercion, we also recognize and confront the more direct and concrete forms of exploitation and violence rooted in state-regulated institutions and economic systems." Cohen, "Punks, Bulldaggers, and Welfare Queens," 442.

6. I am drawing on Kimberly Springer's theorization of black feminist politics in the 1970s as being forged "in the cracks," or the interstices, between gender-based and race-based movements. See Springer, "Interstitial Politics of Black Feminist Organizations," 155.

7. For an account of the "get tough" movement in the 1970s that emphasizes its relationship to welfare policy, see Kohler-Hausmann, *Getting Tough*.

8. Burnham, "Wellspring of Feminist Theory." On social movements and knowledge production, see also Kelley, *Freedom Dreams*, introduction.

9. "All Our Trials" is drawn from a 1980 issue of the Boston feminist newspaper *Sojourner*. I use the phrase to convey a politics of both alliance and intersectionality. It was the heading editors gave to a letter by feminist writer and activist Adrienne Rich on behalf of the defense committee for Juanita Thomas, an African American woman convicted of murder and sentenced to life without parole for killing her long-abusive partner (see chapter 3 of this book for more on the case).

10. Crenshaw, "Demarginalizing the Intersection of Race and Sex."

11. On black women's radicalism as a crucible for intersectionality theory, see especially Burnham, "Wellspring of Black Feminist Theory"; Gore, *Radicalism at the Crossroads*; Randolph, *Florynce "Flo" Kennedy*; Farmer, *Remaking Black Power*. For genealogies of this theoretical framework that emphasize its relationship to the activism of women of color feminists, see Hill Collins and Bilge, *Intersectionality*; Carastathis, *Intersectionality*. "Interlocking" is quoted from the Combahee River Collective's "Black Feminist Statement."

12. Peter Wagner and Wendy Sawyer, "Mass Incarceration: The Whole Pie 2018," *Prison Policy Initiative*, March 14, 2018, https://www.prisonpolicy.org/reports/pie2018 .html (accessed on March 20, 2018); National Research Council, *Growth of Incarceration in the United States*, eds. Travis, Western, and Redburn; Gilmore, *Golden Gulag*; Western, *Punishment and Inequality*.

13. For analyses that emphasis the role of the drug war in precipitating the prison crisis, see, e.g., Alexander, *New Jim Crow*; Provine, *Unequal under Law*.

14. On the LEAA and the 1960s war on crime, see Flamm, *Law and Order*; Hinton, *From the War on Poverty*; Murakawa, *First Civil Right*, ch. 3; Parenti, *Lockdown America*, ch. 1; Simon, *Governing Through Crime*; Weaver, "Frontlash."

15. Hinton, *From the War on Poverty*, 2.

16. On the dialectical relationship between antiracist social movements and the racial state, see Omi and Winant, *Racial Formation in the United States*.

17. Gilmore, "Globalisation and US Prison Growth," 175.

18. For general accounts of COINTELPRO, see Cunningham, *There's Something Happening Here*; Churchill and Vander Wall, *Agents of Repression*. On FBI repression of the Black Panther Party, see Bloom and Martin, *Black against Empire*; Spencer, *Revolution Has Come*. For a discussion of FBI surveillance of the women's liberation movement, see Rosen, *World Split Open*, 239–252.

19. Berger, *Struggle Within*.

20. On the LEAA and the rape crisis center and battered women's shelter movements, see especially Gottschalk, *Prison and Gallows*, 124–130, 145–147. See also Bevacqua, *Rape on the Public Agenda*; Matthews, *Confronting Rape*; Schecter, *Women and Male Violence*.

21. Gottschalk, *Prison and Gallows*, ch. 5 and 6; Bumiller, *In an Abusive State*; Richie, *Arrested Justice*, ch. 3; Kim, "Dancing the Carceral Creep." These scholars demonstrate that the combined expansion of punitive social control and dismantling of the social safety net facilitated this carceral turn in feminist antiviolence work. Bumiller and Richie both emphasize the cultural politics of this process of neolib-

eral state appropriation. On the importance of cultural politics to the making of the neoliberal state, see especially Duggan, *Twilight of Equality?*

22. Marjory D. Fields of Brooklyn Legal Services, testifying in the 1978 hearings on battered women sponsored by the U.S. Commission on Civil Rights, quoted in Gottschalk, *Prison and Gallows*, 144.

23. Richie, "Black Feminist Reflection on the Antiviolence Movement," 1134–1135; Richie, *Arrested Justice*, 91–94.

24. Critical ethnic studies scholar Chandan Reddy theorizes this kind of contradiction of the neoliberal state as *freedom with violence*. See Reddy, *Freedom with Violence.*

25. Sociologist Elizabeth Bernstein coined the term *carceral feminism* in her 2007 article, "Sexual Politics of the New Abolitionism," which provides a critique of feminist campaigns against sex trafficking. Since then, numerous scholars and activists have employed it in the context of advocacy around rape and domestic violence. See, for example, Law, "Against Carceral Feminism"; Davis, *Freedom Is a Constant Struggle*, 138–139.

26. I borrow the formulation *liberal law-and-order* from Murakawa, *First Civil Right*, 9.

27. The term *incorporative reforms* is from Omi and Winant, *Racial Formation in the United States*, 149. For other accounts that also emphasize nonstatist strategies employed by feminist antiviolence activists in the 1970s, see Jacquet, "Fighting Back"; Law, "Protection without Police"; Law, "Where Abolition Meets Action."

28. The growing literature on 1960s–1980s prison and jail rebellions, prison activist cultures, and the writings of imprisoned radicals includes Rodríguez, *Forced Passages*; Hames-García, *Fugitive Thought*; James, *Imprisoned Intellectuals*; Berger, *Captive Nation*; Cummins, *Rise and Fall of California's Prison Movement*; Thompson, *Blood in the Water*; Bernstein, *America Is Prison*; Losier, "Prison House of Nations"; Gómez, "Resisting Living Death"; Kunzel, *Criminal Intimacy*. Formative works on organizing and everyday resistance in women's prisons in the 1970s and 1980s include Faith, *Unruly Women*; Díaz-Cotto, *Gender, Ethnicity, and the State*. Law, *Resistance behind Bars*, is an important contemporary account of imprisoned women's everyday and organized forms of resistance. See Stanley and Smith, *Captive Genders*, and Spade, *Normal Life*, for contemporary accounts of trans resistance within and against the carceral state.

29. Díaz-Cotto, *Gender, Ethnicity, and the State*; Gross, *Colored Amazons*; Haley, *No Mercy Here*; Hicks, *Talk with You Like a Woman*; Kunzel, *Criminal Intimacy*; LeFlouria, *Chained in Silence*; Ross, *Inventing the Savage*.

30. Hewitt, Introduction, in *No Permanent Waves*, 3; Blackwell, *¡Chicana Power!*; Breines, *Trouble between Us*; Carroll, *Mobilizing New York*; Cobble, *Other Women's Movement*; Enke, *Finding the Movement*; Farmer, *Remaking Black Power*; Gore, *Radicalism at the Crossroads*; Nadasen, *Welfare Warriors*; Nelson, *Women of Color*; Randolph, *Florynce "Flo" Kennedy*; Roth, *Separate Roads*; Springer, *Living for the Revolution*; Valk,

Radical Sisters; Thompson, "Multiracial Feminism"; Ward, "Third World Women's Alliance"; Heaney, "Women-Identified Women." Recent scholarship on LGBT activist history has also illuminated lesbian feminisms that challenge conventional narratives and chronologies; see Hanhardt, *Safe Space*; Hobson, *Lavender and Red*.

31. See especially Valk, *Radical Sisters*; Randolph, *Florynce "Flo" Kennedy*; Enke, *Finding the Movement*; Gore, *Radicalism at the Crossroads*. This book also draws methodological inspiration from Regina Kunzel's study of the interactions between the gay and lesbian left and the prison in the 1970s (see *Criminal Intimacy*, ch. 6, and "Lessons in Being Gay") as well as from Christina Hanhardt's *Safe Space*, a study of LGBT antiviolence activism since the 1960s that attends to the making of a mainstream movement in relation to its radical queer discontents.

32. Enke, *Finding the Movement*, 4.

33. Blackwell, *¡Chicana Power!*, 134. See also Blackwell, "Contested Histories," 59.

34. Historian Dan Berger theorizes this as a "strategy of visibility"; Berger, *Captive Nation*, 6.

35. The Sophia Smith Collection's Voices of Feminism Oral History Project was an especially invaluable archive of oral history interviews for this project.

36. Scott, *Domination and the Arts of Resistance*.

37. See especially Richie, *Arrested Justice*; INCITE!, *Color of Violence*; "CONVERGE! Reimagining the Movement."

38. See, for example, Reddy, *Freedom with Violence*; Gottschalk, *Caught*; Hanhardt, *Safe Space*; Meiners, *For the Children?*

39. Gordon, *Ghostly Matters*, 127.

Chapter 1. Lessons in Self-Defense

1. Barbara Holtzman, "'Free Our Sisters,' Prison Protesters Cry," *Daily Tar Heel* (Chapel Hill, N.C.), November 18, 1974, 1; Action for Forgotten Women, "Fact Sheet on the Women's Correctional Institute," n.d., SBC; Barbara Holtzman, "Women Will Protest Overcrowded Prison," *Daily Tar Heel*, November 16, 1974, 2; Celine Chenier interview with James Reston Jr., Audiotapes 1–2, JR; "Miss Little Defense Aid Set Up," *Greensboro Daily News* (Greensboro, N.C.), October 1, 1974 (clipping), box 6, Sara M. Evans Papers, SBC.

2. The medical examiner's report is quoted in "State of North Carolina vs. Joanne Little Fact Sheet," 1975, Prisons Vertical File, LHA.

3. Testimony of Joan Little, transcript, folders 1 and 2, box 1, JR.

4. The *Chicago Tribune* declared it the "trial of the decade." Quoted in McGuire, *At the Dark End of the Street*, 217.

5. Bevacqua, *Rape on the Public Agenda*; Gagné, *Battered Women's Justice*; Schneider, *Battered Women and Feminist Lawmaking*; Coker and Harrison, "Story of *Wanrow*."

6. Hill, *Men, Mobs, and Law*, 15.

7. Victoria Law discusses these four cases in an essay that argues feminist activists were more reluctant to rally around domestic violence survivors who killed their

abusers than they were to support women who killed perpetrators of rape. Law, "Sick of the Abuse." In her study of the nexus of black liberation and feminist organizing in Washington, D.C., Anne Valk remarks that all four cases "symbolically put women of color at the center of the antiviolence movement" and helped to engender a distinctive U.S. Third World feminist consciousness. Valk, *Radical Sisters*, 173.

8. Crenshaw, "Demarginalizing the Intersection." I draw on a range of primary sources as well as on existing scholarship on the case and campaign: Fergus, *Liberalism*, 132–165; Greene, "She Ain't No Rosa Parks"; McGuire, *At the Dark End of the Street*, 202–228; McNeil, "Body, Sexuality, and *Self*-Defense"; McNeil, "Joanne Is You."

9. Ashley Futrell, "Brutal Murder," *Washington Daily News* (Washington, N.C.), August 28, 1974 (clipping), box 93, Minnie Bruce Pratt Papers, SBC.

10. McGuire, *At the Dark End of the Street*, 210.

11. Ibid.; Greene, "She Ain't No Rosa Parks," 433–434; McNeil, "Body, Sexuality, and *Self*-Defense," 241.

12. Greene, "She Ain't No Rosa Parks," 431; McGuire, *At the Dark End of the Street*, 206–208; McNeil, "Body, Sexuality, and *Self*-Defense," 241.

13. Greene, "She Ain't No Rosa Parks," 430, 432.

14. Ibid., 439–440.

15. French, "Incarcerated Black Female."

16. Chenier, interview with Reston; "Miss Little Defense Aid Set Up."

17. "State of North Carolina vs. Joanne Little Fact Sheet"; Julian Bond, fund-raising appeal letter, n.d., box 5, folder 17, Violence Against Women Collection, SSC.

18. Jerry Paul and Karen Galloway to Defense Fund mailing list, February 1975, box 93, Minnie Bruce Pratt Papers, SBC; Marjory Nelson, journal, 1975–1976, Marjory Nelson Papers (unprocessed collection), SSC.

19. Paul and Galloway to Defense Fund mailing list.

20. Danielle McGuire points out that the Superior Court Judge, Henry A. McKinnon, did so on the basis of the media onslaught, rather than the claims of ubiquitous racial bias (*At the Dark End of the Street*, 217). Devin Fergus has shown that a crucial defense strategy was to make North Carolina's reputation as a "racially moderate" southern state hang in the balance of the trial (*Liberalism*, 142–146).

21. "State of North Carolina vs. Joanne Little Fact Sheet"; Bond, fund-raising appeal letter; Paul and Galloway to Defense Fund mailing list. On the Black Women's United Front and its support of Little, see Farmer, *Remaking Black Power*, 123–124.

22. McGuire, *At the Dark End of the Street*. See page 215 for a discussion of Rosa Parks's involvement in the Little campaign.

23. On the State of Georgia's long-standing practice of criminalizing and incarcerating black women for using self-defensive violence, see Haley, *No Mercy Here*.

24. McDuffie, "New Freedom Movement of Negro Women," 83.

25. Gore, *Radicalism at the Crossroads*, 77. In addition to Gore, see also on the Ingram case: Martin, "Race, Gender, and Southern Justice"; McDuffie, "New Freedom Movement of Negro Women"; McGuire, *At the Dark End of the Street*.

26. On Concerned Women for Justice, see McNeil, "JoAnne Is You," 271–272;

for more on black women's civil rights–era activism in Durham more broadly, see Greene, *Our Separate Ways*. On the overlap with the Ingram campaign, see Gore, *Radicalism at the Crossroads*, 153.

27. See Haley, *No Mercy Here*, 119–155.

28. Lee, *For Freedom's Sake*, 45–60. See also McGuire, *At the Dark End of the Street*, 156–173; Colley, *Ain't Scared of Your Jail*.

29. MacMillan, "Joanne Little: No Escape Yet," *off our backs* 5, no. 1 (Jan 1975): 4.

30. Frances B. Kent, "Joan Little's Lawyers to Show Jailer Made Frequent Sexual Advances," *Los Angeles Times*, August 8, 1975.

31. "Women in Southern Jails: Situation Still Explosive," *Raleigh News and Observer*, November 9, 1975 (clipping), box 6, Sara M. Evans Papers, SBC.

32. Ibid.; Chenier, interview with Reston.

33. Chenier, interview with Reston.

34. Singh, *Black Is a Country*, 57.

35. Emphasis added. Quoted in *Negroes with Guns*. Williams and his wife, Mabel, also a black radical activist, fled to postrevolutionary Cuba in 1961 to escape government persecution, and from there they continued their political organizing. See Tyson, *Radio Free Dixie*.

36. Baldwin, "In the Shadow of the Gun"; Murch, *Living for the City*; Nelson, *Body and Soul*; Spencer, *Revolution Has Come*; and Bloom and Martin, *Black against Empire*.

37. Juan González, "The Vote or the Gun," in Enck-Wanzer, *Young Lords*, 81–82. On the Young Lords, see also Fernández, "Denise Oliver and the Young Lords Party." On the American Indian Movement, see Smith and Warrior, *Like a Hurricane*.

38. On the making of the U.S. Third World Left, see especially Pulido, *Black, Brown, Yellow, and Left*; Young, *Soul Power*.

39. James, "Introduction," 7. On Ida B. Wells, see Giddings, *Ida: Sword among Lions*.

40. On the politics of masculinist protection within black nationalist movements, see especially Griffin, "Ironies of the Saint"; Taylor, *Promise of Patriarchy*. On BPP women rejecting this politics, see Matthews, "No One Ever Asks," 244–245; Spencer, "Engendering the Black Freedom Struggle," 93–94.

41. Third World Women's Alliance, "Women in the Struggle," *National SNCC Monthly* 1, no. 6 (Mar 1971): 8. For more on the TWWA, see Farmer, *Remaking Black Power*, 159–192; Roth, *Separate Roads*, 89–93; Springer, *Living for the Revolution*; Ward, "Third World Women's Alliance." On women and gender politics in the Young Lords, see Fernández, "Denise Oliver and the Young Lords Party"; Nelson, "Abortion under Community Control."

42. "Is a Third World Women's Group Divisive to the Liberation Struggle?" *Triple Jeopardy* 1, no. 1 (1971): 8–9.

43. Frances Beal interview, VOFOHP.

44. Examples of coverage of political prisoners and prison activism include "Prisons Everywhere," *Triple Jeopardy* 1, no. 2 (1971): 4; Charlene Mitchell, "We Can Defeat

Repression," *Triple Jeopardy* 2, no. 3 (1973): 14; and "Political Prisoners Held 20 Years," *Triple Jeopardy* 3, no. 2 (1974). "Prison Project" and "Triple Jeopardy: Distribution," box 4, Third World Women's Alliance Records, SSC.

45. "Woman Inmate Kills Would-Be Rapist," *Triple Jeopardy* 4, no. 2 (1975): 7.

46. Letter from Jerome Paul to Charlene Mitchell, September 30, 1975, box 23, folder 13, NAARPR records, 20th Century Organizational Files, SCLSSR; Nelson, interview with author; McNeil, "Joanne Is You," 268–269.

47. The guilty verdicts were thrown out by a federal court judge in 1980 after the prosecution's evidence was linked to the FBI's COINTELPRO against the black liberation movement. See Janken, *Wilmington Ten.*

48. "Death Penalty Protested, Raleigh March Peaceful," *Daily Times-News* (Burlington, N.C.), July 5, 1974, 1; "10,000 March on North Carolina," NAARPR, pamphlet, 1974, box 23, folder 13, NAARPR records, 20th Century Organizational Files, SCLSSR.

49. Fergus, *Liberalism*, 156.

50. Edward Tivnan, "Jury by Trial," *New York Times*, November 16, 1975; Nelson, interview with author; Alice Price, "'I Am Somebody!' The Case of Joanne Little," *Guild Notes* (National Lawyers Guild), series 2, JR.

51. Joan Little Solidarity Day Committee, "Demonstrate on Saturday, FREE JOANN LITTLE!" June 1975, Prisons Vertical File, LHA.

52. Southern Organizing Committee for Social & Economic Justice, "Free Joann Little! Mobilize for her Trial July 14," box 10, ALFAA.

53. Carlton Jones, "East Bay Supports Joan Little," *Sun Reporter* (San Francisco), July 19, 1975, 13.

54. Davis, "JoAnne Little." According to Jerry Paul, Little had "many opportunities to escape the area, even the country, but had declined." See MacMillan, "Joanne Little: No Escape Yet." McNeil also emphasizes this point in "Body, Sexuality, and *Self*-Defense," 236–237.

55. From a poem entitled, "Joanne Walks with Dignity," published in the *Poverty Law Report* 3, no. 2 (May 1975): 3.

56. Danny Meyers, "Joan Little's Trial to Open Next Month," *Sun Reporter*, June 21, 1975, 37.

57. Ibid.; "A Conversation with Joanne Little," *Tri-State Defender* (Memphis, Tenn.), September 13, 1975, 1.

58. Quoted from *Jet Magazine* in McNeil, "Body, Sexuality, and *Self* Defense," 246.

59. For a discussion of prisoner rebellions at NCCCW in previous decades, see Shirley and Stafford, *Dixie Be Damned*, 224–226.

60. Holtzman, "'Free Our Sisters,' Prison Protesters Cry"; Chenier, interview with Reston; "Miss Little Defense Aid Set Up."

61. Triangle Area Lesbian Feminists, ed., *Break de Chains of Legalized U.$. Slavery* (Durham: North Carolina Women's Prison Book Project, 1976), Freedom Archives, San Francisco.

62. Karen Lindsey, "Women in North Carolina," n.d., box 14, folder 298, CSIVR.

63. *Break de Chains*; Mecca Reliance, Marsha Segerberg, and Anne Williams, "Ra-

leigh Women Lose," *off our backs* 5, no. 6 (July 1975): 26–27. For a more extensive chronicle of the uprising, see Shirley and Stafford, *Dixie Be Damned*, 219–247.

64. Kathy Hyatt, "News from Women's Prison in Raleigh," *Feminary* 6, no. 13 (1975): 5, box 30, MBP.

65. "Joann Little Rally, July 2," *Feminary* 6, no. 15 (1975): 1, box 30, MBP.

66. Chenier, interview with Reston.

67. "Letter from Prison," *Feminary* 6, no. 19 (1975): 6–7, box 30, MBP.

68. Lindsey, "Women in North Carolina"; "Women in Southern Jails."

69. Lindsey, "Women in North Carolina."

70. "Letters from the Inside," *Feminary* 6, no. 18 (1975): 4, box 30, MBP.

71. Marsh, "Contradiction," in *Break de Chains*, 17–18.

72. For more on the significance of Reagon's song and her involvement in the campaign more generally, see McNeil, "Joanne Is You," 261, 271–272. For a compelling reading of Reagon's "Joanne Little" in relation to contemporary racial justice movements, see Redmond, "As Though It Were Our Own."

73. Marjory Nelson interview, VOFOHP.

74. Bond, fund-raising appeal letter.

75. Richie, "Black Feminist Reflection," 1134–1135; Richie, *Arrested Justice*, 91–94.

76. Davis, "JoAnne Little," 149, 154–157.

77. Socialist Women's Caucus of Louisville, "The Racist Use of Rape and the Rape Charge: A Statement to the Women's Movement from a Group of Socialist Women" (Louisville, Ky.: Socialist Women's Caucus of Louisville, 1975), SBC.

78. Anne Braden, "A Second Open Letter to Southern White Women," *Southern Exposure* 4, no. 4 (1976): 50. Tibbs was hitchhiking in Florida in early 1974 when he was arrested and charged with the rape and murder of a white woman. Widespread protests brought scrutiny to the legal process, and in 1976 the case was thrown out of the Florida Supreme Court due to weak evidence. On the Tibbs case, see "An Innocent Man CAN Be Freed," *Southern Exposure* 4, no. 4 (1976).

79. *Feminary* 6, no. 14 (1975): 1, box 30, MBP.

80. *Feminary* is more widely known for its late 1970s/1980s iteration as a lesbian literary journal with a regional scope and distribution. See Powell, "Look What Happened Here."

81. "Triangle Women's Union—Structure," *Feminary* 7, no. 5 (1976): 3–4, box 30, MBP.

82. *Break de Chains*. For a compelling close reading of this text in relation to several other writing projects collaboratively authored by imprisoned activists, see Hames-García, *Fugitive Thought*, 219–247.

83. Nelson, journal; Marjory Nelson interview, VOFOHP.

84. Ibid.; Nelson, interview by author.

85. Alison Edwards, *Rape, Racism, and the White Women's Movement: An Answer to Susan Brownmiller* (Chicago: Sojourner Truth Organization, 1976), SBC.

86. Davis, "Racism and the Contemporary Literature on Rape," 26.

87. Nan Blitman and Robin Green, "Inez Garcia on Trial," *Ms.* (May 1975): 50.

88. Danny Meyers, "Inez Garcia Wins Appeal for New Trial," *Sun Reporter*, January 10, 1976, 17.

89. Ann Senechal, "Justice: A Political Case of Rape," *San Francisco Bay Guardian*, August 15, 1974; "The Trial: Inez Garcia," *Plexus* (Oct 1974) (clipping), box 6, Sara M. Evans Papers, SBC; Lacey Fosburgh, "Trial Raises Questions on Rape Victims' Rights," *New York Times*, October 3, 1974 (clipping), box 5, folder 12, Violence Against Women Collection, SSC.

90. Fosburgh, "Trial Raises Questions."

91. Inez Garcia Defense Committee Fact Sheet, box 2, folder 21, Rosalyn Baxandall: Women's Liberation Research Files, TL; Jean Horan and Fran Moira, "Executing the Enemy," *off our backs* 4, no. 10 (Oct 1974): 8.

92. Jim Wood, "Women Chant 'Freedom'; Inez Gets 5-to-Life," *San Francisco Examiner*, October 22, 1974 (clipping); IGDC letter, October 7, 1974; IGDC, "Fight Goes On!"; statements from Margo St. James, Gloria Steinem, Kate Millet, Simone de Beauvoir, and Marge Piercy (all in box 2, LM).

93. Ibid. On the involvement of Combating Sexism, see Hobson, *Lavender and Red*, 73–74. See Hobson also for an analysis of the campaign in the context of the history of the gay and lesbian left in the San Francisco Bay Area.

94. del Drago, "Pride of Inez Garcia," *Ms.* (May 1975): 54, 84.

95. "Viva Inez!" information sheet, n.d., box 2, LM.

96. Interview with Liberation News Service reprinted in *La Razon Mestiza III* (Summer 1976), Chicano Studies Newsletters Collection, Ethnic Studies Library, University of California, Berkeley.

97. Susan Weiss to Governor Brown, February 19, 1975; "The 6 Free-Inez Demonstrators," flier, n.d., both in box 2, LM.

98. Statement from Inez Garcia, recorded by Shiane Summer and Judith Graywoman at CIW, September 20, 1975, box 2, LM.

99. Inez Garcia Defense Committee Fact Sheet; "Trial: Inez Garcia"; Senechal, "Justice"; Inez Garcia Defense Committee, "Free Inez!" *FAAR News* (Sept/Oct 1974).

100. Letter from Louise Merrill for the IGDC, June 28, 1977, box 2, LM.

101. Woods's name occasionally appeared as "Dessie X. Woods." She later went by the name Rashida Mustafa Muhammad.

102. "Victimized," *Midnight Special* 5, no. 7 (Dec 1975/Jan 1976): 5–6, Interference Archive, Brooklyn; "Dear Sisters," open letter from Dykes for the Second American Revolution, Atlanta, Ga., n.d., box 20, ALFAA.

103. "The Story of Dessie Woods: A Close-Up Look at Justice in the 'New South,'" pamphlet, 1977, box 33, Printed Ephemera Collection on Individuals, TL.

104. Nkenge Touré and Deirdre Wright, "Dialogue with Dessie," *Aegis* (July/Aug 1978): 10.

105. The robbery conviction was overturned in June 1981, resulting in her early release.

106. For more on the African People's Socialist Party, see its website: http://apspu huru.org/about/apsp-history/ (accessed September 1, 2017).

107. Letter from Carrie Joy for the Dessie Woods Support Committee, August 11, 1980, box 10, ALFAA.

108. National Committee to Defend Dessie Woods, "Help Keep the Struggle to Free Dessie Woods Alive!" mailer, 1979, box 10, ALFAA; Touré and Wright, "Dialogue with Dessie," 9–13.

109. "Dessie Woods Speaks Out!" *off our backs* 11, no. 10 (Nov 1981): 11.

110. "We Did It!" *Newsletter of the National Committee to Defend Dessie Woods*, (Nov 1977), box 10, ALFAA; "Smash Colonial Violence/Free Dessie Woods March on July 4 in San Francisco," poster, Interference Archive, Brooklyn.

111. July 4th Movement to Free Dessie Woods press release, 1978, Prisons Vertical File, LHA.

112. "Forward to Atlanta!" *Newsletter of the National Committee to Defend Dessie Woods* (Summer 1977), box 10, ALFAA; Willow Katz to Inez Garcia, November 2002, in the possession of Cathy Cade; Block, interview with author.

113. For a genealogy of "internal colonialism as an American theory of race" in the second half of the 20th century, see Gutiérrez, "Internal Colonialism."

114. "We Did It!"; "Woods Rally Sparks Controversy," *Plexus* 5, no. 6 (Aug 1978) (clipping), box 6, Sara M. Evans Papers, SBC. See also Law, "Sick of the Abuse," 44–45.

115. "Story of Dessie Woods."

116. Touré and Wright, "Dialogue with Dessie," 9–13.

117. Wanrow testimony in Russell and Van de Ven, "Crimes against Women," 71.

118. On the judicial history of the Wanrow case, see especially Coker and Harrison, "Story of *Wanrow*," and Schneider, *Battered Women*.

119. Wanrow testimony in Russell and Van de Ven, "Crimes against Women," 70.

120. Coker and Harrison, "Story of *Wanrow*," 234–235.

121. Swan, interview with author; Debbie Richards and Yvonne Wanrow interviewed on the KPFA program, "Freedom Is a Constant Struggle," March 15, 1978, Berkeley, Freedom Is a Constant Struggle collection, Freedom Archives, San Francisco. Yvonne Swan (formerly Wanrow) continues to advocate for the freedom of Leonard Peltier today.

122. Letter from Wanrow to Nelson and Taylor, June 14, 1978, Marjory Nelson Papers (unprocessed collection), SSC; Swan, interview with author.

123. Margaret Tarter, "Wanrow Conviction Is Reversed," *Bay State Banner*, February 3, 1977, 10.

124. Richards and Wanrow on "Freedom Is a Constant Struggle."

125. Swan, interview with author; Sherrie Cohen, "Native Women's Benefit to Free Yvonne Wanrow," *off our backs* 9, no. 4 (Apr 1979): 6.

126. Jaimes and Halsey, "American Indian Women"; O'Sullivan, "More Destruction to These Family Ties."

127. Correspondence between Center for Constitutional Rights, Yvonne Wanrow, Marjory Nelson, and Polly Taylor, 1977–1978, in the possession of Marjory Nelson; Women of All Red Nations, grant application to the Women's Foundation, July 1, 1983, box 51, folder 23, San Francisco Women's Building Records, GLBTHS; "Free

Yvonne Wanrow," *Aegis* (Mar/Apr 1979): 17–18; Richards and Wanrow on "Freedom Is a Constant Struggle"; Fran Moira, "Let This Be a WARNing," *off our backs* 8, no. 11 (Dec 1978): 9.

128. Talking points for NOW-Spokane meeting, Nov 3, 1977, Marjory Nelson Papers (unprocessed collection), SSC.

129. Touré interview, VOFOHP.

130. On the LEAA and the rape crisis center and battered women's shelter movements, see especially Gottschalk, *Prison and the Gallows*, 124–130, 145–147. See also Bevacqua, *Rape on the Public Agenda*; Matthews, *Confronting Rape*; Schecter, *Women and Male Violence*.

131. Hill, *Men, Mobs, and Law*, 20.

132. "NY Women Discuss Rape," *Militant*, May 7, 1971, box 20, folder 3, Women's Liberation Collection, SSC.

133. Russell, *Politics of Rape*, 276.

134. Block, *Arm the Spirit*, 53.

135. Sarita Cordell, "Self Confidence, Self Defense," 1973; Sue Lenaerts and Christine Murphy, "Why Women Need Self-Defense—A Theoretical Discussion"; Susan Pascale, Rachel Moon, and Leslie Tanner, "Karate as Self-Defense for Women," *Women: A Journal of Liberation* (Winter 1970) (all clippings in box 8, ALFAA).

136. Pascale, Moon, and Tanner, "Karate as Self-Defense," 69.

137. Haag, "Putting your Body on the Line," 41.

138. Fran Moira, "Coming to Terms," *off our backs* 5, no. 1 (Jan 1975): 2.

139. On the centrality of self-defense in 1970s antirape activism, see also Bevacqua, *Rape on the Public Agenda*, 66–69; Delacoste and Newman, *Fight Back!*; Jacquet, "Fighting Back."

140. Feminist Alliance Against Rape to subscribers, June, 1974, box 5, folder 43, Rosalyn Baxandall: Women's Liberation Research Files, TL.

141. Jackie MacMillan and Freada Klein, "FAAR Editorial," *FAAR News* (Sept/Oct 1974): 2.

142. San Francisco Women Against Rape and Feminist Alliance Against Rape, "Readers' Responses," *FAAR News* (Nov/Dec 1974): 7–8.

143. Ibid., 8.

144. *FAAR News* brochure, n.d., box 5, folder 14, Violence Against Women Collection, SSC.

145. FAAR, "The Case of Joann Little," *FAAR News* (Nov/Dec 1974): 1–2.

146. MacMillan and Klein, "FAAR Editorial."

147. Marlene Schmitz, "On Violence," *off our backs* 5, no. 2 (Feb 1975): 8.

148. Robin McDuff, Deanne Pernell, and Karen Saunders, "Feminists Critique Anti-Rape Movement," *FAAR News* (Jan/Feb 1977): 4. *FAAR News* also helped to circulate Angela Davis's editorial on the Little case in *Ms.* by publishing a review of her essay.

149. Brochure for *The Confrontation: Latinas Fight Back Against Rape* (1983), box 1, folder 13, Cherríe Moraga Papers, Green Library, Stanford University.

150. IGDC, "Inez Garcia: Womanpride Fighting Back," pamphlet, 1976, box 2, LM.

151. Delacoste and Newman, *Fight Back!*, vii, 30, 78, 215.

152. See, for example: Joan Little Solidarity Day Committee, "Demonstrate on Saturday, FREE JOANN LITTLE!" June 1975, Prisons Vertical File, LHA; Southern Organizing Committee for Social & Economic Justice, "Free Joann Little! Mobilize for Her Trial July 14," box 10, ALFAA; and Correspondence between Center for Constitutional Rights, Wanrow, Nelson, and Taylor, 1977–1978, in the possession of Marjory Nelson.

153. Sue Lenaerts, "Killing with Just Cause," *FAAR News* (July/Aug 1976): 8.

154. Feminist Alliance Against Rape to subscribers.

155. Block, *Arm the Spirit*, 53.

156. Ibid., 56.

157. Block, interview with author; Willow Katz to Inez Garcia, November, 2002, in the possession of Cathy Cade.

158. Ross, interview with author.

159. Letter from NCDDW to Loretta Ross, July 16, 1981; "Hear Dessie Woods," Anti-Rape Week flier, September 25, 1981, both in box 9, folder 16, NT. Touré and Wright, "Dialogue with Dessie."

160. For more on the center's development and the process by which it became black feminist–centered, see ch. 4 of this book; Valk, *Radical Sisters*, 162; Bevacqua, "Reconsidering Violence against Women," 166, 170.

161. Loretta Ross, Kathy Powell, and Nkenge Touré, "Report From the First National Conference on Third World Women and Violence," 1980, box 5, folder 2, Loretta Ross Papers, SSC.

162. Coker and Harrison, "Story of *Wanrow*," 244.

163. Lynora Williams, "Third World Women Decry Violence," *Guardian*, September 10, 1980, 9 (clipping), box 100, MBP.

164. Bay Area Defense Committee for Battered Women, Vanguard Application Form, May 14, 1979, box 134, folder 14, Phyllis Lyon and Del Martin Papers, GLBTHS.

165. Ibid.

166. Anderson, *Imagined Communities*, 27.

Chapter 2. Diagnosing Institutional Violence

1. CSIV, "Dear Sisters," letter addressed to feminist activists in Greater Boston, August 20, 1977, box 1, folder 12; "Worcester Unit Background," n.d., box 6, folder 112; Letter, Boston Movement Bail Fund to Human Services Committee, March 22, 1976, box 1, folder 12 (all in CSIVR).

2. The quotation is borrowed from Lipsitz, *Life in the Struggle*, 10.

3. Cohen, "Deviance as Resistance."

4. Gómez, "Resisting Living Death," 60.

5. Metzl, *Protest Psychosis*, xii.

6. Gómez, "Resisting Living Death"; Mitford, *Kind and Usual Punishment*; Samuels, "Improvising on Reality"; Berger, *Captive Nation*.

7. Mitford, *Kind and Usual Punishment*, 231.

8. Gómez, "Resisting Living Death," 59. In addition, see Committee to End the

Marion Lockdown, "From Alcatraz to Marion to Florence"; Mitford, *Kind and Usual Punishment*.

9. Nelson, *Body and Soul*, 155.

10. Mark, Sweet, and Ervin,"Role of Brain Disease in Riots."

11. Mason, "Brain Surgery to Control Behavior," 63.

12. CSIV, "An Annotated Chronology of the Events Surrounding the Development of the Proposed 'Center for Violent Women' at Worcester State Hospital," November 1977, box 1, folder 2, CSIVR; Jean Dietz, "Senate Urged to Kill 'Brain Study,'" *Boston Globe*, September 24, 1972, 38. Deitz reported that studies were carried out at Walpole, Bridgewater, and Framingham to collect blood samples and fingerprints and chromosomal analyses "to determine if inmates possess unique characteristics."

13. Duster, *Backdoor to Eugenics*; Nelson, *Body and Soul*; Washington, *Medical Apartheid*; Hornblum, *Acres of Skin*.

14. Nelson, *Body and Soul*, 153–180.

15. Women Against Prison, "Dykes behind Bars," *Dyke, A Quarterly* 1, no. 1 (1975): 15; Personal statement by a Bedford Hills prisoner, June 2, 1974, box 1, Inmate Misbehavior Case Files (1964–1974), New York State Archives, Albany.

16. Quoted in Nicholas, "August Rebellion," https://www.villagevoice.com/2016/08/30/august-rebellion-new-yorks-forgotten-female-prison-riot/ (accessed August 31, 2016).

17. Díaz-Cotto, *Gender, Ethnicity, and the State*, 324–327; "Behavior Modification," *No More Cages* 2, no. 3 (1979): 8–17, WHCC. On the August Rebellion, see also ibid. and Law, *Resistance behind Bars*, 11–12.

18. "Bedford Hills," *Through the Looking Glass* 2, no. 3 (1977), box 41, ALFAPC; "Behavior Modification."

19. Díaz-Cotto, *Gender, Ethnicity, and the State*, 327.

20. "Bedford Hills."

21. "Updates," *Through the Looking Glass* 1, no. 1 (1976), box 41, ALFAPC.

22. Women's Prison Coalition, press release, April 6, 1976, box 52, folder 14, San Francisco Women's Building Records, GLBTHS.

23. "Women Rally to Protest State Prison Program," *Sacramento Bee*, March 20, 1976, box 52, folder 14, San Francisco Women's Building Records, GLBTHS.

24. Women's Prison Coalition, press release; "Women Protest Behavior Modification," 1973 (clipping), box 3, folder 8, Flora Haas Papers, SL-NU.

25. Faith, *Unruly Women*, 275–315; Faith, "Reflections on Inside/Out Organizing"; "Santa Cruz Women's Prison Project Progress Report—October 1973," box 4, folder 46, Rosalyn Baxandall: Women's Liberation Research Files, TL.

26. Shakur, *Assata*, 253.

27. U.S. Department of Justice. *Interstate Transfer of Prison Inmates in the United States*. Longmont, Colorado: National Institute of Corrections Information Center, 2006.

28. Shakur, *Assata*, 253. For analyses of Shakur's activism and writings, see James, "Framing the Panther"; Hames-García, *Fugitive Thought*, 95–140; Dillon, "Possessed by Death."

29. National Prison Project, press release, October 20, 1978, box 11, folder 217, CSIVR.

30. Norman A. Carlson (director, Bureau of Prisons), "Policy Statement on the Maximum Security Unit at FCI, Alderson, West Virginia," September 22, 1977, box 11, folder 217; CSIV, "'Violent Women' Slammed in New Jails," n.d., box 6, folder 110; National Prison Project, press release, October, 20, 1978, box 11, folder 217 (all in CSIVR).

31. Freedman, *Their Sisters' Keepers*, 185.

32. Freedman, *Maternal Justice*, 186; League of Women Voters of Massachusetts, "Why We Need Changes in the Penal Laws Affecting Women Offenders," June 7, 1949, box 2, folder 16, Friends of Framingham Papers, SL-HU.

33. Freedman, *Maternal Justice*, 313–339. On state-sponsored homophobia in the mid–twentieth century, see Johnson, *Lavender Scare*; Canaday, *Straight State*.

34. Freedman, *Maternal Justice*, 330–335.

35. Kay Bourne, "Framingham Site of Peaceful Revolt," *Bay State Banner*, March 30, 1972, 1; Women's Prison Collective, "Framingham," *off our backs* 2, no. 8 (Apr 1972): 7; Joseph Rosenbloom, "Violence Erupts at Framingham," *Boston Globe*, January 2, 1972, 49, 64.

36. Bourne, "Framingham Site of Peaceful Revolt."

37. Tina Williams, "Our Fight Is Not Over," *off our backs* 2, no. 8 (Apr 1972): 6.

38. "Framingham Protest Still On," *Boston Globe*, March 22, 1972, 16.

39. "Women Inmates Stage Sit-in," *Boston Globe*, March 21, 1972, box 1, folder 4, CPRS; Women's Prison Collective, "At Framingham Prison, the Women Fight Back," *Boston After Dark*, March 28, 1972, box 1, folder 4, CPRS; Kathleen Kilgore, "The Trouble with Framingham Women's Prison Is Men," *Boston Phoenix*, May 17, 1972, box 1, folder 4, CPRS; Rhonda Zangwill, "An Ivy Covered Prison Is Still a Jail," *Equal Times*, August 28, 1978, box 2, folder 43, CSIVR; CSIV, "Annotated Chronology."

40. Women's Prison Collective, "At Framingham Prison"; Jean Dietz, "Supt. Cuzzi Apologizes to Framingham Inmates," *Boston Globe*, March 28, 1972, 7.

41. Bourne, "Framingham Site of Peaceful Revolt."

42. Samuels, "Improvising on Reality"; Thompson, *Blood in the Water*.

43. The state system also included three forestry camps at Plymouth, Monroe, and Warwick.

44. "Walpole Tensions Still High," *Burlington Free Press* (Burlington, VT), March 21, 1972, 2; "Routine Returns Slowly at Walpole Prison," *Lowell Sun*, March 21, 1972, 3; Jeff Northrup, "Billerica Jail Unrest Put Down with Tear Gas," *Lowell Sun*, March 23, 1972, 51.

45. Coleman, "Prison Reform in Massachusetts."

46. Ibid., 176.

47. "Guards Still 'Out Sick' at Framingham," *Boston Globe*, April 30, 1972, 29; Ray Richard, "Superintendent Suspends 16 for Walpole Sick-in," *Boston Globe*, May 5, 1972, 1.

48. Coleman, "Prison Reform in Massachusetts," 251.

49. Bissonette, *When the Prisoners Ran Walpole*.

50. Coleman, "Prison Reform in Massachusetts," 353.

51. For a discussion of transfers from MCI-Walpole to Bridgewater State Hospital, see Bissonette, *When the Prisoners Ran Walpole,* 26–29, 33–36; CSIV, "Annotated Chronology"; "Ward for Violent Women Opens in Worcester," *Sister Courage* (Dec 1976), box 1, folder 12, CSIVR.

52. Bridgewater Alternatives Project, "The Children of Bridgewater: A Report on Adolescents at Bridgewater State Hospital," December 16, 1974, 1, box 1, folder 16, Flora Haas Papers, SL-NU.

53. Anderson and Benson, *Documentary Dilemmas.*

54. Daniel Connolly, "An Insider's Look at Maximum Security," *Boston Globe*, April 9, 1972, D32.

55. Women's Prison Collective, "At Framingham Prison"; CSIV, "Annotated Chronology"; "Ward for Violent Women Opens."

56. Robinson, interview with author; CSIV, "Annotated Chronology."

57. CSIV, "Annotated Chronology"; "Ward for Violent Women Opens"; Sally Challant, Freada Klein, and Sunny Robinson, "Women in Prison," *FAAR News* (Nov/Dec 1976): 4, Periodicals Collection, SSC.

58. The term *therapeutic state* was coined by Thomas Szasz. See Szasz, *Law, Liberty, and Psychiatry.* The intellectual movement of antipsychiatry predated and informed the ex-patient activism and theorizing of the 1970s. Key figures included R. D. Laing, Erving Goffman, Thomas Szasz, and Michel Foucault. For a nuanced cultural and intellectual history of antipsychiatry from the 1940s to the 1970s, see Staub, *Madness Is Civilization.*

59. Bluestone and Stevenson, *Boston Renaissance.*

60. On the history of black community organizing for educational equality in Boston, see Theoharis, "'We Saved the City.'" For a critique of the "busing crisis" frame, see Delmont and Theoharis, "Rethinking the Boston 'Busing Crisis.'"

61. CSIV, newsletter, n.d., box 2, folder 27, CSIVR.

62. Bevacqua, *Rape on the Public Agenda*; Morgen, *Into Our Own Hands*; Schecter, *Women and Male Violence.*

63. Breines, *Trouble between Us*, 101–102.

64. CSIV newsletter, March 1979, box 2, folder 27, CSIVR. The history of sterilization abuse is long and well-documented. See, e.g., Roberts, *Killing the Black Body*; Briggs, *Reproducing Empire*; Smith, *Conquest*; Carpio, "Lost Generation." On feminist campaigns against sterilization abuse, see Silliman et al., *Undivided Rights*; Nelson, *Women of Color.* On the persistence of coercive sterilization in U.S. women's prisons today, see Roth and Ainsworth, "If They Hand You a Paper."

65. "Ella Ellison . . . Imprisoned for Five Lifetimes, Why?" poster, Ella Ellison Support Committee, n.d.; "High Court Reverses Ella Ellison's Murder Conviction," *Boston Globe*, July 19, 1978 (clipping); and Letter from Ella Ellison Support Committee to supporters, April 16, 1976 (all in box 2, folder 23, BS).

66. On the Combahee River Collective, see ch. 4 of this book; Breines, *Trouble Between Us*; Gumbs, "We Can Learn to Mother Ourselves"; Harris, "All of Who I

Am," and *Black Feminist Politics*, 1–54; Springer, *Living for the Revolution*; Taylor, *How We Get Free*.

67. CSIV newsletter, March 1979, box 2, folder 27, CSIVR.

68. Boston Bail Project, "Boston Bail Fund," *Bar None* no. 7 (1976): 9–13, box 4, ALFAPC.

69. *Inmates of Suffolk County Jail et al. v. Thomas S. Eisenstadt et al.*, 360 F. Supp. 676 (United States District Court, D. Mass., 1973).

70. "Crisis! And The Boston Bail Project/Funds Presents a Community Workshop," flier, box 1, folder 12, SGS.

71. Letter from the Boston Bail Project/Bail Funds to prospective supporters, January 14, 1980, box 1, folder 2, SGS.

72. Boston Bail Project, "Women, Bail, and Repression," *Sister Courage* (Apr 1977): 9 (clipping), CB (unprocessed collection).

73. *Doing Time* (Feb 1975): 1, CB.

74. Ibid. (Sept 1979): 3, CB.

75. "Dorchester International Women's Day Celebration," *Doing Time* (Mar/Apr 1981): 19, CB.

76. "Family Center," *Doing Time* (Feb 1975): 3; "Doing Time" and "Survival Center Update," *Doing Time* (Mar 1975): 4, 5 (both in CB).

77. "Dorchester International Women's Day Celebration."

78. Memo by Connie Breece and Linda Dirocco, 1977, CB.

79. UMass Boston/Framingham Prison Project for Women Offenders, Public Service Announcement, July 30, 1976, CB. On the defense campaign for Susan Saxe, see Hobson, *Lavender and Red*, 42–68.

80. Breece, interview with author.

81. CSIV newsletter, March 1979, box 2, folder 27, CSIVR; Prison Research Education Action Project, *Instead of Prisons*; Ronna Bolante, "Promoting Hope, Healing in the Justice System," September 9, 2015, AFSC website, https://www.afsc.org/story/promoting-hope-healing-justice-system (accessed September 15, 2016).

82. Elizabeth Stone House brochure, box 2, Feminist Ephemera Collection, SL-HU; Chamberlin, *On Our Own*.

83. Pelka, *What We Have Done*, 286–287.

84. Chamberlin, "Ex-Patients' Movement"; Staub, *Madness Is Civilization*.

85. Staub, *Madness Is Civilization*, 10.

86. "21 Reasons for Our Opposition to the Worcester Unit for 'Violent' Women," broadsheet, 1977, box 1, folder 24; Challant, Klein, and Robinson, "Women in Prison," 2; CSIV, "The Worcester Ward: Violence Against Women," *Science for the People* 10, no. 6 (1978): 10; CSIV, "We Stopped the Women's Unit," flier, October 1979, box 2, folder 27 (all in CSIVR).

87. "Women in Fight Against Prison/Hospital Unit," *FAAR News* (Mar/Apr 1977): 12–13, Periodicals Collection, SSC.

88. Special Consultation and Treatment Program for Women Advisory Committee, meeting minutes, March 22, 1978, box 6, folder 108, CSIVR.

89. CSIV press release, December 20, 1977, box 2, folder 29, CSIVR.

90. CSIV, "Workshop Schedule for October 2," conference program, 1977, box 12, folder 278, CSIVR.

91. "Framingham Goes Max," n.d., box 2, folder 27, CSIVR.

92. Marian J. Meyers, "A Ward for Violent Women: A Controversy without End," *Worcester: The Magazine for Central Massachusetts* (Feb 1978): 12–13, box 6, folder 101, CSIVR.

93. DeCourcy Squire (spokesperson for the Boston Bail Fund), "Oral Testimony Given Opposing the Application for a Certificate of Need for a Unit for Violent Women at Worcester State Hospital," April 26, 1978, box 6, folder 113, CSIVR.

94. Ibid.

95. Testimony for DoN Hearing, March 8, 1978, box 8, folder 135, CSIVR; Freedman, "Prison Lesbian"; Kunzel, *Criminal Intimacy*, 77–110.

96. Wendi E. Weinshel (spokesperson for Western Massachusetts Residents against the Worcester Unit), "Testimony Regarding the DMH Worcester State Hospital Project #2-2723," box 8, folder 135, CSIVR.

97. "Testimony for Determination of Need Hearing Regarding the Department of Mental Health Worcester State Hospital Project," March 8, 1978, box 8, folder 135; Letter, Boston Bail Fund to Human Services Committee of the Massachusetts General Court, March 22, 1976, box 1, folder 12 (both in CSIVR).

98. "We Stopped the Women's Unit."

99. See, e.g., Blumenthal, *Law and the Modern Mind*.

100. "21 Reasons for Our Opposition."

101. CSIV, "The Truth behind the Bars," *No More Cages* 2, no. 4 (1981): 13, box 31, ALFAPC.

102. On progressive mobilization against indeterminate sentencing in the 1970s, see especially Garland, *Culture of Control*, 53–73; Kohler-Hausmann, *Getting Tough*, 211–249.

103. CSIV, "Worcester Ward," 12.

104. Sen, "Naming Myself," 31.

105. Challant, Klein, and Robinson, "Women in Prison," 2.

106. Alberta James, Sheila Liles, and Irma Jean Mitchelle, "Behavior Modification," *off our backs* 8, no. 2 (Feb 1978): 11.

107. CSIV, "Worcester Ward," 15.

108. Bayer, *Homosexuality and American Psychiatry.*

109. Kunzel, "Rise of Gay Rights."

110. For a discussion of radical critiques of psychiatry within the gay liberation movement in the years surrounding the APA decision, see Lewis, "We Are Certain."

111. Cookie Dean, "An Editorial Opinion," *Turning Point* (1977): 3, CB.

112. "21 Reasons for Our Opposition to the Worcester Unit."

113. Breece, interview with author.

114. CSIV, "Worcester Ward," 14.

115. "Women in Fight against Prison/Hospital Unit," 13.

116. "21 Reasons for Our Opposition"; Letter from CSIV to CORE Collective at the Cambridge Women's Center, October 28, 1976, box 1, folder 5, CSIVR.

117. CSIV, "We Stopped the Women's Unit."

118. CSIV, "Worcester Ward," 16.

119. Minutes from an organizational retreat, n.d., box 1, folder 17, CSIVR.

120. On prefigurative politics in late-twentieth-century and early-twenty-first-century radical social movements in North America, including prison abolitionism, see Dixon, *Another Politics*; Polletta, *Freedom Is an Endless Meeting*.

121. While its origins lay in postwar international human rights discourse, the concept of transformative justice has been taken up in the past decade by antiracist feminist activists working on issues of interpersonal violence and seeking noncarceral intervention and prevention strategies. See, for example, Bierria, Rojas, and Kim, "Community Accountability"; Chen, Dulani, and Piepzna-Samarasinha, *Revolution Starts at Home*.

122. Gordon, *Ghostly Matters*, 127.

123. CSIV, "Worcester Ward," 16.

124. CSIV, "Truth behind the Bars," 19.

125. Ibid., 18.

126. Arlene Sen, "Arlene," personal essay, n.d., CB.

127. Grob, *Mad Among Us*, 249–312; Nielson, *Disability History*, 163–164; Rembis, "New Asylums."

128. CSIV, "Worcester Ward," 11.

129. CSIV, "Truth Behind the Bars," 18.

130. Joseph, *Against the Romance of Community*, ix.

131. Ibid., 19.

132. CSIV, "Worcester Ward," 17.

133. CSIV, "Truth behind the Bars," 18.

134. CSIV, "Principles of Unity," n.d., box 1, folder 22, CSIVR.

135. Ibid.

136. Ibid.; Robinson, interview with author.

137. Statement on internal process, n.d., box 12, folder 276, CSIVR.

138. CSIV, "Principles of Unity."

139. Enke, *Finding the Movement*, 4.

140. Margo Schulter, "Transsexophobia: Old Arguments against New People," *Gay Community News* no. 40 (Mar 1974): 6.

141. "Open Letter," n.d., box 1, folder 22, CSIVR; Meeting minutes, n.d., box 12, folder 276, CSIVR.

142. Meeting minutes, n.d., box 12, folder 276, CSIVR.

143. "Statement on Transsexualism," *Sojourner* 4, no. 2 (Oct 1978): 3.

144. Ibid.

145. Emily Culpepper and Jean MacRae, "Dealing with Difference: A Case Study," *Sojourner* 4, no. 3 (Nov 1978): 13.

146. Cambridge Women's Center, "A Space for All Women," *Sojourner* 4, no. 3 (Nov 1978): 3.

147. Ibid.; Karen Lindsey, "Alarming Attitudes," *Sojourner* 4, no. 3 (Nov 1978): 2–3; Socialist-Feminist Group: Minutes, 1979–1980, box 3, folder 5, SGS.

148. Meeting minutes, n.d., box 12, folder 276, CSIVR.

149. Heaney, "Women-Identified Women," 140. For a brief genealogy of antitransgender feminisms, transfeminist interventions, and transfeminist solidarities since the early 1970s, see Stryker and Bettcher, "Introduction: Trans/Feminisms."

150. Memorandum, "Action Alert," November 17, 1986, box 2, folder 41, CSIVR.

151. Robinson, interview with author.

152. Ibid.; Breece, interview with author; Aid to Incarcerated Mother, "Where Words Fail Action Speaks: Aid to Incarcerated Mothers 1983 Annual Report," CB; Barry, "Women Prisoners on the Cutting Edge."

153. Ben-Moshe, "Disabling Incarceration," 399.

154. Cohen, *Boundaries of Blackness*, 13–16.

Chapter 3. Printing Abolition

1. *Through the Looking Glass* 1, no. 1 (May 1976): 1, WSL.

2. "Statement of Purpose," *No More Cages* 1, no. 3 (Aug 1979): 1–2, WHCC.

3. "TTLG . . . and Us," *No More Cages* 2, no. 1 (1980): 25; "Where We're At," *No More Cages* 2, no. 3 (1980): 2–3, WHCC; "What's Happening with TTLG," *Through the Looking Glass* 5, no. 6 (July 1980): 1–2, box 41, ALFAPC.

4. Beins, "Revolution in Ephemera."

5. Ibid., 48.

6. Berlant and Warner, "Sex in Public." On queer worldmaking, see also Muñoz, *Disidentifications* and *Cruising Utopia*.

7. Berlant and Warner, "Sex in Public."

8. Anderson, *Imagined Communities*.

9. Blackwell, "Contested Histories," 59.

10. Berger, *Captive Nation*, 94–95.

11. Goffman, *Asylums*.

12. Morgan's anthology included many pamphlets and selections from short-lived journals. Jaime Harker and Cecilia Konchar Farr made Morgan's opening line the title of their 2015 edited collection on feminist print culture. See especially Beins, "Revolution in Ephemera," in that collection.

13. McMillian, *Smoking Typewriters*, 6–7.

14. On the Liberation News Service, see Slonecker, *New Dawn for the New Left*. See also McMillian, *Smoking Typewriters*.

15. McMillian, *Smoking Typewriters*, 6.

16. For a history of officially sanctioned prison newspapers and prisoner journalism, see Morris, *Jailhouse Journalism*.

17. Berger, *Captive Nation*, 236.

18. On black nationalist prison publications, see ibid., 236–244. On *Join Hands*, see Kunzel, *Criminal Intimacy*, 191–224.

19. Adams, "Built out of Books," 118.

20. Ibid.; Beins, "Revolution in Ephemera"; Beins, *Liberation in Print*; Hogan, *Feminist Bookstore Movement*; Klinger, "Paper Uprisings."

21. Resources for Community Change, *Women behind Bars*, 49; "Free to Prisoners," *No More Cages* 4, no. 3 (Apr–May 1983): 28, SL-NU.

22. "Dear Sisters Inside," *No More Cages* 4, no. 5 (Oct–Nov 1983): 2, SL-NU.

23. Burton-Rose, *Guerilla USA*, 98.

24. Ibid., 95–103; Ottey, interview with author.

25. "Purdy Treatment Center for Women," memo, May 8, 1975; and "Treatment Center," clipping from *Perspective*, n.d., both in box 1, Department of Corrections, Purdy, Administrative Series, WA State Archives, Olympia, Wash.

26. "Treatment Center."

27. "The George Jackson Brigade: Where Did They Come From?" *Through the Looking Glass* 3, no. 4 (May 1978): 7–8, box 41, ALFAPC.

28. Burton-Rose, *Guerrilla USA*; Ottey, interview with author.

29. Ottey, interview with author.

30. Women Out Now Prison Project, open letter, August 28, 1975, box 4, folder 46, Rosalyn Baxandall: Women's Liberation Research Files, TL.

31. Quoted in Burton-Rose, *Guerrilla USA*, 105–106.

32. Rita Brown, or "Bo" Brown, was released from prison in 1987. She has remained active in prison movements. See "White North American Political Prisoners," in James, *Imprisoned Intellectuals*, 214–226; and rita d. brown, "a short autobiography," 71–74.

33. For a chronicle of the history of the Brigade, see Burton-Rose, *Guerrilla USA*.

34. Miller, interview with author; Ottey, interview with author; TTLG, "Dear Folks," fund-raising appeal, box 4, folder 46, Rosalyn Baxandall and Linda Gordon Research Files on Women's Liberation, TL; "Bail Fund," *Through the Looking Glass* 3, no. 6 (1978): 5, box 41, ALFAPC.

35. Coffin, interview with author; Miller, interview with author; Ottey, interview with author.

36. Ottey, interview with author; "KRAB Seeks 1976 Funding," *Pandora* (December 1975): 14, Archives of Sexuality & Gender, http://tinyurl.galegroup.com /tinyurl/6dqpM2 (accessed March 15, 2017).

37. "Bail Fund," *Through the Looking Glass* 3, no. 6 (1978): 5; Preliminary matter, *Through the Looking Glass* 12, no. 2 (1987): 1, both in box 41, ALFAPC.

38. Women Against Prison, "Dykes behind Bars," *Dyke, A Quarterly*, no. 1 (1975): 14–17, 63–68, box 10, ALFAPC.

39. Ibid.

40. Díaz-Cotto, *Gender, Ethnicity, and the State*, 330.

41. New York Department of Corrections records show that at least one African American prisoner was threatened with a transfer to Matteawan in 1966; see box 1, Inmate Misbehavior Case Files (1964–1974), New York State Archives, Albany, N.Y.

42. Everett S. Landers, "7 Female Inmates at Fishkill Claim Forced Use of Drugs," *Poughkeepsie Journal* (Poughkeepsie, N.Y.), November 14, 1976, 4.

43. Díaz-Cotto, *Gender, Ethnicity, and the State*, 331; "Behavior Modification: Victory for the Matteawan Sisters," *No More Cages* 1, no. 3 (Aug 1979): 8–15, WHCC.

44. Dontopoulos, interview with author.

45. Ibid.

46. Díaz-Cotto, *Gender, Ethnicity, and the State*, 342–349.

47. Solidarity with Sisters Inside, "Bedford Hills Prison Strike," *Big Mama Rag* 6, no. 8 (Sept 1978): 4.

48. Charoula, "Women in Prison," n.d., Prisons Vertical File, LHA.

49. "Statement of Purpose"; Dontopoulos, interview with author.

50. Charoula, "Prison Work and the Lesbian Issue," 44.

51. On Dykes Against Racism Everywhere, see Hanhardt, *Safe Space*, 117–154.

52. "Women inside Prisons and Psychiatric Institutions: A Benefit for No More Cages," flier, n.d., Prisons Vertical File, LHA.

53. Berlant and Warner, "Sex in Public."

54. "Mailbag," *No More Cages* 5, no. 1 (Feb–Mar 1984): 3, SL-NU.

55. On MOVE, see Boyette and Boyette, *Let It Burn*; Wagner-Pacifici, *Discourse and Destruction*; and Assefa and Wahrhaftig, *MOVE Crisis in Philadelphia*.

56. *No More Cages* 4, no. 1 (Dec–Jan 1981–1982), box 31, ALFAPC.

57. *Through the Looking Glass* 2, no. 6 (July 1977), WSL.

58. "Letters from Inside," *No More Cages* 4, no. 3 (1983): 13, SL-NU.

59. At Bedford Hills, for instance, monolingual Spanish-speaking immigrants comprised nearly 25 percent of the prison population by the mid-1980s. Díaz-Cotto, *Gender, Ethnicity, and the State*, 271–294.

60. "Communications?" *Through the Looking Glass* 6, no. 3 (May–June 1981): 5–7, box 41, ALFAPC.

61. "Letters," *No More Cages* 4, no. 3 (1983): 2–3, SL-NU.

62. "Pine Bluff Women's Prison," *Through the Looking Glass* 1, no. 4 (1976), WSL; "Rebellious Women Shaken Down," *Women's Press* 7, no. 1 (Feb/Mar 1977): 4.

63. "California Institution for Women: Negligence = Murder," *No More Cages* 3, no. 6 (Oct–Nov 1982): 6, SL-NU.

64. "Stagnant Waters," *No More Cages* 4, no. 4 (June–July 1983): 8, SL-NU.

65. Neil Miller, "Gay Press Barred From All Federal Prisons," *Gay Community News* 4, no. 26 (Dec 1976) (clipping), Prisons Vertical File, LHA.

66. See Kunzel, *Criminal Intimacy*, 206.

67. "Lesbian Publications Banned," *Through the Looking Glass* 2, no. 2 (Feb 1977), WSL; "Fear for Queers," *Through the Looking Glass* 2, no. 6 (June 1977), WSL.

68. *Through the Looking Glass* 2, no. 4 (Apr 1977), WSL.

69. "Equal Rights for Whom? Vocational Training in Women's Prisons," *No More Cages* 2, no. 3 (1980): 17–19, WHCC.

70. "Prisoner Fights Homosexual Magazine Ban," *Washington Post*, May 14, 1977, C3; Kunzel, *Criminal Intimacy*, 207.

71. "Mailbag," *No More Cages* 3, no. 6 (Oct–Nov 1982): 9, SL-NU.

72. Rodríguez, *Forced Passages*, 14.

73. Scott, *Domination and the Arts of Resistance*; Gordon, "Methodologies of Imprisonment," 654.

74. "Edna Louise Pipkin," *No More Cages* 2, no. 3 (Dec 1980): 26, WHCC; Gerald Demeusy, "Battered-Woman Argument Frees Defendant in Manslaughter Case," *Hartford Courant*, November 1, 1980, A1, A20.

75. "Paula Three Stars," *No More Cages* 5, no. 1 (Feb–Apr 1984): 7, SL-NU.

76. "Paula Three Stars," *Through the Looking Glass* 9, no. 2 (Apr 1984): 7, box 41, ALFAPC.

77. "Victory for Bulesa Gibbs," *Through the Looking Glass* 4, no. 8 (Sept 1979): 26, box 41, ALFAPC.

78. "Anna Small Acquitted," *off our backs* 12, no. 1 (Jan 1982): 15.

79. "Anna Small Fights Back and Wins!" *No More Cages* 3, no. 1 (Nov–Dec 1981): 16, box 31, ALFAPC.

80. "Why Do Men Batter Women?" *No More Cages* 2, no. 5 (1981): 17, box 31, ALFAPC; "Update: Juanita Thomas," *No More Cages* 4, no. 4 (June–July 1983): 6, SL-NU.

81. Lyon, Hughes, and Thomas, "People v. Juanita Thomas," 45. Juanita Thomas served nearly 20 years in prison before being paroled in 1998.

82. "Update: Juanita Thomas."

83. "Robin Anderson, Convicted Self-Defender, Comes Up for Clemency," *No More Cages* 2, no. 1 (1980): 33, WHCC.

84. "Rita Silk Nauni," *Through the Looking Glass* 5, no. 5 (May 1980): 17–20, box 41, ALFAPC.

85. "Defend Rita Silk-Nauni," *No More Cages* 1, no. 6 (Nov 1976): 3, WHCC.

86. Ibid.

87. "Bulesa Gibbs: Judge Rockoff Gets his Rocks Off!" *No More Cages* 1, no. 3 (Aug 1979): 21–23, WHCC.

88. Carol Ann Wilds, "Sexual Harassment," *No More Cages* 2, no. 5 (May 1981): 38–41, box 31, ALFAPC; "Sexual Harassment = Cruel and Usual Punishment," *Through the Looking Glass* 6, no. 3 (May–June 1981): 34–37, box 41, ALFAPC.

89. Ann Jones, "One Woman Who Chose to Say No," *Nation*, April 17, 1982, 456–459.

90. Wilds, "Sexual Harassment."

91. See chapter 2 in this book. Kunzel also makes this point in *Criminal Intimacy*, 202.

92. "Florida," *off our backs* 6, no. 5 (May 1976): 12.

93. "Rape: Letter from Alderson," *Through the Looking Glass* 4, no. 11 (Dec 1979): 30–31, box 41, ALFAPC.

94. "Sisters of Unity," *Through the Looking Glass* 4, no. 5 (May 1979): 18–19, box 41, ALFAPC.

95. "Free Alejandrina Torres: An Open Letter to the Women's Community," *No More Cages* 5, no. 4 (1984): 26–27, SL-NU.

96. "Clinton, NJ," *Through the Looking Glass* 2, no. 6 (July 1977): 20–21, WSL.

97. "Nightmare at Maryland Correctional Institution for Women," *Through the Looking Glass* 4, no. 7 (Aug 1979): 6–7, box 41, ALFAPC.

98. "Bedford Hills Again," *Through the Looking Glass* 3, no. 8 (1978): 18, box 41, ALFAPC.

99. On the Nation of Islam and Muslim prisoners' leading roles in prisoner rights organizing and litigation in the 1960s, see Losier, "For Strictly Religious Reason[s]"; and Felber, "Those Who Say Don't Know."

100. "Victory," *Through the Looking Glass* 2, no. 8 (Sept 1977): 6, WSL; "The Fight Goes On at Bedford Hills," *Through the Looking Glass* 4, no. 5 (May 1979): 6–7, box 41, ALFAPC.

101. "Bedford Hills: Male Guards in Women's Prisons," *No More Cages* 2, no. 1 (Aug 1980): 27–29, WHCC. Upon its reclassification from medium- to maximum-security in the early 1980s, Bedford Hills became a guard training facility, which meant it received a constant influx of new male custodial officers, still overwhelmingly from white, rural, upstate communities. On this point, see Díaz-Cotto, *Gender, Ethnicity, and the State*, 271–294.

102. "Sexual Harassment in Frontera," *No More Cages* 3, no. 6 (Oct–Nov 1982): 11, SL-NU.

103. Kunzel, *Criminal Intimacy*, 81–82. On the "Daddy Tank" at the Sybil Brand Institute, see ibid., 204–205; "Down on Dykes," *Through the Looking Glass* 2, no. 8 (Sept 1977): 4, WSL; and Córdova, *When We Were Outlaws*.

104. "Who's Doing the Touching . . .," *No More Cages* 1, no. 6 (1980): 11, WHCC.

105. "Homophobia at Purdy," *Through the Looking Glass* 7, no. 4 (1982), box 41, ALFAPC. One woman incarcerated at Purdy characterized the uneven and arbitrary enforcement of prison rules—from those prohibiting physical affection to those prohibiting prisoners to store food in their rooms—along with the "omnipresent threats of reprisals" for insubordination as "invisible bars" that worked just as well as "shackles of steel." "Guard Threatens Woman," *No More Cages* 4, no. 6 (Dec 83–Jan 84): 16, SL-NU.

106. "Racism in Purdy," *Through the Looking Glass* 5, no. 8 (1980): 18, box 41, ALFAPC.

107. Hammonds, "Toward a Genealogy."

108. "Guard Threatens Woman," *No More Cages* 4, no. 6 (Dec 83–Jan 84): 16, SL-NU.

109. "Behavior Modification: The Ordeal and the Victory of the Matteawan Sisters," *No More Cages* 1, no. 3 (Aug 1979): 8–15; "Drugs: Who Needs Guards?" *No More Cages* 1, no. 3 (Aug 1979): 15, both in WHCC. "Women Organizing, Part Two," *Through the Looking Glass* 2, no. 7 (Aug 1977): 1; "Max in Mass," *Through the Looking Glass* 2, no. 10 (Nov 1977), both in WSL. "Behavior Mod," *Through the Looking Glass* 3, no. 3 (1978): 4–6; "Rapists of the Mind," *Through the Looking Glass* 6, no. 4 (July 1981): 8–10, both in box 41, ALFAPC.

110. Alberta James, Sheila Liles, and Irma Jean Mitchelle, "Behavior Modification," *off our backs* 8, no. 2 (Feb 1978): 11.

111. Donna Radford Murphy, "Word from CIW," *No More Cages* 2, no. 4 (Mar 1981), box 31, ALFAPC.

112. "Behavior Modification."

113. "Word From CIW," *No More Cages* 2, no. 5 (1981): 27, box 31, ALFAPC.

114. "Carol Crooks Tells It Like It Is at Bedford Hills," *Through the Looking Glass* 4, no. 8 (Sept 1979): 7, box 41, ALFAPC.

115. The history of sterilization abuse is long and well-documented. See, e.g., Roberts, *Killing the Black Body*; Briggs, *Reproducing Empire*; Smith, *Conquest*; Carpio, "Lost Generation." On feminist campaigns against sterilization abuse, see: Silliman et al., *Undivided Rights*; Nelson, *Women of Color and the Reproductive Rights Movement*. On the persistence of coercive sterilization in U.S. women's prisons today, see Roth and Ainsworth, "If They Hand You a Paper."

116. "To Whom it May Concern," *No More Cages* 3, no. 6 (Oct–Nov 1982): 7, SL-NU.

117. "Women in Prison—Organizing," *Through the Looking Glass* 2, no. 6 (1977): 1–3, WSL.

118. "Lockdown at CIW," *Through the Looking Glass* 3, no. 5 (1978): 16, box 41, ALFAPC.

119. "Muncy: Struggle Continues," and "Incarcerated People," *No More Cages* 1, no. 6 (1980): 6–7, 8–9, WHCC.

120. "The Politics of Anti-Prison Work," *Through the Looking Glass* 6, no. 3 (May/June 1981): 2–7, box 41, ALFAPC.

121. "Statement of Purpose."

122. "Battered and Raped: The Physical/Sexual Abuse of Women: Part II," *No More Cages* 2, no. 3 (Dec 1980): 27–35, WHCC; "Dykes behind Bars."

123. "Visiting Womyn in Jail," leaflet, Prisons Vertical File, LHA.

124. Women Free Women in Prison, "Lesbians and Gay Men Behind Bars," 1981, Prisons Vertical File, LHA.

125. "Battered and Raped."

126. Ibid.

127. "Solidarity with Sisters Inside," *off our backs* 8, no. 2 (Feb 1978): 10.

128. "Violence against Women: Victories in Court," *Through the Looking Glass* 3, no. 9 (Dec 1978): 15, box 41, ALFAPC.

129. "Battered and Raped."

130. Kim, "Dancing the Carceral Creep."

131. Women Free Women in Prison, "Lesbians and Gay Men Behind Bars."

132. Reigle is quoted in Kunzel, *Criminal Intimacy*, 223.

133. "Who We Are," *Through the Looking Glass* 4, no. 10 (Nov 1979): 1–2, box 41, ALFAPC; Dontopoulos, interview with author; Ottey, interview with author; Miller, interview with author; Coffin, interview with author.

134. Thompson, *Promise and a Way of Life*, 117.

135. TTLG, "Racism in the Prison System," 134.

136. Carrillo Rowe, *Power Lines*; Cohen, "Punks, Bulldaggers, and Welfare Queens," 458.

137. "Communications?" *Through the Looking Glass* 6, no. 3 (1981): 19, box 41, ALFAPC; "Bedford Goes to Court," *No More Cages* 1, no. 3 (1979): 5–7, WHCC.

138. "Statement of Purpose."

139. Quotations are from the Combahee River Collective, "Black Feminist State-ment." On feminist activism and lesbian separatism in the 1970s and 1980s, see Enke, *Finding the Movement*; Enke, "Smuggling Sex through the Gates"; Taylor and Rupp, "Women's Culture and Lesbian Feminist Activism"; Valk, *Radical Sisters*, ch. 6.

140. Charoula, "Prison Work and the Lesbian Issue," 45.

141. Bennett and Gibbs, "Racism and Classism in the Lesbian Community," 1.

142. "Where We're At," *No More Cages* 2, no. 3 (1980): 2–3, WHCC.

143. Miller, interview with author; Coffin, interview with author; Ottey, interview with author.

144. "Greetings from TTLG," *Through the Looking Glass* 10, no. 1 (1985): 1, box 41, ALFAPC.

145. Kelley, *Freedom Dreams*, 8.

Chapter 4. Intersecting Indictments

1. Nkenge Touré, "Report on the First National Third World Women's Conference on Violence," *Aegis* (Summer/Autumn 1980): 70.

2. Loretta Ross, Kathy Powell, and Nkenge Touré, "Third World Women and Rape," Report from the First National Conference on Third World Women and Violence, Rape Crisis Center, Washington, D.C., 1981, box 5, folder 2, LR.

3. Ibid.

4. Ibid. Conference brochure, 1980, box 100, MBP.

5. Nkenge Touré, "An Overview of Third World Women and Violence," Report from the First National Conference on Third World Women and Violence, Rape Crisis Center, Washington, D.C., August 1980, box 5, folder 3, LR.

6. Nkenge Touré interview, VOFOHP; Touré, "Overview of Third World Women."

7. Other accounts of the coalitional organizing around the 1979 Boston murders include Breines, *Trouble between Us*; Grant, "Who's Killing Us?"; Barbara Smith, Black Feminism: A Movement of Our Own," *Sojourner* 10, no. 4 (Dec 1984): 13–14; Smith, "Interview with Kimberly Springer"; Williamson, "Who Is Killing Us?" For more on the Combahee River Collective, see Gumbs, "We Can Learn to Mother Ourselves"; Harris, "All of Who I Am," and *Black Feminist Politics*, 1–54; Springer, *Living for the Revolution*; Taylor, *How We Get Free*. Other accounts of the D.C. Rape Crisis Center in the 1970s and early 1980s include Bevacqua, *Rape on the Public Agenda*, and "Reconsidering Violence against Women"; Valk, *Radical Sisters*, 158–180.

8. The term *coalitional moments* is from Chávez, *Queer Migration Politics*, 8–9.

9. Support Group for CWS information packet (news clippings), box 2, SGS. The women and girls who were killed included Christine Ricketts, Andrea Foye, Gwendolyn Stinson, Caren Prater, Daryal Ann Hargett, Desiree Denice Etheridge, Darlene Rogers, Lois Hood Nesbitt, Valyric Holland, Sandra Boulware, Bobbie Jean Graham, and Lilly Mae Nesbitt. In April, the body of a white woman from the Boston suburb of Newton, Faye Polner, was also found in a car in Dorchester. All thirteen killings were sometimes aggregated in the media.

10. Gayle Pollard, Carmen Fields, and Viola Osgood, "Six Slain Women, and Those Who Loved Them," *Boston Globe*, April 1, 1979; Lonnie Isabel and Dave Wood, "5th Black Woman Slain in South End," *Boston Globe*, February 22, 1979 (clippings in box 4, SGS); Smith, "Twelve Black Women," 68.

11. Aimee Sands, "Rape and Racism in Boston: An Open Letter to White Feminists," *off our backs* 11, no. 1 (1981): 16–17.

12. Catherine Avril, "Media on Violence: Taking the Easy Way Out," *Sojourner* 4, no. 7 (Mar 1979): 4.

13. Willie Sanders Defense Committee, "A Rush to Judgment in the Case of Willie Sanders," leaflet, 1979, box 2, SGS; Willie Sanders Defense Committee, "The Willie Sanders Case: The Facts," one-sheet, n.d., box 2, folder 17, BS.

14. According to Sanders and his legal team, Sanders was the only man with a beard in several of the lineups, and only one of two men with a thin build.

15. Fund-raising letter from the Willie Sanders Defense Committee, November 21, 1979, box 2, folder 17, BS.

16. Smith, "Twelve Black Women," 68.

17. On the National Black Feminist Organization, see Springer, *Living for the Revolution*; and Randolph, *Florynce "Flo" Kennedy*, 205–211.

18. Springer, *Living for the Revolution*, 59, 124–128.

19. Combahee River Collective, "Black Feminist Statement."

20. Springer, *Living for the Revolution*, 106–111.

21. Combahee River Collective, "Black Feminist Statement." Robin D. G. Kelley argues that this statement is "one of the most important documents of the black radical movement in the twentieth century." See Kelley, *Freedom Dreams*, 148–150. As a testament to the statement's legacy in feminist studies and activism, the National Women's Studies Association's 2017 president, Barbara Ransby, selected as that year's annual meeting theme: "Forty Years after Combahee: Feminist Scholars and Activists Engage the Movement for Black lives." The fortieth anniversary of the statement also inspired a special issue of *Souls: A Critical Journal of Black Politics, Culture and Society*, as well as Keeanga-Yamahtta Taylor's book of essays and interviews, *How We Get Free*.

22. Quoted in Grant, "Who Is Killing Us?" 153.

23. Ibid., 147.

24. For other analyses of this pamphlet and its significance, see Hanhardt, *Safe Space*, 126; Hong, *Ruptures of American Capital*, xxxi–xxxiv; Williamson, "Why Did They Die?"

25. "Coalition for Women's Safety: Who We Are," box 1, SGS.

26. Letter from Demita Frazier to Combahee River Collective retreat participants, April 18, 1979, box 2, folder 7, BS.

27. Miriam Kenner, Linda Stein, and Deb Gallagher, "Interview with the Coalition for Women's Safety," *Second Wave* 5, no. 4 (Summer 1980): 8–11, box 2, SGS.

28. CWS meeting minutes, March 5, 1980, box 1, SGS.

29. CWS meeting minutes, August 15, 1979, box 1, SGS.

30. Letter from Barbara Smith to Sandi Stein, June 26, 1979, box 1, SGS; CWS

meeting minutes from March 1979 through May 1981 (box 1, SGS); Kenner, Stein, and Gallagher, "Interview with the Coalition"; Okazawa-Rey, interview with author.

31. Smith, "Black Feminism"; Letter from Barbara Smith to Debora Gay, November 25, 1979, box 2, folder 7, BS.

32. Support Group meeting minutes, June 28, 1979; Support Group Resource List, n.d., both in box 2, SGS.

33. Kenner, Stein, and Gallagher, "Interview with the Coalition"; Tacie Dejanikus and Janis Kelly, "Roxbury Organizing," *off our backs* 9, no. 9 (Oct 1979): 7, 26.

34. Speight, *People United*; Agenda for CWS Community Meeting, January 28, 1980, box 1, SGS; Margaret Neville, "Where Do We Go From Here?" *Equal Times* 3, no. 64 (May 1979): 8.

35. CWS, "Who We Are," n.d., box 1, SGS.

36. Dejanikus and Kelly, "Roxbury Organizing"; Crisis, "CRISIS! Wave of Violence on Black Women," pamphlet, May 1979, box 2, folder 7, BS. On Dorchester Green Light Program, see also Law, "When Abolition Meets Action."

37. "Proposal for Mass Street Education Campaign by Coalition for Women's Safety," handwritten notes, 1979; and CWS meeting minutes, November 7, 1979, both in box 1, SGS.

38. CWS meeting minutes, April 2, 1980, June 4, 1980, and July 9, 1980, box 1, SGS. At the time the working title for Speight's film was *Roxbury's Response*. The finished version was released in 1985 under the title *The People United*.

39. Dejanikus and Kelly, "Roxbury."

40. Draft description of the Freedom Stride, 1979, box 4, SGS.

41. "Running for Safety," *Boston Phoenix*, August 14, 1979 (clipping), box 4, SGS.

42. "Women's Freedom Stride," flier, 1979, box 4, SGS.

43. National Black Students Association, "Black Woman Beat Up by Police Officer," leaflet, box 1, SGS; Speight, *People United*; Viola Osgood, "Boston Blacks Decry Police Brutality," *Boston Globe*, February 29, 1980, 16.

44. Event flier, August 24, 1979, box 2, folder 17, BS.

45. Breines, *Trouble between Us*, 165–166.

46. Barbara Smith, presentation notes, 1979, box 2, folder 17, BS.

47. "Partial List of Endorsers," n.d., box 2, folder 17, BS.

48. Willie Sanders Defense Committee, "Free Willie Sanders Drop the Charges!" brochure, box 2, folder 17, BS. The *Boston Globe*'s Spotlight Team "published the results of a survey documenting persistent and pervasive discrimination against Black defendants by the Massachusetts courts" on April 4, 1979.

49. Willie Sanders Defense Committee, "A Rush to Judgment in the Case of Willie Sanders," leaflet, 1979, box 2, SGS.

50. Johnson, "Commonwealth vs. Willie Sanders," 82.

51. Willie Sanders Defense Committee, "A Racist Frame-Up," one-sheet, n.d., box 2, folder 17, BS.

52. The ACLU helped the group fight the subpoena for its records.

53. Willie Sanders Defense Committee, "Racist Frame-Up."

54. Willie Sanders Defense Committee, "From Scottsboro 1930 to Boston 1980: The Frame-Up Continues," pamphlet, 1980, box 2, SGS.

55. Williams, "Violence against Women," 24.

56. Sands, "Rape and Racism in Boston."

57. Sunny Robinson, "And Justice for All," letter, *off our backs* 11, no. 4 (Apr 1981): 30.

58. "Take Back the Night—History," 1979, box 2, SGS.

59. CWS meeting minutes, June 27, 1979, box 1, SGS.

60. Fund-raising letter from the Willie Sanders Defense Committee, November 21, 1979, box 2, folder 17, BS.

61. "Women Unite: Take Back the Night—August 18, 1979," brochure, June 1979, box 2, SGS.

62. "5,000 Women March to Take Back the Night," *Sojourner* 5, no. 1 (Sept 1979): 13.

63. CWS meeting minutes, May 28, 1980, box 1, SGS.

64. Smith, "Interview with Alexis Pauline Gumbs," 278.

65. CWS meeting minutes, May 28, 1980, and July 9, 1980, box 1, SGS.

66. Ross interview, VOFOHP.

67. Robnett, *How Long? How Long?*

68. Ross interview, VOFOHP.

69. Valk, *Radical Sisters*, 162; Bevacqua, "Reconsidering Violence against Women," 166, 170.

70. D.C. Rape Crisis Center, *How to Start a Rape Crisis Center*; Touré interview, VOFOHP.

71. Valk, *Radical Sisters*, 162–163; "High School Pamphlet," *Rape Crisis Center Newsletter* (May/June 1974): 3, box 12, folder 11, Center for Women's Studies and Services Records, Malcolm A. Love Library, San Diego State University.

72. Boston Area Rape Crisis Center, "Rape: Medical and Legal Information" (Boston, Mass: Rape Crisis Center, 1973).

73. D.C. RCC, *How to Start*, 7–8, 24.

74. Ibid., 7–8.

75. Bevacqua, "Reconsidering Violence against Women," 167.

76. RCC representatives quoted in Valk, *Radical Sisters*, 165.

77. Ibid., 166–167.

78. Crenshaw, "Demarginalizing the Intersection."

79. D.C. RCC, *How to Start*, 2.

80. Ross, interview with author.

81. Touré was originally from Baltimore and had been an antiracist activist since high school. Before cofounding Save the People, she was a member of the D.C. chapter of the Black Panther Party.

82. Ibid.; Touré interview, VOFOHP; Ross interview, VOFOHP.

83. Touré interview, VOFOHP.

84. Touré, "Organizing Now and for the Future," paper presented at a symposium

entitled "Feminism and the Critique of Capitalism," April 25, 1981, box 7, folder 20, NT; Touré interview, VOFOHP.

85. Valk, *Radical Sisters*, 175.

86. Touré interview, VOFOHP; Ross, interview with author; Ross interview, VOFOHP.

87. Ross interview, VOFOHP.

88. For a history of the interchanges between feminist and black liberation struggles in Washington, D.C., in the 1960s and 1970s, see Valk, *Radical Sisters*.

89. Marcy Rein and Carol Anne Douglas, "Women Unite: Reclaim the Night," *off our backs* 8, no. 6 (June 1978): 9.

90. DCAFA newsletter 1, no. 2 (Apr 1978), box 2, Julie LaValle Jones Papers, SBC.

91. On Dupont Circle's construction as "gay ghetto," see Holmes, "Chocolate to Rainbow City." Loretta Ross lived in Adams-Morgan in the mid-1970s, helping to battle the tide of developer-initiated gentrification by becoming her apartment building's tenant organizer. Hers was one of several cases in which tenants successfully used a 1974 rent control law to purchase the building and hence stave off displacement. For Ross's reflections on this effort, see her interview with VOFOHP. For a history of antigentrification activism in Adams-Morgan in the 1970s, see Lloyd, "Fighting Redlining and Gentrification in Washington, D.C." For histories of postwar tenant organizing that center women, see especially Gold, *When Tenants Claimed the City*; Williams, *Politics of Public Housing*.

92. DCAFA meeting minutes, May 10, 1978, box 2, Julie LaValle Jones Papers, SBC; Valk, *Radical Sisters*, 178–179.

93. Rein and Douglas, "Women Unite," 9.

94. Photograph of Deirdre Wright, Nkenge Touré, and Dessie Woods, 1978, box 3, folder 2, NT; Nkenge Touré and Deirdre Wright, "Dialogue with Dessie," *Aegis* (July/Aug 1978): 9–13.

95. DCAFA meeting minutes, May 10, 1978, box 2, Julie LaValle Jones Papers, SBC.

96. DCAFA, "DC's First 'March to Stop Violence Against Women,'" *Aegis* (July/Aug 1978): 5; DCAFA outreach letter for March to Stop Violence Against Women, March 17, 1978, box 2, Julie LaValle Jones Papers, SBC; Rein and Douglas, "Women Unite," 8.

97. Touré interview, VOFOHP; Lynora Williams, "Third World Women Decry Violence," *Guardian*, September 10, 1980, 9 (clipping), MBP.

98. Nkenge Touré, Michelle Plate, Jackie MacMillan, and Sue Lenaerts, "Black Women Organizing against Rape," *FAAR News* (Nov/Dec 1976); reprinted in the 1977 edition of *How to Start a Rape Crisis Center*.

99. Deb Friedman, "Conferences Evoke Concerns of 'Special' Populations," *FAAR News* (May/June 1977): 1–8; Touré, "Overview of Third World Women."

100. Letter from Loretta Ross to participants at the 1980 Third World Women and Violence conference, June 11, 1981, box 3, folder 11, NT.

101. Touré interview, VOFOHP; Touré, "Overview of Third World Women."

102. All Souls, Unitarian had served as a center for the March on Washington in 1963. In 1969, African American civil rights activist David Eaton was hired as senior pastor. In the early 1970s, the church participated actively in the War on Poverty, and Eaton was a vocal and visible opponent of the 1970 D.C. Crime Bill that authorized the district's police department to employ "no-knock" searches and preventative detention. The number of African American congregants climbed throughout the 1970s. By the end of the decade, the church was a hub of social justice work in the city (see Howe, "David Eaton.").

103. Conference brochure.

104. Ibid.; Touré interview, VOFOHP; Ross interview, VOFOHP.

105. Tacie Dejanikus, "First National Conference on Third World Women and Violence," *off our backs* 10, no. 11 (1980): 13; Touré, "Report," 70–71.

106. Dejanikus, "First National Conference," 13.

107. Touré interview, VOFOHP.

108. Young, *Soul Power*, 13.

109. Loretta Ross, "Third World Women and Violence," August 1980, box 5, folder 3, LR.

110. Ibid.; Ross, Powell, and Touré, "Third World Women and Rape."

111. Ross, Powell, and Touré, "Third World Women and Rape."

112. Loretta Ross, "Working with Minority Men Committing Violence against Women," Report from the First National Conference on Third World Women and Violence, August 1980, Rape Crisis Center, Washington, D.C., box 5, folder 12, LR; Loretta Ross, "Domestic Violence and the Black Community," 1980, box 4, folder 7, LR; Loretta Ross, "Black Women: Why Feminism?" 1981, box 3, folder 15, LR.

113. Larry Cannon and William Fuller, "Prisoners Against Rape," *FAAR News* (Sept–Oct 1974): 7.

114. William Fuller, "Working with Men Who Have Committed Violence," letter to conference participants, August 17, 1980, box 34, folder 10, LR.

115. Ross, interview with author; Ross interview, VOFOHP; Ross, "Working with Minority Men"; Lazarus and Wunderlich, *Rape Culture*.

116. Ross, "Working with Minority Men."

117. Touré, "Overview of Third World Women."

118. Williams, "Third World Women Decry Violence."

119. Dejanikus, "First National Conference"; Bay Area Defense Committee for Battered Women, Vanguard Application Form, May 14, 1979, box 134, folder 14, Phyllis Lyon and Del Martin Papers, GLBTHS.

120. Molly Ivins, "An Eclectic Crowd Gathers to Save the Black Hills," *New York Times*, July 28, 1980, A12; Dejanikus, "First National Conference."

121. Ross interview, VOFOHP.

122. Touré, "Overview of Third World Women"; Dejanikus, "First National Conference."

123. Moraga, "Preface," xiv.

124. Touré, "Report," 71.

125. "A Movement of New World Women," conference flier and proposal, 1985, box 1, folder 15, Cherríe Moraga Papers, Green Library, Stanford University.

126. Fullwood, interview with author.

127. Ron Klain, "The Strange Case of Yulanda Ward," *Washington Tribune* 5, no. 6 (Mar 27–Apr 9, 1981): 7 (clipping), box 58, folder 4, LR.

128. "Two Men Are Charged in Slaying," clipping, box 58, folder 4; and Loretta Ross, untitled essay draft, n.d., box 58, folder 8, both in LR.

129. "Community Bulletin from the Yulanda Ward Memorial Fund," n.d., box 58, folder 9, LR.

130. Quotation is from Ross interview, VOFOHP; Yulanda Ward Memorial Fund (YWMF), "Spatial Deconcentration in D.C.," 1981, Libcom.org.

131. Partial list of endorsers, n.d., box 7, folder 16, NT.

132. YWMF, press release, January 9, 1981, box 58, folder 8, LR.

133. YWMF, press release, March 20, 1981, box 58, folder 4, LR; Ross interview, VOFOHP.

134. Support Committee Roster, n.d.; and "YWMF Support Committee Preliminary Statement of Purpose," February 9, 1981, both in box 58, folder 8, LR.

135. Loretta Ross, "The Connections Are Clear," March 5, 1981, box 58, folder 8, LR.

136. Ibid.; Touré, "Overview of Third World Women"; "Support New Afrikan Freedom Fighters!" event flier, 1981, box 7, folder 16, NT.

137. Klain, "The Strange Case of Yulanda Ward," 7.

138. YWMF Support Committee, untitled document, 1981, box 7, folder 16, LR. Letter from Loretta Ross to participants at the 1980 Third World Women and Violence conference, June 11, 1981, box 3, folder 11, NT.

139. YWMF Support Committee meeting minutes, April 1981, box 58, folder 8, LR.

140. "Peoples Court of the District of Columbia Criminal Division" indictment forms, box 58, folder 9, LR.

141. "The People Investigate State Complicity in Yulanda Ward's Death," box 58, folder 8, LR.

142. Arleen Rogan, "Some Thoughts on Violence—Testimony before 'The People's Grand Jury Hearing,'" June 6, 1981, D.C. RCC, box 58, folder 9, LR.

143. "Community Bulletin."

144. Letter from Loretta Ross to Tyrone W. Miller (subject: returned contribution), October 20, 1982, box 58, folder 9, LR.

145. Ross, interview with VOF.

146. Ibid. See also Valk, *Radical Sisters*, 176.

147. At the April 1, 1979, memorial walk, longtime civil rights activist and faith leader Mrs. Sarah Small posed the question, "Who Is Killing Us?" to the crowd. Mrs. Small was the aunt of one of the slain women, Daryal Ann Hargett. For other discussions of the rhetorical significance of this question, see Grant, "Who Is Killing Us?"; Williamson, "Who Is Killing Us."

148. The term *right to the city* was originated by Marxist geographer and philosopher Henri Lefebvre in a 1968 book titled as such (*Le Droit a la Ville*). Its popularity among geographers, urbanists, and grassroots activists surged in the context of the global economic recession of 2008. See, for example, Harvey, *Rebel Cities*. As of 2018, the U.S.-based Right to the City Alliance is comprised of more than thirty social justice organizations working in sixteen different states, www.righttothecity.org (accessed August 20, 2017).

149. Loretta Ross interview, VOFOHP.

Epilogue

1. Scholar-activist Mike Davis coined the term *prison-industrial complex* in 1995. See Davis, "Hell Factories in the Field." The organizing work of the prison abolitionist organization Critical Resistance and the writings of several of its scholar-activist cofounders, especially Angela Davis and Ruth Wilson Gilmore, fueled the increasing circulation of this term.

2. INCITE!, "Introduction."

3. Angela Davis, "Color of Violence Against Women."

4. This work includes, and is documented in, several anthologies: Chen, Dulani, and Piepzna-Samarasinha, *Revolution Starts at Home*; CR-10 Publications Collective, *Abolition Now!*; Bierria, Rojas, and Kim, "Community Accountability"; INCITE!, *Color of Violence*; Sudbury, *Global Lockdown*.

5. INCITE! Color of Violence 4 Conference, March 26–29, 2015, www.colorof violence.org (accessed March 1, 2018).

6. Ibid. For some of Kaba's reflections on the plenary discussion, see Kaba, "Free Us All." In 2014, Kaba conceived and edited *No Selves to Defend,* a short anthology of writing and artwork that situated Marissa Alexander's case in relation to nearly a dozen others (including those of McDonald and the New Jersey 4), reaching back to the 1940s. Proceeds went to Alexander's legal defense fund.

7. An archive of press releases, public statements and letters by Alexander, and campaign materials along with a detailed timeline of her legal case are available at freemarissanow.org (accessed March 20, 2018).

8. Pasulka, "Case of CeCe McDonald"; *FREE CeCe!* Directed by Jacqueline Gares. Jac Gares Media Inc., 2016.

9. Mogul, Ritchie, and Whitlock, *Queer (In)Justice*, 42–43; Richie, *Arrested Justice*, 12–14, 140–141; *Out in the Night*. Directed by Blair Doroshwalther, 2014.

10. Ibid.; "Free the New Jersey 4 Campaign," http://freenj4.wordpress.com (accessed March 20, 2018); INCITE! and FIERCE!, "Re-Thinking 'The Norm.'"

11. See, for example, Benjamin Mueller, "Marissa Alexander Case Emerges as Symbol After Zimmerman Verdict," *LA Times*, July 20, 2013; Imani Henry, "Jail Zimmerman. Free Marissa Alexander and CeCe McDonald!" *Workers World*, July 24, 2013; Sabrina Rubin Erdely, "The Transgender Crucible: How CeCe McDonald Became a Folk Hero," *Rolling Stone*, July 30, 2014. For scholarly analyses of the contemporary politics of self-defense law that bring these cases into the same frame, see Cacho,

"Presumption of White Innocence"; "Stand Your Ground," Special Issue. For an analysis of Alexander's case as a contemporary manifestation of a long history of black women's criminalization and exclusion from state protection, see Gross "African American Women." For a long genealogy of the racial and gender politics of lethal self-defense in the United States, see Light, *Stand Your Ground*.

12. *Survived and Punished* website, survivedandpunished.org (accessed March 20, 2018).

13. Crenshaw et al., "#SayHerName." See also Ritchie, *Invisible No More*.

14. Janet Burkitt, "Turning Point for Crisis Centers," *Seattle Times*, July 4, 1999; Bierria, "Pursuing a Radical Anti-Violence Agenda"; CARA brochure, 2002, in the author's possession.

15. See, for example, Dayton Martindale, "Anti-jail Demonstrators Seek 'Care not Cages,'" *Oakland North*, October 12, 2015, https://oaklandnorth.net/2015/10/12/anti -jail-demonstrators-seek-care-not-cages/ (accessed March 20, 2018).

Bibliography

Archival Collections

Center for the Study of Political Graphics, Culver City, Calif.
Freedom Archives, San Francisco
    Freedom Is a Constant Struggle Audio Collection
Gay, Lesbian, Bisexual, and Transgender Historical Society, San Francisco
    Louise Merrill Papers
    Phyllis Lyon and Del Martin Papers
    San Francisco Women's Building Records
Green Library, Stanford University, Palo Alto
    Cherríe Moraga Papers
Healey Library, University of Massachusetts, Boston
    Connie Breece Papers
Interference Archive, Brooklyn
Lesbian Herstory Archives, Brooklyn
    Barbara Smith Papers
    Combahee River Collective organization file
    Dykes Against Racism Everywhere organization file
    Prisons vertical file
Malcolm A. Love Library, San Diego State University
    Center for Women's Studies and Services Records
New York State Archives, Albany
    Bedford Hills Inmate Misbehavior Files, 1964–1974
ONE National Gay and Lesbian Archives, Los Angeles
    Lesbian Legacy Subject Files
Sallie Bingham Center, David M. Rubenstein Rare Book and Manuscript Library, Duke University, Durham
    Atlanta Lesbian Feminist Alliance Archives Collection

Atlanta Lesbian Feminist Alliance Periodicals Collection
Julie LaValle Jones Papers
Minnie Bruce Pratt Papers
Sara M. Evans Papers
Schlesinger Library, Radcliffe Institute, Harvard University, Cambridge
Feminist Ephemera Collection
Friends of Framingham
Women's Newsletter and Periodical Collection
Shields Library, Special Collections Dept., University of California, Davis
Women's History and Culture Collection
Snell Library, Archives and Special Collections Dept., Northeastern University,
Boston
Bromfield Educational Center Prison Newsletter Collection
Coalition to Stop Institutional Violence Records
Flora Haas Papers
Sondra Gayle Stein Papers
Sophia Smith Collection, Smith College, Northampton
Crime, Prisons, and Reform Schools Collection
Loretta Ross Papers
Marjory Nelson Papers
Nkenge Touré Papers
Third World Women's Alliance Records
Violence Against Women Collection
Women's Liberation Collection
Southern California Library for Social Studies and Research, Los Angeles
20th Century Organizational Files
Southern Historical Collection, Library of the University of North Carolina,
Chapel Hill
James Reston Jr., Collection of Joan Little Trial Materials
Tamiment Library, New York University, New York
Printed Ephemera Collection
Rosalyn Baxandall: Women's Liberation Research Files
Washington State Archives, Olympia, Wash.
Department of Corrections, Purdy, Administrative Series
Washington State Library, Olympia, Wash.
Journals Collection

Digital Collections

Archives of Sexuality and Gender: LGBTQ History and Culture since 1940, Part II.
Gale, A Cengage Company.
Independent Voices: An Open Access Collection of an Alternative Press. Reveal
Digital.

Private Collections

Cathy Cade, San Francisco
Marjory Nelson, San Francisco

Interviews

Frances Beal interview, Voices of Feminism Oral History Project, Sophia Smith Collection, Smith College, Northampton (hereafter VOFOHP).
Diana Block, interviewed by author, San Francisco, March 8, 2011.
Connie Breece, interviewed by author, Jamaica Plain, Mass., September 15, 2015.
Linda Burnham interview, VOFOHP.
Fai Coffin, telephone interview by author, February 1, 2011.
Charoula Dontopoulos, telephone interview by author, January 28, 2017, and April 4, 2017.
P. Catlin Fullwood, telephone interview by author, March 4, 2011.
Anne Miller, telephone interview by author, February 23, 2011.
Cherríe Moraga interview, VOFOHP.
Marjory Nelson, interviewed by author, San Francisco, November 2, 2010.
Marjory Nelson interview, VOFOHP.
Margo Okazawa-Rey, telephone interview by author, January 30, 2018.
Shan Ottey, telephone interview by author, February 14, 2011.
Sunny Robinson, telephone interview by author, December 22, 2010.
Loretta Ross, telephone interview by author, January 9, 2018.
Loretta Ross interview, VOFOHP.
Barbara Smith interview, VOFOHP.
Yvonne Swan, telephone interview by author, February 6, 2017.
Nkenge Touré interview, VOFOHP.

Selected Newsletters, Newspapers, and Periodicals

Aegis: Magazine on Ending Violence Against Women
Bar None
Big Mama Rag
Boston Globe
Distaff
Doing Time
Dyke, A Quarterly
Feminary
Feminist Alliance Against Rape Newsletter
Gay Community News
Lesbian Tide
New York Times
No More Cages
off our backs

Poverty Law Report
Science for the People
Sojourner
Southern Exposure
Through the Looking Glass
Triple Jeopardy

Moving Image Sources

Negroes with Guns: Rob Williams and Black Power. Directed by Sandra Dickson, Churchill Roberts, and Terrence Blanchard. California Newsreel, 2005.

Rape Culture. Directed by Margaret Lazarus and Renner Wunderlich. Cambridge Documentary Films, 1975.

The Confrontation. Directed by Anne Irving. Iris Films/Iris Feminist Collective, 1983.

The People United. Directed by Alonzo Rico Speight. Third World Newsreel, 1985.

Titicut Follies. Directed by Frederick Wiseman. Zipporah Films, 1967.

Books, Book Chapters, Articles, and Dissertations

Adams, Kate. "Built out of Books: Lesbian Energy and Feminist Ideology in Alternative Publishing." *Journal of Homosexuality* 34, nos. 3–4 (1998): 113–141.

Alexander, Michelle. *The New Jim Crow: Mass Incarceration in the Age of Colorblindness.* New York: The New Press, 2010.

Anderson, Benedict. *Imagined Communities: Reflections on the Origin and Spread of Nationalism.* New York: Verso, 1983.

Anderson, Carolyn, and Thomas W. Benson. *Documentary Dilemmas: Frederick Wiseman's Titicut Follies.* Carbondale: Southern Illinois University Press, 1991.

Assefa, Hizkias, and Paul Wahrhaftig. *The MOVE Crisis in Philadelphia: Extremist Groups and Conflict Resolution.* New York: Praeger, 1988.

Baldwin, Bridgette. "In the Shadow of the Gun: The Black Panther Party, the Ninth Amendment, and Discourses of Self-Defense." In *In Search of the Black Panther Party: New Perspectives on a Revolutionary Movement*, edited by Jama Lazerow and Yohuru Williams, 67–95. Durham: Duke University Press, 2006.

Barry, Ellen. "Women Prisoners on the Cutting Edge: Development of the Activist Women's Prisoners' Rights Movement." *Social Justice* 27, no. 3 (Fall 2000): 168–175.

Baxandall, Rosalyn, and Linda Gordon, eds. *Dear Sisters: Dispatches from the Women's Liberation Movement.* New York: Basic Books, 2000.

Bayer, Ronald. *Homosexuality and American Psychiatry: The Politics of Diagnosis.* New York: Basic Books, 1981.

Beckett, Katherine. *Making Crime Pay: Law and Order in Contemporary American Politics.* New York: Oxford University Press, 1997.

Beins, Agatha. "A Revolution in Ephemera: Feminist Newsletters and Newspapers of the 1970s." In *This Book Is an Action: Feminist Print Culture and Activist Aesthetics*, edited by Jaime Harker and Cecilia Konchar Farr, 46–65. Urbana: University of Illinois Press, 2016.

——. *Liberation in Print: Feminist Periodicals and Social Movement Identity*. Athens: University of Georgia Press, 2017.

Ben-Moshe, Liat. "Disabling Incarceration: Connecting Disability to Divergent Confinements in the USA." *Critical Sociology* 39, no. 3 (2013): 385–403.

Bennett, Sara and Joan Gibbs. "Racism and Classism in the Lesbian Community: Towards the Building of a Radical Autonomous Lesbian Movement." In *Top Ranking: A Collection of Articles on Racism and Classism in the Lesbian Community*, edited by Sara Bennett and Joan Gibbs, 1-30.

Berger, Dan. *Captive Nation: Black Prison Organizing in the Civil Rights Era*. Chapel Hill: University of North Carolina Press, 2014.

——. *The Struggle Within: Prisons, Political Prisoners, and Mass Movements in the United States*. Oakland, Calif.: PM Press, 2014.

Berlant, Lauren, and Michael Warner. "Sex in Public." *Critical Inquiry* 24, no. 2 (1998): 547–566.

Bernstein, Elizabeth. "Militarized Humanitarianism Meets Carceral Feminism: The Politics of Sex, Rights, and Freedom in Contemporary Antitrafficking Campaigns." *Signs: Journal of Women in Culture and Society* 36, no. 1 (2010): 45–71.

Bernstein, Lee. *America Is the Prison: Arts and Politics in Prison in the 1970s*. Chapel Hill: University of North Carolina Press, 2010.

Bevacqua, Maria. *Rape on the Public Agenda: Feminism and the Politics of Sexual Assault*. Boston: Northeastern University Press, 2000.

——. "Reconsidering Violence against Women: Coalition Politics in the Anti-rape Movement." In *Feminist Coalitions: Historical Perspectives on Second-Wave Feminism in the United States*, edited by Stephanie Gilmore, 163–177. Urbana: University of Illinois Press, 2008.

Bierria, Alisa. "Pursuing a Radical Anti-Violence Agenda inside/outside of a Non-Profit Structure." In *The Revolution Will Not Be Funded: Beyond the Non-Profit Industrial Complex*, edited by INCITE! Women of Color against Violence, 151–164. Brooklyn: South End Press, 2009.

Bierria, Alisa, Clarissa Rojas, and Mimi Kim, eds. "Community Accountability: Emerging Movements to Transform Violence." Special Issue, *Social Justice* 37, no. 4 (2010).

Bissonette, Jamie. *When the Prisoners Ran Walpole: A True Story in the Movement for Prison Abolition*. Brooklyn: South End Press, 2008.

Blackwell, Maylei. *¡Chicana Power!: Contested Histories of Feminism in the Chicano Movement*. Austin: University of Texas Press, 2011.

——. "Contested Histories: Las Hijas de Cuauhtémoc, Chicana Feminisms, and Print Culture in the Chicano Movement, 1968–1973." In *Chicana Feminisms: A Critical Reader*, edited by Gabriela F. Arredondo, Aída Hurtado, Norma Klahn, Olga Nájera-Ramírez, and Patricia Zavella, 59–89. Durham: Duke University Press, 2003.

Block, Diana. *Arm the Spirit: A Woman's Journey Underground and Back*. Oakland, Calif.: AK Press, 2009.

Bloom, Joshua, and Waldo E. Martin. *Black against Empire: The History and Politics of the Black Panther Party*. Oakland: University of California Press, 2013.

Bluestone, Barry, and Mary Huff Stevenson. *The Boston Renaissance: Race, Space, and Economic Change in an American Metropolis*. New York: Russell Sage Foundation, 2000.

Blumenthal, Susanna L. *Law and the Modern Mind: Consciousness and Responsibility in American Legal Culture*. Cambridge: Harvard University Press, 2016.

Boyette, Michael, and Randi Boyette. *Let It Burn: MOVE, the Philadelphia Police Department, and the Confrontation That Changed a City*. San Diego, Calif.: Quadrant Books, 2013.

Breines, Winifred. *The Trouble between Us: An Uneasy History of White and Black Women in the Feminist Movement*. New York: Oxford University Press, 2006.

Briggs, Laura. *Reproducing Empire: Race, Sex, Science, and U.S. Imperialism in Puerto Rico*. Los Angeles: University of California Press, 2002.

Brown, Rita Bo. "White North American Political Prisoners." In *Imprisoned Intellectuals: America's Political Prisoners Write on Life, Liberation, and Rebellion*, edited by Joy James, 214–226. Lanham, Md.: Rowman and Littlefield, 2003.

brown, rita d. "A Short Autobiography." In *Creating a Movement with Teeth: A Documentary History of the George Jackson Brigade*, edited by Daniel Burton-Rose, 71–74. Oakland, Calif.: PM Press, 2010.

Bumiller, Kristin. *In an Abusive State: How Neoliberalism Appropriated the Feminist Movement against Sexual Violence*. Durham: Duke University Press, 2008.

Burnham, Linda. "The Wellspring of Black Feminist Theory." *Southern University Law Review* 28 (2001): 265–270.

Burton-Rose, Daniel. *Guerrilla USA: The George Jackson Brigade and the Anti-capitalist Underground of the 1970s*. Los Angeles: University of California Press, 2010.

Cacho, Lisa Marie. "The Presumption of White Innocence." *American Quarterly* 66, no. 4 (2014): 1085–1090.

Canaday, Margot. *The Straight State: Sexuality and Citizenship in Twentieth-Century America*. Princeton, N.J.: Princeton University Press, 2009.

Carastathis, Anna. *Intersectionality: Origins, Contestations, Horizons*. Lincoln: University of Nebraska Press, 2016.

Carpio, Myla Vicenti. "The Lost Generation: American Indian Women and Sterilization Abuse." *Social Justice* 31, no. 4 (2004): 40–53.

Carrillo Rowe, Aimee. *Power Lines: On the Subject of Feminist Alliances*. Durham: Duke University Press, 2008.

Carroll, Tamar W. *Mobilizing New York: AIDS, Antipoverty, and Feminist Activism*. Chapel Hill: University of North Carolina Press, 2015.

Chamberlin, Judi. *On Our Own: Patient-Controlled Alternatives to the Mental Health System*. Portland, Ore.: Hawthorne Books, 1978.

———."The Ex-Patients' Movement: Where We've Been and Where We're Going." *Journal of Mind and Behavior* 11, no. 3 (1990): 323–336.

Charoula. "Prison Work and the Lesbian Issue: A Personal Statement." In *Top Ranking: A Collection of Articles on Racism and Classism in the Lesbian Community*, edited by Sara Bennett and Joan Gibbs, 44–48. New York: Come! Unity Press, 1980.

Chávez, Karma R. *Queer Migration Politics: Activist Rhetoric and Coalitional Possibilities*. Urbana: University of Illinois Press, 2013.

Chen, Ching-In, Jai Dulani, and Leah Lakshmi Piepzna-Samarasinha, eds. *The Revolution Starts at Home: Confronting Intimate Violence within Activist Communities*. Brooklyn: South End Press, 2011.

Churchill, Ward, and Jim Vander Wall. *Agents of Repression: The FBI's Secret Wars against the Black Panther Party and the American Indian Movement*. Brooklyn: South End Press, 1988.

Cobble, Dorothy Sue. *The Other Women's Movement: Workplace Justice and Social Rights in Modern America*. Princeton, N.J.: Princeton University Press, 2004.

Cohen, Cathy J. "Deviance as Resistance: A New Research Agenda for the Study of Black Politics." *Du Bois Review* 1, no. 1 (2004): 27–45.

———. "Punks, Bulldaggers, and Welfare Queens: The Radical Potential of Queer Politics?" *GLQ: A Journal of Lesbian and Gay Studies* 3, no. 4 (1997): 437–465.

———. *The Boundaries of Blackness: AIDS and the Breakdown of Black Politics*. Chicago: The University of Chicago Press, 1999.

Coker, Donna, and Lindsay C. Harrison. "The Story of *Wanrow*: The Reasonable Woman and the Law of Self-Defense." In *Criminal Law Stories*, edited by Donna Coker and Robert Weisberg, 213–262. New York: Foundation Press, 2013.

Coleman, Paulette. "Prison Reform in Massachusetts: A Study of the Politics of Institutional Change." PhD Dissertation, Massachusetts Institute of Technology, 1977.

Colley, Zoe A. *Ain't Scared of Your Jail: Arrest, Imprisonment, and the Civil Rights Movement*. Gainesville: University Press of Florida, 2012.

Combahee River Collective. "A Black Feminist Statement." In *This Bridge Called My Back: Writings by Radical Women of Color*, edited by Cherríe Moraga and Gloria Anzaldúa, 4th ed., 210–218. Albany: The State University of New York Press, 2015.

———. *The Combahee River Collective Statement: Black Feminist Organizing in the Seventies and Eighties*. Freedom Organizing Series no. 1. New York: Kitchen Table: Women of Color Press, 1986.

"CONVERGE! Reimagining the Movement to End Gender Violence." Symposium issue, *University of Miami Race and Social Justice Law Review* 5, no. 2 (2015).

Córdova, Jeanne. *When We Were Outlaws: A Memoir of Love & Revolution*. Tallahassee, Fla.: Spinsters Ink, 2011.

CR10 Publications Collective, ed. *Abolition Now! Ten Years of Strategy and Struggle against the Prison Industrial Complex*. Oakland, Calif.: AK Press, 2008.

Crenshaw, Kimberlé. "Demarginalizing the Intersection of Race and Sex: A Black Feminist Critique of Antidiscrimination Doctrine, Feminist Theory and Antiracist Politics." *University of Chicago Legal Forum* no. 1 (1989): 139–167.

———. "Mapping the Margins: Intersectionality, Identity Politics, and Violence against Women of Color." *Stanford Law Review* 43, no. 6 (1991): 1241–1299.

Crenshaw, Kimberlé, Andrea J. Ritchie, Rachel Anspach, Rachel Gilmer, and Luke Harris. "Say Her Name: Resisting Police Brutality against Black Women." African American Policy Forum, Center for Intersectionality and Social Policy Studies, Columbia Law School, 2015.

Cummins, Eric. *The Rise and Fall of California's Radical Prison Movement.* Palo Alto: Stanford University Press, 1994.

Cunningham, David. *There's Something Happening Here: The New Left, the Klan, and FBI Counterintelligence.* Berkeley: University of California Press, 2004.

Davis, Angela Y. *Freedom Is a Constant Struggle: Ferguson, Palestine, and the Foundations of a Movement.* Chicago: Haymarket Books, 2016.

———. "JoAnne Little: The Dialectics of Rape." In *The Angela Y. Davis Reader*, edited by Joy James, 149–160. Malden, Mass.: Blackwell Publishers, 1998.

———. "Racism and Contemporary Literature on Rape." *Freedomways* 16, no. 1 (Winter 1976): 25–33.

———. "The Color of Violence against Women." *Colorlines*, October 10, 2000.

Davis, Mike. "Hell Factories in the Field." *The Nation* 260, no. 7 (1995): 229–233.

D.C. Rape Crisis Center. *How to Start a Rape Crisis Center.* Washington, D.C.: D.C. Rape Crisis Center, 1972.

Delacoste, Frédérique, and Felice Newman, eds. *Fight Back! Feminist Resistance to Male Violence.* Minneapolis: Cleis Press, 1981.

Del Drago, Maria. "The Pride of Inez Garcia." *Ms.*, May 1975.

Delmont, Matthew, and Jeanne Theoharis. "Rethinking the Boston 'Busing Crisis.'" *Journal of Urban History* 43, no. 2 (2017): 191–203.

Díaz-Cotto, Juanita. *Gender, Ethnicity, and the State: Latina and Latino Prison Politics.* Albany: State University of New York Press, 1996.

Dillon, Stephen. "Possessed by Death: The Neoliberal-Carceral State, Black Feminism, and the Afterlife of Slavery." *Radical History Review* 112 (2012): 113–125.

Dixon, Chris. *Another Politics: Talking across Today's Transformative Movements.* Oakland: University of California Press, 2014.

Dowker, Fay, and Glenn Good. *From Alcatraz to Marion to Florence: Control Unit Prisons in the United States.* Chicago: Committee to End the Marion Lockdown, 1992.

Duggan, Lisa. *The Twilight of Equality? Neoliberalism, Cultural Politics, and the Attack on Democracy.* Boston: Beacon Press, 2003.

Duster, Troy. *Backdoor to Eugenics.* New York: Routledge, 1990.

Enck-Wanzer, Darrel, ed. *The Young Lords: A Reader.* New York: New York University Press, 2010.

Enke, A. Finn. *Finding the Movement: Sexuality, Contested Space, and Feminist Activism.* Durham: Duke University Press, 2007.

———. "Smuggling Sex through the Gates: Race, Sexuality, and the Politics of Space in Second-Wave Feminism." *American Quarterly* 55, no. 4 (2003): 635–667.

Faith, Karlene. *Unruly Women: The Politics of Confinement and Resistance*. Vancouver: Press Gang Publishers, 1993.

Farmer, Ashley D. *Remaking Black Power: How Black Women Transformed an Era*. Chapel Hill: University of North Carolina Press, 2017.

Felber, Garrett. "'Those Who Say Don't Know and Those Who Know Don't Say': The Nation of Islam and the Politics of Black Nationalism in the Civil Rights Era." PhD Dissertation, University of Michigan, 2016.

Fergus, Devin. *Liberalism, Black Power, and the Making of American Politics, 1965–1980*. Athens: University of Georgia Press, 2009.

Fernández, Johanna. "Denise Oliver and the Young Lords Party: Stretching the Boundaries of Struggle." In *Want to Start a Revolution? Radical Women in the Black Freedom Struggle*, edited by Dayo F. Gore, Jeanne Theoharis, and Komozi Woodard, 271–293. New York: New York University Press, 2009.

Flamm, Michael W. *Law and Order: Street Crime, Civil Unrest, and the Crisis of Liberalism in the 1960s*. New York: Columbia University Press, 2007.

Foucault, Michel. "About the Concept of the Dangerous Individual in Nineteenth-Century Legal Psychiatry." In *Power: Essential Works of Foucault, 1954–1984*, vol. 3, edited by James D. Faubion, 176–200. New York: New York Press, 1994.

Freedman, Estelle B. *Maternal Justice: Miriam Van Waters and the Female Reform Tradition*. Chicago: University of Chicago Press, 1996.

———. *Their Sisters' Keepers: Women's Prison Reform in America, 1830–1930*. Ann Arbor: University of Michigan Press, 1981.

———. "The Prison Lesbian: Race, Class, and the Construction of the Aggressive Female Homosexual, 1915–1965." *Feminist Studies* 22, no. 2 (1996): 397–423.

French, Laurence. "The Incarcerated Black Female: The Case of Social Double Jeopardy." *Journal of Black Studies* 8, no. 3 (1978): 321–335.

Gagné, Patricia. *Battered Women's Justice: The Movement for Clemency and the Politics of Self*. Woodbridge, Conn.: Twayne, 1998.

Garland, David. *The Culture of Control*. Oxford: Oxford University Press, 2001.

Giddings, Paula J. *Ida: A Sword among Lions: Ida B. Wells and the Campaign against Lynching*. New York: HarperCollins, 2008.

Gilmore, Ruth Wilson. "Globalisation and US Prison Growth: From Military Keynesianism to Post-Keynesian Militarism." *Race & Class* 40, nos. 2–3 (1998/99): 171–188.

———. *Golden Gulag: Prisons, Surplus, Crisis, and Opposition in Globalizing California*. Berkeley: University of California Press, 2007.

Gilmore, Stephanie, ed. *Feminist Coalitions: Historical Perspectives on Second-Wave Feminism in the United States*. Urbana: University of Illinois Press, 2008.

Goffman, Erving. *Asylums: Essays on the Social Situation of Mental Patients and Other Inmates*. Garden City, N.Y.: Anchor Books, 1961.

Gold, Roberta. *When Tenants Claimed the City: The Struggle for Citizenship in New York City Housing*. Urbana: University of Illinois Press, 2014.

Gómez, Alan Eladio. "Resisting Living Death at Marion Federal Penitentiary, 1972." *Radical History Review* no. 96 (2006): 58–86.

Gordon, Avery F. *Ghostly Matters: Haunting and the Sociological Imagination.* Minneapolis: University of Minnesota Press, 1997.

———. "Methodologies of Imprisonment." *PMLA* 123, no. 3 (2008): 651–657.

Gore, Dayo F. *Radicalism at the Crossroads: African American Women Activists in the Cold War.* New York: New York University Press, 2011.

Gottschalk, Marie. *Caught: The Prison State and the Lockdown of American Politics.* Princeton, N.J.: Princeton University Press, 2015.

———. "Money and Mass Incarceration: The Bad, the Mad, and Penal Reform." *Criminology & Public Policy* 8, no. 1 (2009): 97–109.

———. *The Prison and the Gallows: The Politics of Mass Incarceration in America.* New York: Cambridge University Press, 2006.

Grant, Jamie. "Who Is Killing Us?" In *Femicide: The Politics of Woman Killing*, edited by Jill Radford and Diana E. H. Russell, 145–160. New York: Maxwell Mac-Millan International, 1992.

Greene, Christina. *Our Separate Ways: Women and the Black Freedom Movement in Durham, North Carolina.* Chapel Hill: University of North Carolina Press, 2005.

———. "'She Ain't No Rosa Parks': The Joan Little Rape-Murder Case and Jim Crow Justice in the Post-Civil Rights South." *Journal of African American History* 100, no. 3 (2015): 428–447.

Griffin, Farah Jasmine. "'Ironies of the Saint': Malcolm X, Black Women, and the Price of Protection." In *Sisters in the Struggle: African American Women in the Civil Rights–Black Power Movement*, edited by Bettye Collier-Thomas and Vincent P. Franklin, 214–229. New York: New York University Press, 2001.

Grob, Gerald. *The Mad among Us: A History of the Care of America's Mentally Ill.* New York: Simon and Schuster, 1994.

Gross, Kali N. "African American Women, Mass Incarceration, and the Politics of Protection." *Journal of American History* 102, no. 1 (2015): 25–33.

———. *Colored Amazons: Crime, Violence, and Black Women in the City of Brotherly Love, 1880–1910.* Durham: Duke University Press, 2006.

Gumbs, Alexis Pauline. "We Can Learn to Mother Ourselves: The Queer Survival of Black Feminism 1968–1996." PhD Dissertation, Duke University, 2010.

Gutiérrez, Ramón A. "Internal Colonialism: An American Theory of Race." *Du Bois Review: Social Science Research on Race* 1, no. 2 (2004): 281–295.

Haag, Pamela. "'Putting Your Body on the Line': The Question of Violence, Victims, and the Legacies of Second-Wave Feminism." *Differences: A Journal of Feminist Cultural Studies* 8, no. 2 (1996): 23–68.

Haley, Sarah. *No Mercy Here: Gender, Punishment, and the Making of Jim Crow Modernity.* Chapel Hill: University of North Carolina Press, 2016.

Hames-García, Michael. *Fugitive Thought: Prison Movements, Race, and the Meaning of Justice.* Minneapolis: University of Minnesota Press, 2004.

Hammonds, Evelynn M. "Toward a Genealogy of Black Female Sexuality: The Problematic of Silence." In *Feminist Theory and the Body: A Reader*, edited by Janet Price and Margrit Shildrick, 93–104. New York: Routledge, 1999.

Hanhardt, Christina B. *Safe Space: Gay Neighborhood History and the Politics of Violence*. Durham: Duke University Press, 2013.

Harris, Duchess. "All of Who I Am in the Same Place: The Combahee River Collective." *Womanist Theory and Research* 2, no. 2 (1999): 1–26.

———. *Black Feminist Politics from Kennedy to Clinton*. New York: Palgrave Macmillan, 2009.

Harvey, David. *Rebel Cities: From the Right to the City to the Urban Revolution*. New York: Verso, 2012.

Heaney, Emma. "Women-Identified Women: Trans Women in 1970s Lesbian Feminist Organizing." *TSQ: Transgender Studies Quarterly* 3, nos. 1–2 (2016): 137–145.

Hewitt, Nancy A., ed. *No Permanent Waves: Recasting Histories of U.S. Feminism*. New Brunswick, N.J.: Rutgers University Press, 2010.

Hicks, Cheryl D. *Talk with You Like a Woman: African American Women, Justice, and Reform in New York, 1890–1935*. Chapel Hill: University of North Carolina Press, 2010.

Hill, Rebecca N. *Men, Mobs, and Law: Anti-Lynching and Labor Defense in U.S. Radical History*. Durham: Duke University Press, 2009.

Hill Collins, Patricia, and Sirma Bilge. *Intersectionality*. Hoboken, N.J.: Wiley, 2016.

Hinton, Elizabeth. *From the War on Poverty to the War on Crime: The Making of Mass Incarceration in America*. Cambridge: Harvard University Press, 2016.

Hobson, Emily K. *Lavender and Red: Liberation and Solidarity in the Gay and Lesbian Left*. Oakland: University of California Press, 2016.

Hogan, Kristen. *The Feminist Bookstore Movement: Lesbian Antiracism and Feminist Accountability*. Durham: Duke University Press, 2016.

Holmes, Kwame A. "Chocolate to Rainbow City: The Dialectics of Black and Gay Community Formation in Postwar Washington, D.C., 1946–1978." PhD Dissertation, University of Illinois at Urbana-Champaign, 2011.

Hong, Grace Kyungwon. *The Ruptures of American Capital: Women of Color Feminism and the Culture of Immigrant Labor*. Minneapolis: University of Minnesota Press, 2006.

Hornblum, Allen M. *Acres of Skin: Human Experiments at Holmesburg Prison*. New York: Routledge, 2013.

Howe, Charles A. "David Eaton." *Dictionary of Unitarian and Universalist Biography*. 2002.

INCITE! Women of Color against Violence, ed. *Color of Violence: The INCITE! Anthology*. Durham: Duke University Press, 2016.

INCITE! Women of Color against Violence and FIERCE!. "Re-Thinking 'The Norm' In Police/Prison Violence & Gender Violence: Critical Lessons from the New Jersey 7." *Left Turn*, October 1, 2008.

Jacquet, Catherine O. "Fighting Back, Claiming Power: Feminist Rhetoric and Resistance to Rape in the 1970s." *Radical History Review* no. 126 (2016): 71–83.

Jaimes, M. Annette, and Theresa Halsey. "American Indian Women: At the Center of Indigenous Resistance in North American." In *The State of Native America: Genocide, Colonization, and Resistance*, edited by Arnette M. Jaimes, 311–344. Cambridge, Mass.: South End Press, 1992.

James, Joy. "Framing the Panther: Assata Shakur and Black Female Agency." In *Want to Start a Revolution? Radical Women in the Black Freedom Struggle*, edited by Dayo F. Gore, Jeanne Theoharis, and Komozi Woodard, 138–160. New York: New York University Press,2009.

——. Introduction. In *The Angela Y. Davis Reader*, edited by Joy James, 1–27. Malden, Mass.: Blackwell, 1998.

James, Joy, ed. *Imprisoned Intellectuals: America's Political Prisoners Write on Life, Liberation, and Rebellion*. New York: Rowman and Littlefield, 2003.

——. *The New Abolitionists: (Neo)Slave Narratives and Contemporary Prison Writings*. Albany: State University of New York Press, 2005.

Janken, Kenneth Robert. *The Wilmington Ten: Violence, Injustice, and the Rise of Black Politics in the 1970s*. Chapel Hill: University of North Carolina Press, 2015.

Johnson, Charles Ray. "Commonwealth vs. Willie Sanders." *The Black Scholar* 11, no. 3 (1980): 82.

Johnson, David K. *The Lavender Scare: The Cold War Persecution of Gays and Lesbians in the Federal Government*. Chicago: The University of Chicago Press, 2004.

Joseph, Miranda. *Against the Romance of Community*. Minneapolis: University of Minnesota Press, 2002.

Kaba, Mariame. "Free Us All: Participatory Defense Campaigns as Abolitionist Organizing." *The New Inquiry*, May 8, 2017.

Kaba, Mariame, ed. *No Selves to Defend: A Legacy of Criminalizing Women of Color for Self-Defense*. Chicago: Chicago Alliance to Free Marissa Alexander, 2014.

Kelley, Robin D. G. *Freedom Dreams: The Black Radical Imagination*. Boston: Beacon Press, 2002.

Kim, Mimi. "Dancing the Carceral Creep: The Anti-Domestic Violence Movement and the Paradoxical Pursuit of Criminalization, 1973–1986." PhD Dissertation, University of California, Berkeley, 2014.

Klinger, Alisa Margaret. "Paper Uprisings: Print Activism in the Multicultural Lesbian Movement." PhD Dissertation, University of California, Berkeley, 1995.

Kohler-Hausmann, Julilly. *Getting Tough: Welfare and Imprisonment in 1970s America*. Princeton, N.J.: Princeton University Press, 2017.

Kunzel, Regina G. *Criminal Intimacy: Prison and the Uneven History of Modern American Sexuality*. Chicago: The University of Chicago Press, 2008.

——. "Lessons in Being Gay: Queer Encounters in Gay and Lesbian Prison Activism." *Radical History Review* no. 100 (2008).

———. "The Rise of Gay Rights and the Disavowal of Disability." In *The Oxford Handbook on Disability History*, edited by Catherine Kudlick, Kim Nielsen, and Michael A. Rembis. New York: Oxford University Press, 2018.

Law, Victoria. "Against Carceral Feminism." *Jacobin*, October 17, 2014.

———. "Protection without Police: North American Community Responses to Violence in the 1970s and Today." *Upping the Anti* no. 12 (2011).

———. *Resistance behind Bars: The Struggles of Incarcerated Women*. Oakland, Calif.: PM Press, 2009.

———. "Sick of the Abuse: Feminist Responses to Sexual Assault, Battering, and Self-Defense." In *The Hidden 1970s: Histories of Radicalism*, edited by Dan Berger, 39–56. New Brunswick, N.J.: Rutgers University Press, 2010.

———. "Where Abolition Meets Action: Women Organizing against Gender Violence." *Contemporary Justice Review* 14, no. 1 (2011): 85–94.

Lee, Chana Kai. *For Freedom's Sake: The Life of Fannie Lou Hamer*. Urbana: University of Illinois Press, 1999.

Lefebvre, Henri. *Le Droit a la Ville* [The Right to the City]. Paris: Anthropos, 1968.

LeFlouria, Talitha L. *Chained in Silence: Black Women and Convict Labor in the New South*. Chapel Hill: University of North Carolina Press, 2015.

Lewis, Abram J. "'We Are Certain of Our Own Insanity': Antipsychiatry and the Gay Liberation Movement, 1968–1980." *Journal of the History of Sexuality* 25, no. 1 (2016): 83–113.

Light, Caroline. *Stand Your Ground: America's Love Affair with Lethal Self-Defense*. Boston: Beacon Press, 2017.

Lipsitz, George. *A Life in the Struggle: Ivory Perry and the Culture of Opposition*. Philadelphia: Temple University Press, 1988.

Lloyd, James M. "Fighting Redlining and Gentrification in Washington, D.C.: The Adams-Morgan Organization and Tenant Right to Purchase." *Journal of Urban History* 42, no. 6 (2016): 1091–1109.

Losier, Toussaint. "'For Strictly Religious Reason[s]': *Cooper v. Pate* and the Origins of the Prisoners' Rights Movement." *Souls: A Critical Journal of Black Politics, Culture, and Society* 15, nos. 1–2 (2013): 19–38.

———. "Prison House of Nations: Police Violence and Mass Incarceration in the Long Course of Black Insurgency in Illinois, 1953–1987." PhD Dissertation, University of Chicago, 2014.

Lyon, Andrea D., Emily Hughes, and Juanita Thomas. "The People v. Juanita Thomas: A Battered Woman's Journey to Freedom." *Women & Criminal Justice* 13, no. 1 (2001): 27–63.

Mark, Vernon H., William H. Sweet, and F. R. Ervin. "Role of Brain Disease in Riots and Urban Violence." *JAMA* 201, no. 11 (1967): 895–896.

Martin, Charles H. "Race, Gender, and Southern Justice: The Rosa Lee Ingram Case." *American Journal of Legal History* 29, no. 3 (1985): 251–268.

Mason, B. J. "Brain Surgery to Control Behavior: Controversial Operations Are Coming Back as Violence Curbs." *Ebony* 28, no.4 (Feb 1973): 63.

Matthews, Nancy. *Confronting Rape: The Feminist Anti-Rape Movement and the State*. New York: Routledge, 1994.

Matthews, Tracye. "'No One Ever Asks What a Man's Role in the Revolution Is': Gender and Sexual Politics in the Black Panther Party, 1966–1971." In *Sisters in the Struggle: African American Women in the Civil Rights-Black Power Movement*, edited by Bettye Collier-Thomas and Vincent P. Franklin, 223–249. New York: New York University Press, 2001.

McDuffie, Erik S. "A 'New Freedom Movement of Negro Women': Sojourning for Truth, Justice, and Human Rights during the Early Cold War." *Radical History Review* no. 101 (2008).

McGuire, Danielle L. *At the Dark End of the Street: Black Women, Rape, and Resistance—A New History of the Civil Rights Movement from Rosa Parks to the Rise of Black Power*. New York: Knopf, 2010.

McMillian, John. *Smoking Typewriters: The Sixties Underground Press and the Rise of Alternative Media in America*. New York: Oxford University Press, 2011.

McNeil, Genna Rae. "'Joanne Is You and Joanne Is Me': A Consideration of African American Women and the 'Free Joan Little' Movement, 1974–75." In *Sisters in the Struggle: African American Women in the Civil Rights–Black Power Movement*, edited by Bettye Collier-Thomas and V. P. Franklin, 259–279. New York: New York University Press, 2001.

———. "The Body, Sexuality, and *Self*-Defense in *State vs. Joan Little*, 1974–1975." *Journal of African American History* 93, no. 2 (2008): 235–261.

Meiners, Erica R. *For the Children? Protecting Innocence in a Carceral State*. Minneapolis: University of Minnesota Press, 2016.

Metzl, Jonathan. *The Protest Psychosis: How Schizophrenia Became a Black Disease*. Boston: Beacon Press, 2009.

Mitford, Jessica. *Kind and Usual Punishment*. New York: Knopf, 1973.

Mogul, Joey, Andrea Ritchie, and Kay Whitlock. *Queer (In)Justice: The Criminalization of LGBT People in the United States*. Boston: Beacon Press, 2011.

Moraga, Cherríe. Preface. In *This Bridge Called My Back: Writings by Radical Women of Color*, edited by Cherríe Moraga and Gloria Anzaldúa, xiii–xx. Watertown, Mass.: Persephone Press, 1981.

Morgan, Robin, ed. *Sisterhood Is Powerful: An Anthology of Writings from the Women's Liberation Movement*. New York: Vintage Books, 1970.

Morgen, Sandra. *Into Our Own Hands: The Women's Health Movement in the United States, 1969–1990*. Piscataway, N.J.: Rutgers University Press, 2002.

Morris, James McGrath. *Jailhouse Journalism: The Fourth Estate behind Bars*. Jefferson, N.C.: McFarland, 1998.

Muñoz, José Esteban. *Cruising Utopia: The Then and There of Queer Futurity*. New York: New York University Press, 2009.

———. *Disidentifications: Queers of Color and the Performance of Politics*. Minneapolis: University of Minnesota Press, 1999.

Murakawa, Naomi. *The First Civil Right: How Liberals Built Prison America*. New York: Oxford University Press, 2014.

Murch, Donna Jean. *Living for the City: Migration, Education, and the Rise of the Black Panther Party in Oakland, California*. Chapel Hill: University of North Carolina Press, 2010.

Nadasen, Premilla. *Welfare Warriors: The Welfare Rights Movement in the United States*. New York: Routledge, 2005.

National Research Council. *The Growth of Incarceration in the United States: Exploring Causes and Consequences*, edited by Jeremy Travis, Bruce Western, and Steve Redburn. Washington, D.C.: The National Academies Press, 2014.

Nelson, Alondra. *Body and Soul: The Black Panther Party and the Fight against Medical Discrimination*. Minneapolis: University of Minnesota Press, 2013.

Nelson, Jennifer. "'Abortions under Community Control': Feminism, Nationalism, and the Politics of Reproduction among New York City's Young Lords." *Journal of Women's History* 13, no. 1 (2001): 157–180.

———. *Women of Color and the Reproductive Rights Movement*. New York: New York University Press, 2003.

Nicholas, J. B. "August Rebellion: New York's Forgotten Female Prison Riot," *Village Voice*, August 30, 2016.

Nielson, Kim. *A Disability History of the United States*. Boston: Beacon Press, 2012.

Omi, Michael, and Howard Winant. *Racial Formation in the United States*. New York: Routledge, 2015.

O'Sullivan, Meg Devlin. "'More Destruction to These Family Ties': Native American Women, Child Welfare, and the Solution of Sovereignty." *Journal of Family History* 41, no. 1 (2016): 19–38.

Parenti, Christian. *Lockdown America: Police and Prisons in the Age of Crisis*. New York: Verso, 1999.

Pasulka, Nicole. "The Case of CeCe McDonald: Murder—or Self-Defense against a Hate Crime?" *Mother Jones*, May 22, 2012.

Pelka, Fred. *What We Have Done: An Oral History of the Disability Rights Movement*. Amherst: University of Massachusetts Press, 2012.

Polletta, Francesca. *Freedom Is an Endless Meeting: Democracy in American Social Movements*. Chicago: University of Chicago Press, 2002.

Powell, Tamara M. "Look What Happened Here: North Carolina's Feminary Collective." *North Carolina Literary Review* 9 (2000): 91–102.

Prison Research Education Action Project. *Instead of Prisons: A Handbook for Abolitionists*. Brooklyn: Faculty Press, 1976.

Provine, Doris Marie. *Unequal under Law: Race in the War on Drugs*. Chicago: University of Chicago Press, 2007.

Pulido, Laura. *Black, Brown, Yellow, and Left: Radical Activism in Los Angeles*. Los Angeles: University of California Press, 2006.

Randolph, Sherie M. *Florynce "Flo" Kennedy: The Life of a Black Feminist Radical*. Chapel Hill: University of North Carolina Press, 2015.

Reddy, Chandan. *Freedom with Violence: Race, Sexuality, and the US State*. Durham: Duke University Press, 2011.

Redmond, Shana. "'As Though It Were Our Own': Against a Politics of Identification." In *Critical Ethnic Studies: A Reader*, edited by Nada Elia, David M. Hernández, Jodi Kim, Shana L. Redmond, Dylan Rodríguez, and Sarita Echavez See, 19–42. Durham: Duke University Press, 2016.

Rembis, Michael. "The New Asylums: Madness and Mass Incarceration in the Neoliberal Era." In *Disability Incarcerated: Imprisonment and Disability in the United States and Canada*, edited by Liat Ben-Moshe, Chris Chapman, and Allison C. Carey, 139–159. New York: Palgrave MacMillan, 2014.

Resources for Community Change. *Women behind Bars: An Organizing Tool*. Washington, D.C.: Resources for Community Change, 1975.

Richie, Beth E. "A Black Feminist Reflection on the Antiviolence Movement." *Signs: Journal of Women in Culture and Society* 25, no. 4 (2000): 1133–1137.

———. *Arrested Justice: Black Women, Violence, and America's Prison Nation*. New York: New York University Press, 2012.

Ritchie, Andrea. *Invisible No More: Police Violence against Black Women and Women of Color*. Boston: Beacon Press, 2017.

Roberts, Dorothy. *Killing the Black Body: Race, Reproduction, and the Meaning of Liberty*. New York: Pantheon, 1997.

Robnett, Belinda. *How Long? How Long? African-American Women in the Struggle for Civil Rights*. New York: Oxford University Press, 1997.

Rodríguez, Dylan. *Forced Passages: Imprisoned Radical Intellectuals and the U.S. Prison Regime*. Minneapolis: University of Minnesota Press, 2005.

Rosen, Ruth. *The World Split Open: How the Modern Women's Movement Changed America*. New York: Viking, 2000.

Ross, Luana. *Inventing the Savage: The Social Construction of Native American Criminality*. Austin: University of Texas Press, 1998.

Roth, Benita. *Separate Roads to Feminism: Black, Chicana, and White Feminist Movements in America's Second Wave*. New York: Cambridge University Press, 2003.

———. "The Making of the Vanguard Center: Black Feminist Emergence in the 1960s and 1970s." In *Still Lifting, Still Climbing: African American Women's Contemporary Activism*, edited by Kimberly Springer, 70–90. New York: New York University Press, 1999.

Roth, Rachel, and Sara L. Ainsworth. "'If They Hand You a Paper, You Sign It': A Call to End the Sterilization of Women in Prison." *Hastings Women's Law Journal* 26, no. 1 (2014): 7–50.

Russell, Diana E. H. *The Politics of Rape: The Victim's Perspective*. New York: Stein and Day, 1975.

Russell, Diana E. H., and Nicole Van de Ven, eds. "Crimes against Women: Proceedings of the International Tribunal." Third edition. Berkeley: Russell Publications, 1990.

Samuels, Liz. "Improvising on Reality: The Roots of Prison Abolition." In *The Hidden 1970s: Histories of Radicalism*, edited by Dan Berger, 21–38. New Brunswick, N.J.: Rutgers University Press, 2010.

Schechter, Susan. *Women and Male Violence: The Visions and Struggles of the Battered Women's Movement*. Cambridge, Mass.: South End Press, 1982.

Schneider, Elizabeth M. *Battered Women & Feminist Lawmaking*. New Haven, Conn.: Yale University Press, 2000.

Scott, James C. *Domination and the Arts of Resistance: Hidden Transcripts*. New Haven, Conn.: Yale University Press, 1990.

Sen, Arlene. "Naming Myself." In *Fight Back! Feminist Resistance to Male Violence*, edited by Frédérique Delacoste and Felice Newman, 31–36. Minneapolis: Cleis Press, 1981.

Shakur, Assata. *Assata: An Autobiography*. Chicago: Lawrence Hill, 1987.

Shirley, Neal, and Saralee Stafford. *Dixie Be Damned: 300 Years of Insurrection in the American South*. Oakland, Calif.: AK Press, 2015.

Silliman, Jael, Marlene Gerber Fried, Loretta Ross, and Elena R. Gutiérrez. *Undivided Rights: Women of Color Organize for Reproductive Justice*. Brooklyn: South End Press, 2004.

Simon, Jonathan. *Governing through Crime: How the War on Crime Transformed American Democracy and Created a Culture of Fear*. Oxford, U.K.: Oxford University Press, 2009.

Singh, Nikhil Pal. *Black Is a Country: Race and the Unfinished Struggle for Democracy*. Cambridge: Harvard University Press, 2004.

Slonecker, Blake. *A New Dawn for the New Left: Liberation News Service, Montague Farm, and the Long Sixties*. New York: Palgrave Macmillan, 2012.

Smith, Andrea. *Conquest: Sexual Violence and American Indian Genocide*. Brooklyn: South End Press, 2005.

Smith, Barbara. "Interview with Alexis Pauline Gumbs." In *Ain't Gonna Let Nobody Turn Me Around: Forty Years of Movement Building with Barbara Smith*, edited by Alethia Jones, Virginia Eubanks, and Barbara Smith, 277–284. Albany: State University of New York Press, 2014.

———. "Interview with Kimberly Springer." In *Ain't Gonna Let Nobody Turn Me Around: Forty Years of Movement Building with Barbara Smith*, edited by Alethia Jones, Virginia Eubanks, and Barbara Smith, 71–74. Albany: State University of New York Press, 2014.

———. Introduction to "Twelve Black Women: Why Did They Die?" In *Fight Back! Feminist Resistance to Male Violence*, edited by Frédérique Delacoste and Felice Newman, 68–69. Minneapolis: Cleis Press, 1981.

Smith, Paul Chaat, and Robert Allen Warrior. *Like a Hurricane: The Indian Movement from Alcatraz to Wounded Knee*. New York: The New Press, 1997.

Spade, Dean. *Normal Life: Administrative Violence, Critical Trans Politics, and the Limits of Law*. Brooklyn: South End Press, 2011.

Spencer, Robyn C. "Engendering the Black Freedom Struggle: Revolutionary Black Womanhood and the Black Panther Party in the Bay Area, California." *Journal of Women's History* 20, no. 1 (2008): 90–113.

———. *The Revolution Has Come: Black Power, Gender, and the Black Panther Party in Oakland*. Durham: Duke University Press, 2016.

Springer, Kimberly. "Black Feminists Respond to Black Power Masculinism." In *The Black Power Movement: Rethinking the Civil Rights–Black Power Era*, edited by Peniel E. Joseph, 105–118. New York: Routledge, 2006.

———. *Living for the Revolution: Black Feminist Organizations, 1968–1980*. Durham: Duke University Press, 2005.

———. "The Interstitial Politics of Black Feminist Organizations." *Meridians* 1, no. 2 (2001): 155–191.

"Stand Your Ground." Special Issue, *University of Miami Law Review* 68, no. 4 (2014).

Stanley, Eric A., and Nat Smith, eds. *Captive Genders: Trans Embodiment and the Prison Industrial Complex*. Oakland, Calif.: AK Press, 2011.

Staub, Michael E. *Madness Is Civilization: When the Diagnosis Was Social, 1948–1980*. Chicago: University of Chicago Press, 2011.

Stryker, Susan, and Talia M. Bettcher. "Introduction: Trans/Feminisms." *Transgender Studies Quarterly* 3, nos. 1–2 (2016): 5–14.

Sudbury, Julia, ed. *Global Lockdown: Race, Gender, and the Prison-Industrial Complex*. New York: Routledge, 2004.

Szasz, Thomas S. *Law, Liberty, and Psychiatry: An Inquiry into the Social Uses of Mental Health Practices*. New York: Macmillan, 1963.

Taylor, Keeanga-Yamahtta, ed. *How We Get Free: Black Feminism and the Combahee River Collective*. Chicago: Haymarket Books, 2017.

Taylor, Ula Yvette. *The Promise of Patriarchy: Women and the Nation of Islam*. Chapel Hill: University of North Carolina Press, 2017.

Taylor, Verta, and Leila J. Rupp. "Women's Culture and Lesbian Feminist Activism: A Reconsideration of Cultural Feminism." *Signs: Journal of Women in Culture and Society* 19, no. 1 (1993): 32–61.

Theoharis, Jeanne F. "'We Saved the City': Black Struggles for Educational Equality in Boston, 1960–1976." *Radical History Review* no. 81 (2001): 61–93.

Thompson, Becky. *A Promise and a Way of Life: White Antiracist Activism*. Minneapolis: University of Minnesota Press, 2001.

———. "Multiracial Feminism: Recasting the Chronology of Second Wave Feminism." *Feminist Studies* 28, no. 2 (2002): 336–360.

Thompson, Heather Ann. *Blood in the Water: The Attica Prison Uprising of 1971 and Its Legacy*. New York: Pantheon, 2016.

Through the Looking Glass. "Racism in the Prison System." In *Top Ranking: A Collection of Articles on Racism and Classism in the Lesbian Community*, edited by Sara Bennett and Joan Gibbs, 134–139. New York: Come! Unity Press, 1980.

Tyson, Timothy B. *Radio Free Dixie: Robert F. Williams and the Roots of Black Power*. Chapel Hill: University of North Carolina Press, 1999.

Valk, Anne M. *Radical Sisters: Second-Wave Feminism and Black Liberation in Washington, D.C.* Urbana: University of Illinois Press, 2008.

Wagner-Pacifici, Robin. *Discourse and Destruction: The City of Philadelphia versus MOVE.* Chicago: University of Chicago Press, 1994.

Ward, Stephen. "The Third World Women's Alliance: Black Feminist Radicalism and Black Power Politics." In *The Black Power Movement: Rethinking the Civil Rights–Black Power Era,* edited by Peniel E. Joseph, 119–144. New York: Routledge, 2006.

Washington, Harriet A. *Medical Apartheid: The Dark History of Medical Experimentation on Black Americans from Colonial Times to the Present.* New York: Harlem Moon, 2006.

Weaver, Vesla M. "Frontlash: Race and the Development of Punitive Crime Policy." *Studies in American Political Development* 21 (2007): 230–265.

Western, Bruce. *Punishment and Inequality in America.* New York: Russell Sage Foundation, 2006.

Williams, Lynora. "Violence against Women." *The Black Scholar* 12, no. 1 (1981): 18–24.

Williams, Rhonda Y. *The Politics of Public Housing: Black Women's Struggles against Urban Inequality.* Oxford, U.K.: Oxford University Press, 2004.

Williamson, Terrion. "Who Is Killing Us?" In *Ain't Gonna Let Nobody Turn Me Around: Forty Years of Movement Building with Barbara Smith,* edited by Alethia Jones, Virginia Eubanks, and Barbara Smith, 65–71. Albany: State University of New York, 2014.

———. "'Why Did They Die?': On Combahee and the Serialization of Black Death." *Souls: A Critical Journal of Black Politics, Culture, and Society* 19, no. 3 (2017): 328–341.

Young, Cynthia A. *Soul Power: Culture, Radicalism, and the Making of a U.S. Third World Left.* Durham: Duke University Press, 2006.

Yulanda Ward Memorial Fund. "Spatial Deconcentration in D.C.," *Libcom.org.* 1981.

Index

EMILY L. THUMA is an assistant professor of gender and sexuality studies at the University of California, Irvine.

Women, Gender, and Sexuality in American History

The University of Illinois Press
is a founding member of the
Association of American University Presses.

University of Illinois Press
1325 South Oak Street
Champaign, IL 61820-6903
www.press.uillinois.edu